The American Slave Narrat
the Victorian Novel

THE AMERICAN SLAVE NARRATIVE AND THE VICTORIAN NOVEL

Julia Sun-Joo Lee

OXFORD
UNIVERSITY PRESS
2010

OXFORD

UNIVERSITY PRESS

Oxford University Press, Inc., publishes works that further
Oxford University's objective of excellence
in research, scholarship, and education.

Oxford   New York
Auckland   Cape Town   Dar es Salaam   Hong Kong   Karachi
Kuala Lumpur   Madrid   Melbourne   Mexico City   Nairobi
New Delhi   Shanghai   Taipei   Toronto

With offices in
Argentina   Austria   Brazil   Chile   Czech Republic   France   Greece
Guatemala   Hungary   Italy   Japan   Poland   Portugal   Singapore
South Korea   Switzerland   Thailand   Turkey   Ukraine   Vietnam

Copyright © 2010 by Oxford University Press, Inc.

Published by Oxford University Press, Inc.
198 Madison Avenue, New York, New York 10016

www.oup.com

Oxford is a registered trademark of Oxford University Press

Library of Congress Cataloging-in-Publication Data
Lee, Julia Sun-Joo, 1976–
The American slave narrative and the Victorian novel / Julia Sun-Joo Lee.
p. cm.
ISBN 978-0-19-539032-2
1. English fiction—19th century—History and criticism. 2. English
literature—American influences. 3. Slave narratives. I. Title.
PR865.L44 2010
823'.8093556—dc22   2009023758

1 3 5 7 9 8 6 4 2
Printed in the United States of America
on acid-free paper

One submits oneself to other minds (teachers) in order to increase the chance that one will be looking in the right direction when a comet makes its sweep through a certain patch of sky.

—Elaine Scarry, *On Beauty and Being Just*

Acknowledgments

Beginning with Professor Scarry, herself, I owe a tremendous debt of gratitude to all the teachers who have helped me "look in the right direction."

This book grew under Elaine Scarry's careful tending and supervision. She not only read and responded to every word, but also served as a model of integrity and humanity at Harvard. The project was first conceived under the guidance of Henry Louis Gates, Jr. and John Picker, in whose graduate seminars I first caught sight of the comet's path. To Skip, in particular, I am deeply grateful for his lavish encouragement, generosity, and sense of humor. My gratitude goes to John Stauffer for his enthusiasm and willingness to engage with my ideas, and to Leah Price for her intellectual rigor and discipline. Jamaica Kincaid offered unwavering conviction in my ideas and a novel point of view, and Werner Sollors performed endless small acts of kindness. At Princeton, Lisa Sternlieb, Deborah Nord, and Maria DiBattista embodied perfectly what I one day hoped to become—a scholar and a teacher.

My colleagues at Loyola Marymount University graciously welcomed me into their community and touched me with their easy camaraderie and warmth. I thank Barbara Rico, K. J. Peters, and John Reilly for giving me the opportunity and privilege to join their department. Juan Mah y Busch, Stuart Ching, Barbara Rico, and John Reilly helped to refine and strengthen the chapter on Dickens. Dermot Ryan, David Killoran, Maria Alterra Jackson, and Deborah Harris made going to work an absolute pleasure.

I would like to thank Brendan O'Neill for so capably shepherding this manuscript through the editing process, and the anonymous readers at Oxford University Press for their comments and suggestions. I would also like to thank the editors and anonymous readers at *Nineteenth-Century Literature* and *Victorian Literature and Culture*, where some of the material in this book first appeared. An earlier version of chapter 1 appeared as "The (Slave) Narrative of *Jane Eyre*" in *Victorian Literature and Culture*

36.2 (2008): 317–29. A slightly modified version chapter 4 appeared as "The Return of the 'Unnative': The Transnational Politics of *North and South*" in *Nineteenth-Century Literature* 61.4 (2007): 449–78.

This project received generous support from the W. E. B. Du Bois Institute for African and African American Research at Harvard University, the Andrew W. Mellon Fellowship in Humanistic Studies, the Mrs. Giles Whiting Foundation Dissertation Fellowship, and the W. M. Keck Foundation Fellowship at the Huntington Library.

To Laura Murphy, Nadine Knight, Chinnie Ding, Meg McDermott, Larry Switzky, Melissa Jenkins, Jen Ohlund, Sharrona Pearl, David Roh, Matt Rubery, Christina Svendson, Namwali Serpell, Seo-Young Chu, Gwen Urdang-Brown, and my other compatriots from graduate school—thank you for the intellectual and emotional sustenance. Lizzy Castruccio, Miki Terasawa, Jennifer Heckart, Bob Chen, Janna Conner, Sharon Gi, Riva Kim, Tarry Payton, Lydia Cho, Rhonda Rockwell, Chris Corey, Sandhya Gupta, and Sharon Lee helped keep things in perspective. Robert and Bonnie Sonneborn welcomed me into their family and cheered me on. Nancy Malkiel edited and encouraged, and Burt Malkiel told me to "stick to my guns."

My mother passed on to me her love of books and her steely discipline. My father taught me patience and humility—"Ever the best of friends."

Finally, this book is dedicated, with love, to Brad and Lucy Sonneborn. "Every limit is a beginning as well as an ending."

Contents

The American Slave Narrative and
the Victorian Novel

Introduction

These are the gifts of art; and art thrives most
Where Commerce has enrich'd the busy coast;
He catches all improvements in his flight,
Spreads foreign wonders in his country's sight,
Imports what others have invented well,
And stirs his own to match them, or excel.
'Tis thus, reciprocating each with each,
Alternately the nations learn and teach;
While Providence enjoins to ev'ry soul
A union with the vast terraqueous whole.
—William Cowper, *Charity* (1782)

On March 17, 1848, Charles Dickens wrote a letter to his friend William Charles Macready, enclosing a copy of Frederick Douglass's 1845 narrative with the brief introduction, "Here is Frederick Douglass."[1] Macready, the famous Irish actor who was soon to embark on a tour of America, was interested in learning more about slavery, and Douglass's slave narrative, which had already gone through nine British editions by 1847, was a transatlantic bestseller.[2] After a few paragraphs expressing concern for Mrs. Macready's health, Dickens continued, "—To return to Frederick Douglass. There was such a hideous and abominable portrait of him in the book, that I have torn it out, fearing it might set you, by anticipation, against the narrative."[3]

Dickens's impulse to tear out Douglass's picture seems jarring given his apparent admiration for the narrative; after all, he had not only read the book himself, but was now sending a copy, with his recommendation, to a friend. The portrait in question is presumably from the first British edition of Douglass's *Narrative* and depicts a slightly bemused-looking Douglass, dressed in the garb of a Victorian gentleman (see figure I.1).[4] The frontispiece is signed by the artist, B. Bell, and the engraver, H. Adlard, and was possibly copied from a painting of Douglass once attributed to Elisha Hammond.[5] Douglass is stiffly posed, with an elongated face and nose, prominent cheekbones, stylized hair, and truncated bust. Following nineteenth-century portrait engraving conventions, the picture is left partially unfinished to emphasize the artifice of the engraving. Ezra Greenspan argues that such portraits served as "particularly appropriate openings to slave narratives, which were confirmations of identity and celebrations of free individuals emerging out of an institution that strove to keep such individuality invisible, blank, and unformed."[6] They routinely appeared in

Figure I.1.   B. Bell, del¹, Henry Adlard, sc., engraved frontispiece from Frederick Douglass, *Narrative of the Life of Frederick Douglass* (Dublin: Webb and Chapman, 1845). Reproduced with permission, New York Public Library.

the opening pages of slave narratives, lending credibility and authenticity to the slave author and protagonist.

The British frontispiece departs significantly from the frontispiece that appeared in the American edition of Douglass's narrative, published earlier that same year (see figure I.2). Marcus Wood dismisses the American frontispiece as a "poor-quality engraved portrait" much different from the "high-quality engraving, the face executed in stipple" that opened the first edition of Douglass's 1855 autobiography, *My Bondage and My Freedom* (see figure I.3).[7] The American portrait is unsigned and also presumably inspired by a painting of Douglass. But while it lacks the technical skill of the British portrait, it does convey a greater sense of movement and vitality. Douglass's tie is slightly awry and his hair less stylized. Most strikingly, Douglass lacks the curious half-smile that appears in the British frontispiece. In the American portrait, he appears somber and resolute, his lips grimly set. His arms are crossed and his hands closed into fists.

What Douglass thought of the American portrait is unknown, but he did voice considerable displeasure with the British portrait, which reappeared in the Quaker abolitionist Wilson Armistead's *A Tribute For the Negro*,

Figure I.2. [Unknown artist], engraved frontispiece from Frederick Douglass, *Narrative of the Life of Frederick Douglass* (Boston: Anti-Slavery Office, 1846). Courtesy of the Trustees of the Boston Public Library. British editions of Douglass's narrative reverted to the American frontispiece after the first Dublin edition.

published in Manchester in 1848 (see figure I.4). Writing in the pages of his abolitionist newspaper, *The North Star*, Douglass excoriates the artist for rendering him with "a much more kindly and amiable expression than is generally thought to characterize the face of a fugitive slave."[8] "Negroes," Douglass laments, "can never have impartial portraits, at the hands of white artists"; their features are "grossly exaggerat[ed]," distorted by "high cheek bones, distended nostrils, depressed nose, thick lips, and retreating foreheads."[9] With his later publications, Douglass was able to

Frederick Douglass

Figure I.3.   J. C. Buttre, engraved frontispiece from Frederick Douglass, *My Bondage and My Freedom* (New York: Miller, Orton & Mulligan, 1855). Reproduced with permission, the University Library, University of North Carolina, Chapel Hill. This engraving was made from a daguerreotype, which may account for its greater detail and quality.

Frederick Douglass

Figure I.4. Wilson Armistead, *A Tribute for the Negro*. (Manchester: William Irwin, 1848). Reproduced with permission, the University Library, University of North Carolina, Chapel Hill.

exert greater control over his image, commissioning daguerreotypes that, he felt, more accurately reflected his appearance and attitude.[10] For now, however, he chafed against what he saw as racist and grotesque caricature. Perhaps as a result of Douglass's disapproval, subsequent

British editions of Douglass's narrative reverted to the original American frontispiece.

Dickens certainly hated the British frontispiece as well, calling it "hideous and abominable." But was his disgust also a result of the portrait's failure to accurately—and aesthetically—represent Douglass? After all, many British men and women were quite admiring of Douglass's physical appearance, even as they simultaneously perpetuated racial typologies. The Cork *Examiner* of October 15, 1845, described his appearance as "singularly pleasing and agreeable," a fact they partially attributed to his mixed race background: "The hue of his face and hands is rather yellow brown or bronze, while there is little, if anything, in his features of that particular prominence of lower face, thickness of lips, and flatness of nose, which peculiarly characterize the Negro type."[11] In a letter to an American colleague, the British abolitionist John Estlin marveled at Douglass's physical attractiveness to the opposite sex: "You can hardly imagine how he [Douglass] is noticed—*petted* I may say—by the ladies. Some of them really a little exceed the bounds of propriety, or delicacy, as far as appearances are concerned."[12] Did the British frontispiece, by depicting a racially caricatured Douglass, offend Dickens's realist and aesthetic sensibilities?

Then again, perhaps Dickens was expressing repugnance not at the portrait, but at Douglass himself. For Dickens, a vocal opponent of slavery since his 1842 visit to America, racial sympathy could not necessarily erase racial prejudice. During this period, Dickens was beginning to refocus his humanitarian efforts from the international to the local realm, turning away from the problem of American slavery to issues of domestic reform. An admirer of Thomas Carlyle, who would publish several inflammatory and racist pieces condoning West Indian and American slavery over the next few years, Dickens may have been expressing the increasing negrophobia of the period. Douglas Lorimer writes, "The 1850s and 1860s saw the birth of scientific racism and a change in English racial attitudes from the humanitarian response in the early nineteenth century to the racialism of the imperialist era at the close of the Victorian age."[13] In tearing out the portrait and calling it "hideous and abominable," was Dickens expressing his revulsion at the "Negro physiognomy"?

Whatever Dickens's intention, his letter to Macready testifies to the slave narrative's ability to make a powerful impression upon its readers. It also exposes some of the ambiguity surrounding the influence of the American slave narrative on the Victorian novel and novelist. Dickens's simultaneous act of defacement (tearing out the portrait) and dissemination (sending the narrative to a friend) seems, at first, deeply contradictory. On the one hand, the slave narrator's frontispiece was de rigueur, proof that Douglass was real—or, in the words of Augusta Rohrbach, *"really* black."[14] By removing the frontispiece, Dickens was eliminating a mark of racial authenticity, an act that materially as well as substantively undermined the narrative's integrity. On the other hand, the frontispiece in question appeared racially distorted, and Dickens claimed to be editing the text in the name of aesthetics as well as accessibility. Stripped of its prefatory portrait, Douglass's narrative could transcend some of its racial constraints to become a story of universal appeal. Dickens becomes both unofficial editor and publisher of Douglass's *Narrative*. Over the course of the next decade, he would become a writer and reviser of the slave narrative, as well.

While critics have begun to historicize the works of William Blake, Samuel Taylor Coleridge, and Mary Shelley against the transatlantic anti-slave trade and abolition movements, their timeline of inquiry generally ends with the British Abolition Act of 1833, which roughly coincided with the waning years of British Romanticism. Postcolonial critics, meanwhile, have investigated the effects of West Indian slavery in the years following British emancipation, but their focus remains nationally circumscribed, overlooking the growing influence of American slavery in the literature of the Victorian period. This book looks at the shaping influence of the American slave narrative on the Victorian novel in the mid-nineteenth century, a period in which British abolitionists redirected their energies to the eradication of American slavery. It examines how four Victorian novelists—Charlotte Brontë, W. M. Thackeray, Elizabeth Gaskell, and Charles Dickens—integrated generic features of the slave narrative, from the emancipatory plot, to the emphasis on literacy as a tool of liberation, to the ethical implications of resistance and rebellion. Reversing the traditional vector of influence from Britain to America, this project places the American slave narrative in transnational context and reveals its profound impact on the British literary imagination.

Each author in this study found the slave narrative compelling for different reasons. For Brontë, the plight of the American slave resonated with her own experience of "governessing-slavery" and offered a structural model for *Jane Eyre*. For Thackeray, the slave narrative was a competing literary genre, one whose conventions could be exploited and irreverently applied to the situation of the British hack writer in *Pendennis* (1848–50). For Gaskell, the slave narrative was a source of inspiration for *North and South* (1855) and its depiction of the English working class and the geographic and economic divisions that plagued the British nation. Gaskell also mined the slave narrative for its suspenseful and sensational plot lines and applied them to problems of gender and class in her short story "The Grey Woman" (1861) and her novella, *My Lady Ludlow* (1858). As for Dickens, the slave narrative provided a model through which to comment on the British class system and its treatment of convicts in *Great Expectations* (1860–61). The editorial license he took with Douglass's narrative reaches its apotheosis here in his multiple revisions of the fugitive plot.

What follows is a historical background of the slave narrative that details its importance to the transatlantic antislavery movement, identifies its generic features, and clarifies its relationship to adjacent genres. It includes an exploration of the material and imaginative networks in which the slave narrative circulated. These metonymic networks reflect the sprawling reach of Atlantic slavery, connecting disparate nations and cultures and providing the imaginative infrastructure to disseminate the slave narrative. Through these networks, the slave narrative, like countless genres before it, comes into contact with the novel and is integrated into the novelistic world. The preface ends with a consideration of the ethical implications of such transcultural exchange, given slavery's unique horror, and proposes a model of transatlantic influence based on metonymic alliance rather than metaphoric appropriation.

"Literary Nigritudes"

The American slave narrative played a critical role in publicizing the anti-slavery cause during the "interabolition" period, or the period between the British Abolition Act of 1833 and the American Emancipation Proclamation of 1863. Providing autobiographical accounts of the violence and privation experienced by African American slaves, slave narratives enjoyed bestseller status on both sides of the Atlantic. Douglass's 1845 narrative, for example, sold 11,000 American copies and went through nine British editions in its first two years. By 1860, it had sold 30,000 copies in England and America. Other bestselling slave narratives included those of Solomon Northup (27,000 copies in England and America in its first two years),[15] Moses Roper (ten British and American editions between 1837 and 1856),[16] and William Wells Brown (11,000 British copies in its first year).[17] Marion Wilson Starling notes that at least ten slave narratives were listed in the *British Catalog of Books, 1835–1863*. In a period when few books sold more than five hundred copies, slave narratives sold in the tens of thousands.[18] The slave narrative's popularity in turn spawned numerous imitators. Charles Nichols writes, "So successful were the narratives from a commercial point of view that free Negroes and whites took up the pen and wrote on similar subjects. . . . Indeed, by 1850 almost any book by or about a Negro was in great demand [in America and England]."[19]

In Britain, the slave narrative's popularity was further fueled by the lecture tours of American fugitive slaves. Among the first slave narrators to flee to England and achieve celebrity there was Moses Roper, a towering man who was so light-complected that he could pass for white.[20] Arriving in England in 1835, Roper was taken under the wing of British abolitionists and educated at boarding schools and the University College in London. In 1837, he published his *Narrative of the Adventures and Escape of Moses Roper from American Slavery* and embarked on a lecture tour of churches in England, Scotland, and Ireland. Frederick Douglass and William Wells Brown, two of the most famous slave narrators, visited England in the late 1840s and were welcomed with unrivaled interest and enthusiasm. R. J. M. Blackett writes, "Douglass delivered fifty lectures in the first four months of his visit, the number rising by the end of his nineteen-month tour, to three hundred. William Wells Brown estimated that he had traveled twenty thousand miles and given over a thousand lectures in five years."[21] Both men were accepted as authors in their own right, mingling with literary celebrities like Dickens, Alfred Lord Tennyson, Edward Bulwer-Lytton, and

Harriet Martineau.[22] Blackett adds, "Almost every major black leader visited Britain during the thirty years before the Civil War,"[23] and "most areas of Britain were at one time or another visited by these [slave] lecturers," from the largest city to the smallest village (see figure I.5).[24]

With the passage of the Fugitive Slave Law in 1850, the number of American slaves seeking refuge in England only increased. William and Ellen Craft, whose daring escape from slavery involved an ingenious cross-dressing scheme, arrived in Liverpool in 1851. They toured England and Scotland with William Wells Brown and even attended the Great Exhibition of 1851 in the hopes of further publicizing the antislavery cause and provoking a response from visiting American tourists.[25] Henry "Box" Brown, who had escaped to freedom by mailing himself to Philadelphia in a dry-goods box, fled to England in the early 1850s. There, he traveled the country with his antislavery panorama, the *Mirror of Slavery*, and recreated for rapt audiences his escape and "resurrection."[26] In London, the streets were filled with Ethiopian serenaders (and various spin-offs like the "South Carolina Serenaders" and the "Kentucky Minstrels"), blackface entertainers, and purported fugitive slaves eager to satisfy the public's appetite for black music, humor, and stories.[27] Henry Mayhew, in *London Labour and the London Poor*, even describes tableaux vivants that recreated the adventures of "Pompey," from his life on a plantation to his whipping by an overseer to his flight to freedom.[28]

The period of greatest popularity for the slave narrative overlapped with the most vigorous years of transatlantic antislavery cooperation. Following the abolition of slavery throughout the British Empire, British abolitionists redirected their energies to the emancipation of American slaves. In 1839, the British and Foreign Anti-Slavery Society (BFASS) was formed.[29] The following year, the first World Anti-Slavery Convention was held in London. Claire Midgley writes, "[it] was largely a transatlantic convention of British and American abolitionists, and it became the arena in which British campaigners' decision to focus primarily on slavery in the United States was clarified."[30] Over the next few years, the British and Foreign Anti-Slavery Society published three pamphlets on America: *Slavery and the Internal Slave Trade in the United States of North America* (London, 1841), *An Epitome of Anti-Slavery Information* (London, 1843), and *American Slavery* (London, 1846).[31] As Howard Temperley points out, the second World Anti-Slavery Convention, held in 1843, was "virtually a conference on American slavery," and by the 1850s "the antislavery struggle [came] to mean simply the sectional controversy in the United States."[32]

British readers responded eagerly to the slave narrative's abolitionist message. With the passage of the British Abolition Act, the country had refashioned itself into the world's antislavery policeman: the Royal Navy regularly patrolled the seas for slavers, and the nation was seized by a culture of humanitarian reform. The slave narrative also appealed to a diverse audience. Audrey Fisch writes that "a white English working-class factory hand might have read *The Narrative of the Life of Frederick Douglass* as an uplifting story of a poor man's struggle to overcome social barriers

FREDERICK DOUGLASS, THE ESCAPED SLAVE, ON AN ENGLISH PLATFORM, DENOUNCING
SLAVEHOLDERS AND THEIR RELIGIOUS ABETTORS.

"I am filled with unutterable loathing when I contemplate the religious pomp and show, together with the horrible inconsistencies, which co-exist in the Slave States. They have men-stealers for ministers, women-whippers for missionaries, and cradle-plunderers for church members. The man who wields the blood-clotted cow's-hide during the week fills the pulpit on Sunday, and claims to be a minister of the meek and lowly Jesus. The man who robs me of my earnings at the end of each week meet me as a class-leader on Sunday morning, to show me the way of life and the path of salvation. He who sells my sister for purposes of prostitution, stands forth as the pious advocate of purity. We see the thief preaching against theft, and the adulterer against adultery. We have men sold to build churches, women sold to support the gospel, and babes sold to purchase Bibles for the poor heathen! all for the glory of God and the good of souls!"

Such is the language of Frederick Douglass. Nor can we wonder at it. The man who thus could speak—whose utterance is thus full of power and truth—yet in America was a slave, the property of another—sold, or whipt, or shot at his master's will. In the above engraving we see him, as, in the fulness of intellectual might, he stood upon a British platform before thousands who listened and admired, while he pleaded his rights as a man. We shall see him, a few pages further on, whipped by the brutal slave-breaker as if he were a beast—he whose genius and eloquence was to win even the applause of a British audience. In America, the boasted land of freedom—priding itself upon its Declaration of Independence—its doctrine of equality—its free political institutions—its love of universal liberty—its religious life and light—there Douglass was a slave. No wonder, then, that he was eloquent. So monstrous a wrong might make even the dumb speak.

Figure I.5.   [Unknown artist], "Frederick Douglass, the Escaped Slave, on an English Platform, Denouncing Slaveholders and Their Religious Abettors" from *The Uncle Tom's Almanack, or, Abolitionist Memento* (London: J. Cassell, 1853). Reproduced with permission, New York Public Library.

and adversity in the quest for selfhood";[33] and John Bugg contends that the intended audience for Olaudah Equiano's *Narrative* "was less the London literati than the anonymous workers of the industrial north."[34] For middle-class readers, the slave narrative became a kind of "pious pornography,"[35] combining a respectable moral message with elements of sensationalism. Fisch writes that slave narratives offered Victorian readers "the excitement for which they were eager: graphic scenes of torture, murder, sexual violence, and the thrill of escape."[36]

Critics have also pointed to the slave narrative's similarity to other popular genres as a way to explain both its origins and its widespread appeal. Blackett argues, "The narratives could all have been subtitled 'The Progress of the Poor Fugitive,' for they employed the traditions of the odyssey so popular in nineteenth-century literature. Like the pilgrims in Bunyan's *Pilgrim's Progress*—a literary staple of the century—the fugitives were continually confronted by obstacles that tested their resolve, strength of will, and character."[37] Frances Smith Foster likewise draws connections to the spiritual narrative, comparing the slave's resolution to escape slavery to the seminal moment of conversion.[38] Other readers see connections to the captivity narrative (William Andrews, Henry Louis Gates, Jr.), the sentimental novel (Foster and Gates), sensation fiction (Fisch), adventure tales (Starling), working-class autobiographies (Alan Richardson), Grimm's fairy tales (Blackett), and even genres such as the Western (Arna Bontemps) and detective fiction (Gates).

The slave narrative's heterogeneous origins should not, however, discount its status as a genre in its own right.[39] James Olney writes: "All the mixed, heterogeneous, hetero*generic* elements in slave narratives come to be so regular, so constant, so indispensable to the mode that they finally establish a set of conventions—a series of observances that become virtually de rigueur—for slave narratives unto themselves."[40] Olney offers a convenient taxonomy of the genre, including such conventions as "an engraved portrait, signed by the narrator," "a handful of testimonials and/or one or more prefaces or introductions," and "a poetic epigraph, by preference from William Cowper."[41] On the level of the narrative itself, Olney is even more specific, including among other things, "a first sentence beginning, 'I was born . . . ,'" a "description of a cruel master, mistress, or overseer" and subsequent whippings, a "record of the barriers raised against slave literacy and the overwhelming difficulties encountered in learning to read and write," descriptions of hypocritical "Christian" slaveholders, accounts of escape and pursuit by men and dogs, a successful escape to the free North and the "taking of a new last name . . . to accord with new social identity as a free man," and "reflections on slavery."[42]

Olney's catalog of features pertains specifically to the "classic" phase of the slave narrative, or roughly the years of the interabolition period.[43] Prior to the 1830s, slave narratives operated in a broader Atlantic context and bore a greater semblance to adventure tales and conversion narratives. The early slave narratives spanned the globe, tracing their narrators' movements around Africa, Europe, and the Americas. In *The Interesting*

Narrative of the Life of Olaudah Equiano, or Gustavus Vassa, the African, first published in 1789, Equiano describes his birth in present-day Nigeria, his kidnapping by fellow Africans and sale to white slave traders, his ensuing travels to the West Indies, America, and England, his participation in major naval battles and expeditions, and his eventual purchase of his freedom.[44] While Equiano does describe his harrowing experience of the Middle Passage, as well as the cruel treatment of slaves in Virginia, his narrative spends as much time detailing his conversion experience and numerous military feats. *A Narrative of the Most Remarkable Particulars in the Life of James Albert Ukawsaw Gronniosaw, an African Prince, as Related by Himself* (1770), similarly emphasizes Christian conversion and high adventure. Like Equiano, Gronniosaw was born in Africa and sold into the slave trade, spending time in Barbados, America, and England. Yet Gronniosaw experienced little ill treatment, describing his masters as "kind" and expressing gratitude to them for teaching him to read and introducing him to Christianity.[45]

The narratives of Equiano and Gronniosaw were popular among English abolitionists, helping to publicize the evils of the slave trade and contributing to the eventual passage of the Slave Trade Act of 1807. Equiano's narrative, for example, went through thirty-six editions in English, Dutch, and German by 1857.[46] Gronniosaw's narrative, first published in England in 1770, went through twelve editions in all by 1814, "including a translation into Celtic in 1779."[47] With the rise of Garrisonian abolitionism in the 1830s, slave narratives began to develop a sharper abolitionist message and experienced a resurgence in popularity.[48] The antislavery press helped publicize the plight of American slaves to an ever wider audience, and Starling writes that "there were as many purchasers of the popular book-length slave narratives of the 1830s to 1860s on one side of the Atlantic as on the other, and as many publishers."[49]

The revival of interest in the slave narrative led to questions of veracity and authenticity. Part autobiography, part abolitionist propaganda, slave narratives were accused by proslavery advocates of being nothing more than fictions. The *Memoirs of Archy Moore*, published in 1836, was discovered to have been authored not by a Virginia slave, as advertised, but by a white abolitionist named Richard Hildreth. And the *Narrative of James Williams, an American Slave*, "Written by John Greenleaf Whittier from the Verbal Narrative of James Williams," was later discredited based on factual discrepancies.[50] Questions of authenticity similarly haunted the publication of Frederick Douglass's narrative, leading Douglass to defend himself publicly in the pages of the *Liberator*. He disparages those who would depict him "as an imposter—a free Negro who had never been south of Mason and Dixon's line—one whom the abolitionists, acting on the Jesuitical principle, that the end justifies the means, had educated and sent forth to attract attention to their faltering cause."[51] As recently as the mid-twentieth century, scholars continued to cast doubt on the slave narrative's historical authenticity.[52]

The slave narrative's status as *literary* artifact underwent a similar period of critical disapprobation. While a few early readers saw the slave narrative as a seminal contribution to American literature—Theodore Parker called it the one "wholly indigenous and original"[53] American genre and Ephraim Peabody described it as a modern-day Iliad and Odyssey[54]— many readers considered it a literary fad. In the 1850s, *Graham's Magazine* complained that the "whole literary atmosphere has become tainted" with "those literary nigritudes—little tadpoles of the press . . . which run to editions of hundreds of thousands."[55] Today, slave narratives such as those of Douglass and Wells Brown are regarded as major works of American literature, and it is easy to forget that it was only in the last few decades that scholars have begun to treat the slave narrative as more than a minor, ephemeral genre. Starling has explored the genre's "germinating influence on American letters in the 1850s and 1860s," especially Harriet Beecher Stowe's *Uncle Tom's Cabin* (inspired at least partly by the life of runaway slave, Josiah Henson).[56] And Charles Nichols, Henry Louis Gates, Jr., and Melvin Dixon have demonstrated the slave narrative's importance to the development of the African American literary tradition. In contrast, the influence of African American literature on the *British* literary tradition has only begun to be explored.

Metonymic Networks

Since the publication of Paul Gilroy's *The Black Atlantic* (1933), scholars have begun to reconceptualize the cultural space in which English and African American literature circulated in the last three centuries. Moving beyond ethnic and national boundaries, Gilroy posits a "transcultural, international formation" that unites Africa, Europe, and the Americas in a "single, complex unit of analysis" known as the black Atlantic.[57] Reflecting the sprawling reach of the Atlantic slave trade, Gilroy's black Atlantic is "rhizomorphic" and "fractal" in structure: a cultural network that maps onto the economic network of slavery.[58] Taking Gilroy's theory as her starting point, Helen Thomas looks at the intersection of British Romanticism and the African diaspora, placing the works of Blake and Coleridge beside those of early slave narrators like Gronniosaw and Equiano. Europe and Africa, she argues, "have for centuries been shaped by each other" in a process she terms "creolisation," compelling us to consider the "intertextual dialogue between Western and African culture within the slave narratives."[59]

Thomas's timeline of inquiry ends with the abolition of slavery throughout the British Empire. As we know, however, British antislavery reformers subsequently redirected their energies to the abolition of slavery in America. Following the movement of fugitive slaves and antislavery discourse across the Atlantic, Audrey Fisch examines how the black abolitionist campaign was "manipulated into pre-existing Victorian discourses of culture and class, the worker/slave, education and exotica, and . . . English nationalism."[60] And Amanda Claybaugh attempts to articulate "a new transatlanticism" that reconciles the material and imagined networks binding America and Britain, focusing in particular on print culture and social reform. Fisch and Claybaugh contribute to the growing interest in nineteenth-century transatlantic studies, building upon works by Joseph Roach, Brent Edwards, Robert Weisbuch, Paul Giles, and others.[61]

Taking as its case study the American slave narrative and the Victorian novel, this book uncovers the preponderance of "metonymic networks" created by Atlantic slavery. These networks were comprised of the historical, economic, social, and literary ties that linked Britain and America to each other and to the larger Atlantic world.[62] For Gilroy, the image of a ship is a "central organizing symbol" of the black Atlantic, a "living, micro-cultural, micro-political system in motion" that embodies the circulation of ideas as well as enslaved bodies.[63] This book proposes an alternative symbol—that of the runaway slave, himself. Traveling through America and England, the fugitive slave disseminated abolitionist discourse and embodied to audiences the history of Atlantic (and American) slavery. The fugitive slave's literary extension, the slave narrative, performed the same function within the realm of print culture. As Meredith McGill has shown, in this age of literary piracy and reprinting, texts circulated widely and often illegally, a fact that infuriated authors such as Dickens but served to empower "socially marginal" figures like slave narrators.[64] Even those British readers who could not attend antislavery lectures were exposed to the lives of American slaves through the evangelical press, local newspapers, and the publication of slave narratives.

The sheer scope of Atlantic slavery introduced many "contact zones" between the slave and the British public. Defined by Mary Louise Pratt as "social spaces where disparate cultures meet, clash, and grapple with each other, often in highly asymmetrical relations of domination and subordination, like colonialism, slavery, or their aftermaths as they are lived out across the globe today,"[65] contact zones become the highly charged sites of cultural exchange. As mentioned earlier, Thomas calls the process by which such cultures are subsequently shaped "creolisation," a term that captures the often racialized nature of such encounters. For Pratt, the contact zone "is an attempt to invoke the spatial and temporal copresence of subjects previously separated by geographic and historical disjunctures, and whose trajectories now intersect."[66] By displacing African slaves from their homes and resituating them in the Americas and Europe, the Atlantic slave trade created the geographic and historical conditions for such coerced transcultural exchange.

If the slave trade made the Atlantic world contiguous, it also made it complicit. As Blackett points out, "Slavery had been introduced to North America under British rule, and even though America was now independent and responsible for her present actions, Britain could not escape the responsibility for the establishment of slavery in her American colonies."[67] Britain may have abolished slavery throughout its empire, but it remained linked to slavery through its historical role in the Atlantic slave trade, as well as its ongoing consumption of American slave-produced goods such as cotton and tobacco. Thus, for the British to censure American slavery was simultaneously an act of moral obligation and an act of atonement. Moreover, the two nations were drawn ever closer by other networks of "contact and communication." In his farewell speech to the British people on March 30, 1847, Douglass enumerates these connections:

> The reciprocity of religious deputations—the interchange of national addresses—the friendly addresses on peace and upon the subject of temperance—the ecclesiastical connections of the two countries— their vastly increasing commercial intercourse resulting from the recent relaxation of the restrictive laws upon commerce of this country—the influx of British literature into the United States as well as of American literature into this country—the constant tourists—the frequent visits to America by literary and philanthropic men—the improvement in the facility for the transportation of letters through the post-office, in steam navigation, as well as other means of locomotion—the extraordinary power and rapidity with which intelligence is transmitted from one country to another—all conspire to make it a matter of the utmost importance that Great Britain should maintain a healthy moral sentiment on the subject of slavery.[68]

Douglass touches upon a dizzying number of Anglo-American networks: religious, political, social reform, commercial, literary, tourist, postal, and technological. All, however, "conspire" to condemn that network that preceded them all: the network of Atlantic slavery.[69]

The slave trade connects the world; it also "infects" it with its moral taint. But fugitive slaves and their narratives take advantage of these self-same networks to purge the transatlantic community of this infection. Douglass, in the same speech, cries, "I expose slavery in this country, because to expose it is to kill it. . . . To tear off the mask from this abominable system, to expose it to the light of heaven . . . is my object in coming to this country."[70] To destroy the system of slavery, Douglass must reveal its very workings. Douglass's language takes on additional meaning when juxtaposed with *Graham's Magazine*'s plaint that the "whole literary atmosphere has become tainted . . . [with] those literary nigritudes." *Graham's Magazine* denounces slave narratives as a literary plague, an epidemic of "nigritudes" (or black things) that threatens to overtake the entire literary scene. The threat of racial miscegenation haunts this passage, coded in the language of infection. Yet the magazine's fear of the unrestricted circulation of slave bodies or slave texts masks the true moral plague that is American slavery. The slave narratives circulate in opposition to the traffic of human beings, cleansing a corrupted system.

But what if a "contact zone" could reside in the very body of the fugitive slave? If the runaway slave becomes a living symbol of the black Atlantic, he also serves as the traveling locus of cultural exchange. Forced to flee the American south, he crosses the Atlantic, opening up contact zones among evangelicals and abolitionists, Chartists and aristocrats, the Irish and the Scottish. These spaces of cultural exchange are no less implicated in slavery than the first interactions between West African slaves and European slave traders. Yet they differ crucially in allowing resistance against the very institution that underwrites their existence. To use a chemical analogy, a runaway slave becomes a kind of free radical, "unbonded" to his master and highly unpredictable, capable of shifting the asymmetrical power relations typical of contact zones.[71] Douglass speaks of this anxiety of American slaveholders during a reception speech in England on May 12, 1846: "Let one of the slaves get loose, let him summon the people of Britain, and make known to them the conduct of the slaveholders toward their slaves, and it cuts them to the quick . . . the power I exert now is something like the power that is exerted by the man at the end of the lever; my influence now is just in proportion to the distance that I am from the United States."[72] History and geography, which had previously conspired to disempower the slave, now work in his favor.

Among those who entered into these new contact zones were Victorian novelists. Some, like Martineau, interacted with fugitive slaves in person. Others, like Dickens, interacted with fugitive slaves *in text*. The slave narrative acts as a metonymic extension of the fugitive slave, a fact that is made clear in Dickens' declaration, "Here is Frederick Douglass," and in his conflation of Douglass's "hideous and abominable portrait" with the contents of the narrative, itself. This slippage becomes particularly fruitful when we consider how slave narratives may have influenced Victorian novels *on a formal level*. For the fugitive slave was not simply a symbol on the historical level; he also operated as a textual chronotope, through the slave narrative. As the embodied intersection of time and space, geography and history, the fugitive slave circulated within a literary, as well as a social, contact zone.

The fugitive slave chronotope becomes one of the "organizing centers for the fundamental narrative events of the novel," marking the places where the "knots of narrative are tied and untied" and the "primary point[s] from which 'scenes' in a novel unfold."[73] Conceived of as a textual network, the novel radiates outward from these narrative nodes. Each chronotope, Mikhail Bakhtin writes, provides "the basis for distinguishing generic types."[74] Thus, the chronotope of the road is attached, variously, to the chivalric romance, the picaresque, and the historical novel; the chronotope of the castle to the Gothic novel; the chronotope of the provincial town to the nineteenth-century realist novel.[75] These chronotopes vividly inhabit the Victorian novel, from the road in Dickens's *Oliver Twist*, to the castle (or manor) in Emily Brontë's *Wuthering Heights*, to the provincial town in Eliot's *Middlemarch*.

Attached to the slave narrative genre, the fugitive slave becomes another "organizing center" around which a novel may coalesce and diffuse. Bakhtin himself decrees, "the image of man is always intrinsically chronotopic,"[76] containing within himself the intersection of the temporal and spatial axes. Like the "threshold"—another chronotope that Bakhtin analyzes—the word "slave" already possesses both metaphorical and literal meaning in everyday usage. It is connected to experiences of oppression and alienation, powerlessness and degradation, natal alienation and social death.[77] These metaphorical meanings cluster around the literal meaning of "slave" as "a person who is owned by another," as well as the contemporaneous historical meaning of "slave" as "a person of African descent owned by another." The "fugitive slave" carries with it additional associations of liberation and escape, terror and anonymity, resurrection and renewal. It creates an all-encompassing "fugitive-time" (akin to Bakhtin's "mystery- and carnival-time") that divides biographical or chronological time into pre- and post-emancipatory stages. The chronotope of the fugitive slave, like that of the threshold, is tied to a moment of crisis, of epiphany, of ontological as well as physical liberation. It is marked by an insistent teleology toward freedom, intersecting with the chronotope of the road and the chronotope of the sea—the avenues by which fugitive slaves fled the South.

The chronotope of the fugitive slave enters the Victorian novel through the slave narrative. It opens up *textual* contact zones, or literary spaces where the novel's heteroglot structure reveals itself. In other words, it enacts on the textual level the transcultural exchange of Pratt's social contact zones. Within these zones, the novel's dialogism can be seen at work, from its assimilation of literary and extraliterary genres, to its exposure to the historical moment, or "contemporary reality."[78] The knots of narrative are tied and untied around these scenes of illicit reading and writing, of physical privation and punishment, of forced displacement and harrowing escape. Yet these textual contact zones are no less fraught for being narratological. The novel, Bakhtin concedes, is omnivorous. It incorporates other genres with such ease that "it might seem as if the novel is denied any primary means for verbally appropriating reality, that it has no approach of its own, and therefore requires the help of other genres to re-process reality."[79] On a literary level, the novel appears to recreate the asymmetrical relations of domination and subordination that characterize the historical contact zones of slavery and colonialism.

This anxiety is perpetuated by the sheer ubiquity of slavery as metaphor, which threatened to diminish the unique horror of the institution. Douglass cautioned against this very tendency in a speech to the British people:

> I have found persons in this country who have identified the term slavery with which I think it is not, and in some instances, I have feared, in so doing, have rather (unwittingly, I know) detracted much from the horror with which the term slavery is contemplated. It is common in this country to distinguish every bad thing by the name of slavery. Intemperance is slavery; to be deprived of the right to vote is slavery, says one; to have to work hard is slavery, says another. . . . But I am here to say that I think the term slavery is sometimes abused by identifying it with that which it is not. Slavery in the United States is the granting of that power by which one man exercises and enforces a right of property in the body and soul of another."[80]

Metaphorizing slavery and loosely applying it to "every bad thing" becomes a politically charged act. The vehicle (slavery) is suborned to the tenor (intemperance, economic exploitation), creating a rhetorical asymmetry that strips slavery of some of its signifying power.[81]

Douglass recognized that the struggle against slavery had to be waged on multiple fronts—including the linguistic front. On the one hand, slavery had to be exposed, because to "expose it is to kill it."[82] On the other hand, slavery risked becoming *over*exposed, devalued by careless usage. This tension exists on the textual level, as well. While the novel's capaciousness made it a uniquely democratic genre, it introduced countless point of friction via textual contact zones. Narrative, itself, becomes a contested space. Were Victorian novels and novelists integrating the slave narrative to disseminate antislavery sentiment? To illuminate alternate forms of injustice? Or simply to cannibalize the verbal and semantic forms of an exceedingly popular genre? Did the Victorian novel and novelist condone and even promote the sloppy metaphorization that Douglass so feared?

Genre Tectonics and the Textual Atlantic

In *Culture and Imperialism*, Edward Said cautions against such overly hasty calls to judgment. Regarding the tendency of some critics to dismiss the novel as a vehicle of imperialist propaganda, Said writes, "I am not trying to say that the novel—or the culture in the broad sense—'caused' imperialism, but that the novel as a cultural artifact of bourgeois society, and imperialism are unthinkable without each other."[83] In his famous analysis of Jane Austen's *Mansfield Park*, he is careful to identify the workings of imperialism in the novel without engaging in a wholesale condemnation of the genre. The following passage is worth quoting in its entirety:

> It would be silly to expect Jane Austen to treat slavery with anything like the passion of an abolitionist or a newly liberated slave. Yet what I have called the rhetoric of blame, so often now employed by subaltern, minority, or disadvantaged voices, attacks her, and others like her, retrospectively, for being white, privileged, insensitive, complicit. Yes, Austen belonged to a slave-owning society, but do we therefore jettison her novels as so many trivial exercises in aesthetic frumpery? Not at all, I would argue, if we take seriously our intellectual and interpretive vocation to make connections, to deal with as much of the evidence as possible, fully and actually, to read what is there or not there, above all, to see complementarity and interdependence instead of isolated, venerated, or formalized experience that excludes and forbids the hybridizing intrusions of human history"[84]

Said's invocation of "complementarity and interdependence" argues against hermetic categories and distinctions. Just as Austen cannot be compartmentalized as "abolitionist" or "slave power," so her novel cannot be reduced to pro- or anti-imperialist document. Instead, the novel is a cultural form that is both "incorporative" and "quasi-encyclopedic," reflecting the broad, permeating forces of imperialism.[85]

The novel serves not only as a textualized imperial space, but also as a textualized *Atlantic* space; it depicts not only the tensions between metropole and colony, but also larger transnational and transcultural tensions. It does so through a range of literary methods, beginning with—but not exclusive to—character and metaphor. Said and other postcolonial critics have already noted how Britain's reliance on the slave trade and slave economy manifests itself in various nineteenth-century novels, from the Antiguan plantocrat Sir Thomas Bartram in Austen's *Mansfield Park* to the Creole Bertha Mason in Brontë's *Jane Eyre* to the West Indian sugar heiress Miss Schwartz in Thackeray's *Vanity Fair*. And Catherine Gallagher has shown how the rhetoric of slavery permeated the debate over industrialism and promulgated the worker-slave metaphor in nineteenth-century English fiction.[86] Atlantic slavery did not, however, influence British literature solely through these channels. With the publication and dissemination of American slave narratives, Atlantic slavery influenced British literature metonymically, through literary form.

Straddling the metaphoric and metonymic axes, Atlantic slavery reorders the literary, as well as economic, world. It is at once a powerfully organizing metaphor ("Intemperance is slavery; to be deprived of the right to vote is slavery") and a powerfully organizing metonym (slavery makes the Atlantic world contiguous).[87] In fact, the two are inseparably linked, for the slave trade's restructuring of the Atlantic world created the material and imaginative networks that allow metaphors of slavery to be transmitted. A large part of abolitionist strategy was to make these metonymic networks visible, from the abolitionist slogan, "Am I not a man and a brother?" which emphasized a global human community, to the boycott of slave-produced goods, which connected items like sugar to their origin in slave labor ("They do say he takes no sugar in his tea, because he thinks he sees spots of blood in it," a character observes in Gaskell's *My Lady Ludlow*).

The slave narrative becomes part of the heteroglot, multigeneric network of the novel. On a formal level, it makes visible how black *literary*, as well as economic, production contributes to British culture. Textual contact zones become contested sites, featuring the asymmetric push and pull of language, of tenor and vehicle, of metaphor. But contact zones are also the sites of metonymic collision—of what I describe as "genre tectonics." At these narrative fault lines, the slave narrative slides against adjacent genres, triggering moments of linguistic, epistemological, and even ontological crisis. The fugitive slave becomes not only an "organizing center," but also an *epi*center for the fundamental narrative events in the novel. Meaning radiates outward from these narrative nodes, across the metonymic, as well as metaphoric, axis.

It is perhaps unsurprising, then, that those common metaphors of transatlantic relations—"matrix," "web," "rhizomes," and "network"—are metaphors of *metonymic* relations. America, Europe, and Africa comprise "parts of the whole" Atlantic world. Each, in its turn, is both inseparable from, and reflective of, the system from which it emerges. On the textual level, this can be seen in the slave narrative's absorption of novelistic tropes—but it can also be seen reciprocally, in the novel's absorption of slave narrative tropes. Douglass read Dickens; Dickens read Douglass. Each genre participates in the textual Atlantic, a single imaginative space that brings together the literary production of its members. Conceived of this way, the novel is a dynamic system characterized by the metonymics, as well as metaphorics, of slavery and its cultural productions. To quote from the Cowper epigraph that begins this chapter, commerce and art together bind nations into "a vast terraqueous whole," a planetary union that reflects the oceanic and tectonic powers of the geographic—and textual—Atlantic world. Recalling Wai Chee Dimock's conception of "deep time" and her call for a broader, planetary scope in assessing American studies, the textual Atlantic gestures to the larger, planetary scope of Atlantic studies, beginning with the fundamental geologic event that created the Atlantic world: the rifting of Pangea. The genre tectonics that emerge in my study find their precedent here, in the originary, tectonic movement of the Atlantic world.

The following chapters comprise one kind of metonymic network, revealing how the American slave narrative influences and interconnects four Victorian novels. Since this project is primarily a generic study, I do not address novels in which slavery appears in metaphoric or literal guise. Thus, novels such as Thackeray's *Vanity Fair* (with its motif of "Oriental" slavery) and *The Virginians* (which takes place in America and features American slaves), or Wilkie Collins's *Woman in White* (with its theme of female imprisonment) and *Armadale* (which features a mulatto protagonist), fall outside the purview of this study.

The first chapter, on Charlotte Brontë's *Jane Eyre*, expands critical readings of the novel to include not just West Indian, but also American slavery. This chapter builds on biographical and historical evidence to establish the Brontës' exposure to antislavery literary sources. It contends that the structural force of *Jane Eyre* can be attributed not only to adjacent genres such as the spiritual narrative, but also to the slave narrative, a genre that takes on material power in scenes of literacy and resistance within the novel.

The second chapter depicts how Thackeray burlesques the slave narrative in *Pendennis* by emptying the genre of its racial and political signification and applying it to the debate over transatlantic copyright and professional authorship. Parodying abolitionist rhetoric and imagery in his account of young Pendennis's journey to authorship, Thackeray equates the life of the writer with that of the slave: both are the victims of free circulation and economic exploitation. Rather than lament this fact, Thackeray depicts the writer as an opportunist hack who benefits from the sale of his own autobiography. Reducing slavery to an empty metaphor, Thackeray realizes Douglass's greatest fears of uncontrolled rhetorical usage.

The third and fourth chapters look at Elizabeth Gaskell's use of the slave narrative in three of her fictions: a gothic short story, "The Grey Woman" (1861); a provincial novella, *My Lady Ludlow* (1859); and an industrial novel, *North and South* (1855). In "The Grey Woman," Gaskell bases her sensational cross-dressing plot on two slave narratives, Harriet Jacobs's *Incidents in the Life of a Slave Girl* and William and Ellen Craft's *Running a Thousand Miles to Freedom*, applying the unique plight of female slaves to her story of sexual oppression and gender "passing." In *My Lady Ludlow*, she explores the class anxieties that beset a provincial English town, linking the fear of working-class literacy to that of slave literacy. And in *North and South*, she deploys the slave narrative in depicting the struggle between master and man while exposing the British textile industry's connection to American cotton-slavery.

The fifth chapter investigates Charles Dickens's revision of the slave narrative in *Great Expectations* (1860–61). Written on the eve of the American Civil War, *Great Expectations* appears a steadfastly national text, advocating prison reform and chronicling English class divisions. Yet its organization around scenes of incarceration, clandestine reading, violence, and illicit escape resonate with events across the Atlantic and point to the preeminence of the fugitive plot. Resituating the slave narrative in England, Dickens applies its generic paradigm to issues of class mobility, literacy, and freedom, ultimately mounting a plea for gradual reform over violent insurrection.

This study concludes with an epilogue on Robert Louis Stevenson and Fanny Stevenson's collection of stories, *The Dynamiter* (1885). Set against the Fenian dynamite bombings in London, *The Dynamiter* revises the slave narrative to expose England's dwindling moral authority in the late-Victorian period. This epilogue addresses the cultural durability of the slave narrative in the years following the Emancipation Proclamation, while considering how issues of authorship and authenticity continued to haunt the genre into the late nineteenth century.

But to return to Frederick Douglass. There may have been a "hideous and abominable portrait of him in the [*Narrative*]," but contrary to Dickens's fears, it would do little to set readers against Douglass's tale. The British rallied around Douglass, offering him "cordiality," "kind hospitality," and "deep sympathy."[88] In a letter to William Lloyd Garrison, written four months after he first arrived in Britain, Douglass admits, "I can truly say, I have spent some of the happiest moments of my life since landing in this country. I seem to have undergone a transformation. I live a new life."[89] Two years later, in his farewell speech to the British public, Douglass would thank his hosts and cry, "I will endeavor to have daguerreotyped on my heart this sea of upturned faces, and portray the scene to my brethren when I reach America."[90] The British had impressed themselves upon Douglass's life as he had on theirs. With this introduction, here is *The American Slave Narrative and the Victorian Novel*.

1

The Slave Narrative of Jane Eyre

In *Imperialism at Home*, Susan Meyer explores Charlotte Brontë's use of race and empire in *Jane Eyre*. In particular, she is struck by the repeated allusions to bondage and slavery and wonders, "Why should Brontë write a novel permeated with the imagery of slavery, and suggesting the possibility of a slave uprising, in 1846, after the emancipation of the British slaves had already taken place?" In an attempt to reconcile this discrepancy, Meyer speculates, "Perhaps the eight years since emancipation provided enough historical distance for Brontë to make a serious and public, although implicit critique of British slavery and British imperialism in the West Indies."[1] Perhaps. More likely is the possibility that Brontë was thinking not only of West Indian slavery, but also of American slavery.

The transatlantic abolitionist movement was at its height in the mid-1840s, as British abolitionists turned their efforts toward the liberation of American slaves. David Turley writes,

[English abolitionists] and their American collaborators were most extensively and vigorously active in the years between the passage of the emancipation law in Britain and the period of the liberation of the American bondsmen and their initial settlement as freedmen. Within this period the decade from the mid-1830s to the mid-1840s was the highpoint of transatlantic abolitionism as a functioning international enterprise. In these years it overshadowed in the minds of many abolitionists preoccupations with slavery and its aftermath elsewhere within the British empire and outside it. American slavery as an object of concern even matched anxiety over the evil of the international slave trade.[2]

Interest in the West Indies had waned, stemming in part from the postemancipatory economic decline of the colonies and the general failure of the apprenticeship system.[3] Into its place stepped the American slave question, which allowed English reformers a convenient distraction from the troubled "West Indian experiment"[4] and a new opportunity to exhibit their country's enlightened attitude toward slavery.[5]

Many critics have delved into the influence of Atlantic slavery and British imperialism on Brontë and her fiction. Meyer, for one, has amassed compelling evidence that even as a child, Brontë "unabashedly revel[ed] in the racial conflicts of empire."[6] And Humphrey Gawthrop, describing slavery as the *idée fixe* of Emily and Charlotte Brontë," speculates broadly as to possible sources of information and influence—from books available at the local library to the West Indian affiliations of some of their neighbors.[7] Despite the Brontës' relative isolation at Haworth Parsonage, they had access to several newspapers and were quite worldly about contemporary politics, both on the domestic and international level.[8] Charlotte was fond of setting her tales in exotic locales, whether real or fictional, and in her juvenile tales of Angria, written with her brother Branwell, she creates an African state with a ruling white aristocracy and a downtrodden black underclass. Many of the details of Charlotte's stories can be traced to articles about African exploration that were published in *Blackwood's Edinburgh Magazine*, a favorite periodical in the Brontë household.[9] In addition to Africa, the Brontë children were fascinated by American politics. In 1827, Branwell wrote a description of the "Battell [sic] of Wshington [sic]" and in 1829, Charlotte wrote "The American Tale," a short sketch about President Jackson's possible repeal of a tariff on English cotton.[10]

Brontë would have been aware of racial conflict and slavery not only through her reading, but also through her father's connection to evangelical Anglicanism. The Reverend Patrick Brontë's education at Cambridge was partially funded by William Wilberforce, the great English abolitionist, and he was on good terms with Wesleyan Methodists, Quakers, and other Nonconformists, all of whom were united in their disapproval of slavery.[11] Brontë was a close friend of Mary Taylor, a Radical Nonconformist whom she met at Miss Margaret Wooler's School at Roe Head. The Taylors were an unorthodox and strong-minded family, and they played a critical role in Brontë's intellectual development, introducing her to alternate political views as well as to continental art and literature. In a letter to Elizabeth Gaskell, Taylor writes: "[Charlotte Brontë] visited us twice or thrice when she was at Miss Wooler's. We used to dispute about politics and religion. She, a Tory and clergyman's daughter, was always in a minority of one in our house of violent Dissent and Radicalism."[12] Despite their differences of opinion, Brontë and Taylor were both "furious politicians" who revered Harriet Martineau, the writer, abolitionist, and feminist.[13]

Through the 1830s, Brontë corresponded regularly with Mary Taylor, and from 1836–1840, she made several trips to the Red House, the Taylors' home in Gomersal.[14] These trips overlapped with Brontë's employment as a teacher and governess, first at Roe Head from 1835–1838, then at Mrs. Sidgwick's in Stonegappe (near Skipton) and Mrs. White's in

Rawdon from 1839–1841. During this time, Brontë became increasingly depressed about the social and economic degradation she felt at the hands of her employers and students. In her Roe Head journal and her letters of the period, Brontë begins to make explicit comparisons between her plight and that of a slave. In a journal entry from August 11, 1836, she writes,

> The thought came over me: am I to spend all the best part of my life in this wretched bondage, forcibly suppressing my rage at the idleness, the apathy and the hyperbolical and most asinine stupidity of those fatheaded oafs, and on compulsion assuming an air of kindness, patience and assiduity? Must I from day to day sit chained to this chair prisoned within these four bare walls.[15]

The fury that would characterize Jane Eyre's voice seems to have found its inspiration here, in Brontë's frustrated tenure at Roe Head. She repeats the metaphor of enslavement in a letter to Ellen Nussey of 30 June 1839: "I hope my term of bondage [as governess to Mrs. Sidgwick] will soon be expired"[16] and she adopts similar language to describe her sisters' situations. On 2 October 1838, Brontë writes to Nussey, "My sister Emily is gone into a Situation as a teacher in a large school of near forty pupils near Halifax. . . .Hard labour from six in the morning until near eleven at night. with [sic] only one half hour of exercise between—this is slavery I fear she will never stand it—"[17] and on 1 July 1841, in another letter to Nussey, she writes, "I have lost the chance of seeing Anne. She is gone back to 'the Land of Egypt and the House of Bondage.'"[18]

What triggered Brontë's sudden proclivity for metaphors of slavery? The Slave Emancipation Act, which freed slaves throughout the British Empire, was passed in August 1833, so issues of human bondage and suffering were certainly in the air. And governessing had been compared to slavery as far back as Jane Austen's *Emma*, in which Jane Fairfax alludes to the "governess-trade."[19] A third possible source of inspiration emerges from the heightened interest in American slavery that followed West Indian emancipation. From 1834 to 1846, or from the year of West Indian emancipation to the year Brontë began writing *Jane Eyre*, the British public was increasingly exposed to the plight of American slaves through the efforts of the British and Foreign Antislavery Society (BFASS), the publication of slave narratives, and the lecture tours of American fugitive slaves. This convergence of events would gradually but dramatically shift the focus away from the West Indies to America, so much so that by the 1850s, the antislavery struggle became synonymous with the internecine conflict in America.[20]

In 1840, the first World Anti-Slavery Convention was held in London, an event at which British abolitionists dedicated themselves to the eradication of American slavery.[21] Among those who attended was Charles Lenox Remond, an African American orator and son of free blacks who had embarked on an antislavery lecture tour of England in 1840.[22] Also traversing the country on a lecture tour was the fugitive slave, Moses Roper, who fled to England in 1835 (see figure 1.1). Aided by several British abolitionists, Roper attended boarding schools and University College in London. In 1837, he published a narrative of his life and began an extensive speaking tour, traveling to halls and churches throughout Wales, Scotland, and England. By 1846, several other slave narratives had been published in England to popular acclaim, among them the narrative of Moses Grandy (1843). Grandy was forced to buy his freedom three times (he was duped twice), and in the early 1840s, he traveled to England to raise money to purchase the rest of his family's freedom. There, he met the abolitionist George Thompson, a former member of the House of Commons. With Thompson's help, Grandy published his narrative in the hopes that "whatever profit may be obtained by the sale of this book, and all donations with which I may be favoured, will be faithfully employed in redeeming my remaining children and relatives from the dreadful condition of slavery."[23] Then there was the most famous fugitive slave of all, Frederick Douglass, whose narrative was first published in America in 1845. He fled immediately afterward to England, where his movements were covered by major newspapers as well as the provincial press. In December 1846, Douglass spoke at the Leeds Music Hall, and his speech, entitled, "England Should Lead the Cause of Emancipation," was reprinted on 26 December 1846 in the Leeds *Mercury*, one of the papers to which the Brontës subscribed.[24]

Did Brontë know about these American slaves? Did she hear them speak? Did she read their narratives? These are difficult questions to answer, but there is some enticing evidence to suggest that she did. In the 1839 edition of his narrative, Moses Roper appends a list of the churches and halls he visited in his lecture tour. Included on the list are the "Independent," or Congregationalist, churches in Gomersal and Skipton, two small towns near Haworth, where Brontë grew up. Mary Taylor was from Gomersal, and we know Brontë visited her several times between 1836 and 1840. We also know the two women attended services at Gomersal Church.[25] Taylor, with her radical sympathies, would have been a likely candidate to hear one of Roper's lectures. Roper also visited the church at Skipton, which was adjacent to Stonegappe Hall, the home of Brontë's employer, Mrs. Sidgwick. It was during Brontë's employ there that her student Benson Sidgwick, the likely inspiration for *Jane Eyre*'s Master Reed, reportedly threw a Bible at her.[26] A. C. Benson, a Sidgwick relative, recalls, "all that another cousin can recollect of [Charlotte Brontë] is that if she was invited to church [at Skipton] with them, she thought she was being ordered about like a slave, if she was not invited, she imagined she was excluded from the family circle."[27]

Even if she did not see Moses Roper speak, Brontë almost certainly would have heard of him or read his narrative, especially given her appetite for news and politics. According to Marion Starling, "Roper was the slave narrator with the distinction of being the first person to achieve publicity as a fugitive who fled all the way to England from the Southern

Moses Roper,

In 1840.

Figure 1.1.   [Unknown artist], frontispiece for Moses Roper, *Narrative
of the Adventures and Escape of Moses Roper, from American Slavery*
(Berwick-upon-Tweed: Warder Office, 1848). Reproduced with permission,
the University Library, University of North Carolina, Chapel Hill.

States in search of safety."[28] After his narrative's initial publication in London in 1837, a new edition appeared almost every year, and by 1844, it had sold at least 30,000 copies in Great Britain, alone.[29] In his narrative, Roper describes an unsuccessful flight attempt in which, surrounded by slave catchers, he is taken to "the Red House, where they confined me in a room the rest of the night, and in the morning lodged me in the gaol of Caswell Court House."[30] The episode strongly recalls the moment early in *Jane Eyre* when, "like any other rebel slave," Jane struggles to escape Mrs. Reed, Bessie, and Miss Abbot as they confine her in the "red-room."[31]

Ultimately, the most compelling evidence that Brontë was influenced by American slave narratives is neither biographical nor historical, but textual. With its emphasis on literacy, its teleological journey from slavery to freedom, and its ethics of resistance over submission, *Jane Eyre* borrows many of the generic features of the slave narrative. Moreover, the young Jane Eyre *sounds like* a slave narrator, using the rhetorical devices so successfully deployed by Frederick Douglass, the slave narrator whose literary voice Jane most closely approximates. What critics have identified as elements of the spiritual autobiography in *Jane Eyre* can be traced to the slave narrative's reinscription of that form. Sandra Gilbert and Susan Gubar, for example, describe the novel as a revision of Bunyan's "Pilgrim's Progress" and point to Jane's journey from "oppression (at Gateshead)" to "starvation (at Lowood)" to "madness (at Thornfield)," to "coldness (at Marsh End)," to the Celestial City, Ferndean.[32] Each location is allegorically linked to some form of physical or mental tyranny, a formulation that nicely lends itself to *Jane Eyre*'s episodic structure. Yet the novel's stages are defined not so much by Jane's arrivals as by her escapes. Her residencies at Gateshead, Lowood, Thornfield, and Marsh End all terminate as a result of Jane's desire for greater freedom, and each "station" of her journey moves her palpably closer to a truly authentic sense of self.

As the next section will reveal, the language of the slave narrative emerges most distinctly at moments of crisis, when Jane desperately grasps for the words to articulate her condition. It is at these moments that the novel's heteroglot formation congeals around its constitutive parts, and the reader can see the language of slave narrative jostle against the language of gothic romance, ghost story, spiritual narrative, and adventure tale. In keeping with the teleology of the slave narrative, the discussion is structured around the stages or stations in Jane's journey toward freedom. This structure is, by necessity, chronological and diachronic, allowing the reader to track Jane's progress. The first section demonstrates literacy's critical role in giving Jane a voice, first at Gateshead and then at Lowood, where she explicitly identifies herself with the defiant slave. The second section looks at Jane's tenure at Thornfield, a place of "false freedom" that initially offers safe refuge but in turn becomes a locus of servitude and subjugation from which she must escape. The chapter ends with an analysis of Jane's liberation, predicated on her flight from Thornfield and her eventual discovery of her inheritance at Marsh End.

Learning to Read

> From this time I was most narrowly watched. If I was in a separate room any considerable length of time, I was sure to be suspected of having a book, and was at once called to give account of myself.
>
> —Frederick Douglass, *Narrative of the Life of Frederick Douglass, an American Slave*

At Gateshead, reading becomes an illicit act. Jane retreats to a "hiding-place" (7) to read Bewick's *History of British Birds* and is struck by John Reed for her "sneaking way" (8).[33] In a fit of proprietorship, he exclaims, "You have no business to take our books," a claim that encompasses both the material form of books and the act of reading itself. Wielded by the master, literacy becomes a weapon of subjugation, a fact made clear when John Reed flings the volume of Bewick at Jane and causes her to fall and hurt her head. Yet in the moments after her injury, Jane wrests the power of literacy from her attacker:

> The volume was flung, it hit me, and I fell, striking my head against the door and cutting it. The cut bled, the pain was sharp: my terror had passed its climax; other feelings succeeded.
>
> "Wicked and cruel boy!" I said. "You are like a murderer—you are like a slave-driver—you are like the Roman emperors!"
>
> I had read Goldsmith's "History of Rome," and had formed my opinion of Nero, Caligula, &c. Also I had drawn parallels in silence, which I never thought thus to have declared aloud.
>
> "What! What!" he cried. "Did she say that to me? Did you hear her, Eliza and Georgina? Won't I tell mamma? but first—"
>
> He ran headlong at me: I felt him grasp my hair and my shoulder: he had closed with a desperate thing. I really saw in him a tyrant: a murderer. I felt a drop or two of blood from my head trickle down my neck, and was sensible of somewhat pungent suffering: these sensations for the time predominated over fear, and I received him in frantic sort. (8–9)

It takes a book to trigger this abrupt change in Jane, from an ethics of endurance and submission to one of defiance and resistance. In that brief moment after she is hurt, Jane discovers the words to articulate her condition, responding to the physical assault of "Bewick's Birds" with the verbal assault of Goldsmith's "History of Rome." In other words, Jane figuratively throws the book back at Master John. She imaginatively transforms him into a "slave-driver," a "murderer" and a "tyrant," characterizations so potent that Jane is finally able to comprehend her own condition and to resist.

Jane's epithets mark the novel's initiation into the language of slave narrative. While she draws parallels between her own situation and that of the slaves in Goldsmith's history, her language, with its "morbidly" realist, first-person accounts of oppression and violence, is evocative of contemporary African American slave narratives. As Jane is dragged to the redroom, she describes, "I resisted all the way: a new thing for me. . .and, like any other rebel slave, I felt resolved, in my desperation, to go to all lengths" (9). Her sudden rebellion evokes Frederick Douglass's famous resistance to Mr. Covey, a moment that is likewise triggered by an act of violence. Thrown to the floor by Covey, Douglass suddenly "resolved to fight" (81):

> From whence came the spirit, I don't know. . .and, suiting my action to the resolution, I seized Covey hard by the throat; and as I did so, I rose. He held on to me, and I to him. My resistance was so entirely unexpected, that Covey seemed taken all aback. . . . He asked me if I meant to persist in my resistance. I told him I did, come what might; that he had used me like a brute for six months, and that I was determined to be used so no longer. (81)

What had begun as an impulsive act of defiance develops into a permanent change of consciousness. Although Jane is punished for her behavior toward John Reed, she remains incorrigible, lashing out whenever she is later provoked:

> John thrust his tongue in his cheek whenever he saw me, and once attempted chastisement; but as I instantly turned against him, roused by the same sentiment of deep ire and desperate revolt which has stirred my corruption before, he thought it better to desist and ran from me, uttering execrations, and vowing I had burst his nose. I had indeed leveled at that prominent feature as hard a blow as my knuckles could inflict; and when I saw that either that or my look daunted him, I had the greatest inclination to follow up my advantage to purpose. (22)

From meekly submitting to abuse, Jane now strikes back, meeting violence with violence and startling her family with her heretofore unexpected rebelliousness.

The language of slave narrative similarly emerges when Jane confronts her aunt following a visit by Mr. Brocklehurst. Chafing at how her character has been maligned, Jane muses, "*Speak* I must; I had been trodden on severely, and *must* turn: but how? What strength had I to dart retaliation at my antagonist?" (30).[34] Although Jane has not, in this particular case, been physically abused, her response is strikingly visceral; she feels "trodden on" and wonders if she has the "strength" to respond. "Shaking from head to foot, thrilled with ungovernable excitement" (30), she passionately disavows Mrs. Reed, an act that exacts a physical toll on her body. Immediately afterward, she describes,

Ere I had finished this reply my soul began to expand, to exult, with the strangest sense of freedom, of triumph, I ever felt. It seemed as if an invisible bond had burst, and that I had struggled out into unhoped-for liberty. . . . I was left there alone—winner of the field. It was the hardest battle I had fought, and the first victory I had gained. (30–31)

From her dramatic account of physical victory over an oppressor to her language of spiritual liberation, Jane channels the voice of Frederick Douglass. In a parallel moment in his narrative, Frederick Douglass describes the aftermath of his seminal struggle with Mr. Covey:

The battle with Mr. Covey was the turning-point in my career as a slave. It rekindled the few expiring embers of freedom, and revived within me a sense of my own manhood. . . .It was a glorious resurrection from the tomb of slavery, to the heaven of freedom. My long-crushed spirit rose, cowardice departed, bold defiance took its place. (82–83)

In Jane's case, she bursts the "invisible bond" of familial oppression; in Douglass, he throws off the "crush[ing]" weight of psychological oppression. The effect of their rebellion on their oppressors is likewise devastating. Mr. Covey "trembled like a leaf" (81); Mrs. Reed "looked frightened," and "was lifting up her hands, rocking herself to and fro, and even twisting her face as if she would cry" (30–31).

Jane channels the voice of the "rebel slave" in moments of despair as well as triumph. Immediately after she defies Master Reed and is relegated to the red-room, she suffers from overwhelming feelings of powerlessness:

"Unjust!—unjust!" said my reason, forced by the agonizing stimulus into precocious though transitory power; and Resolve, equally wrought up, instigated some strange expedient to achieve escape from unsupportable oppression—as running away, or, if that could not be effected, never eating or drinking more, and letting myself die.

What a consternation of soul was mine that dreary afternoon! How all my brain was in tumult, and all my heart in insurrection! Yet in what darkness, what dense ignorance was the mental battle fought. I could not answer the ceaseless inward question—why I thus suffered; now, at the distance of—I will not say how many years, I see it clearly. (12)

Marcus Wood argues that Jane's feelings are analogized here with "the emotions of slave rebellion" and that her "thought processes and language form a startling alignment with those of a fugitive slave autobiography."[35] "The domestic life of the Reeds," Wood continues, is figured as a "microcosmic planter household," with Jane designated a social "other" because of her subordinate status.[36] Awakened to the injustice of her situation,

Jane enters a period of ontological crisis. Her situation is, in many ways, untenable: having risen up, she can no longer submit quietly to her fate. And though her sentiments may appear overwrought—she is, after all, a young girl who has been disciplined—they reveal a significant shift in perception and action, from the role of quiescent victim to intractable rebel.

Douglass, too, struggles to reconcile himself to his enslaved status. He writes, "I often found myself regretting my own existence, and wishing myself dead; and but the hope of being free, I have no doubt but that I should have killed myself, or done something for which I should have been killed" (56). Later, in his famous apostrophe to the ships in Chesapeake Bay, he cries, "'O that I were free. . . .Why am I a slave? I will run away. I will not stand it. Get caught, or get clear, I'll try it. I had as well die with ague as the fever. I have only one life to lose'" (76). Douglass's queries and resolutions resonate with Jane's, and he similarly considers killing himself or running away. His mental anguish predicts Jane's "consternation of soul," as he writes, "Thus I used to think, and thus I used to speak to myself; goaded almost to madness at one moment, and at the next reconciling myself to my wretched lot" (77). In accordance with Orlando Patterson's definition of slavery, Jane and Douglass seek liberation from social death in the only two ways available to them: through physical death, or through escape.[37]

Jane's juvenile embrace of the language of slave narrative is not without its complications, for she ultimately replaces one form of imaginative excess with another. While she pays tribute to Douglass at these moments of resistance, she also confirms Douglass's greatest fears. As Douglass had said, "I have found persons in this country who have identified the term slavery with which I think it is not, and in some instances, I have feared, in so doing, have rather (unwittingly, I know) detracted much from the horror with which the term slavery is contemplated."[38] In comparing her experience of childhood misery and frustrated literacy to that of slavery, Jane betrays an imaginative extravagance that reflects her own intellectual immaturity. Yet this overzealous adoption of the slave narrative genre is an important part of Jane's maturation, revealing her struggle to find her narrative voice. At these moments of "genre tectonics," we see the collision of generic modes, as Jane experiments with alternate epistemologies, from the gothic to the romantic to the spiritual. This narrative friction is most evident in these early chapters of the novel, when we see more clearly Jane's clumsy "genre-switching," her attempts to channel a new imaginative medium.

One such transitional moment occurs when Jane is imprisoned in the red-room. She observes, "Superstition was with me at that moment; but it was not yet her hour for complete victory: my blood was still warm; the mood of the revolted slave was still bracing me with its vigor; I had to stem a rapid rush of retrospective thought before I quailed to the dismal present" (11). The drastic swing of emotions reflects Jane's incomplete epistemological development, as she subscribes to "superstition," on the one hand, and "the mood of the revolted slave," on the other. Her response is appropriately adolescent: she simply replaces one imaginative extravagance (rebel slave) for another (gothic victim). As the sun sets, Jane describes: "I grew by degrees cold as stone, and then my courage sank. My habitual mood of humiliation, self-doubt, forlorn depression, fell damp on the embers of my decaying ire" (13). Jane's subsequent bout of hysteria represents her definitive return to the realm of the gothic. From hot-blooded slave, Jane now shifts to the opposite extreme, becoming like a corpse—cold, passive, insensate.[39]

The gothic is only one of many genres that Jane experiments with during this childhood period. She recalls how easily frightened and seduced she is by the ghost stories and romances related by Bessie, and she eagerly absorbs the "passages of love and adventure taken from old fairy tales and older ballads; or (as at a later period I discovered) from the pages of 'Pamela,' and 'Henry, Earl of Moreland'" (7). Through such reading, Jane situates herself in the world through the lens of light Romantic fiction, finding easy fictional cognates in the passive gothic victim, the improbably virtuous Pamela, the lonely orphan child of popular songs. Even Bewick's *History of British Birds* is, for Jane, a genre of supernatural fantasy: "Each picture told a story; mysterious often to my undeveloped understanding and imperfect feelings, yet ever profoundly interesting; as interesting as the tales Bessie sometimes narrated on winter evenings" (7). Gazing at one picture, she writes, "I cannot tell what sentiment haunted the quiet solitary churchyard with its inscribed headstone," slipping effortlessly into gothic conjecture. John Reed's arrival, however, forces Jane to abandon her imaginary world for the physical realities of her existence. Fictional terror gives way to the very real terror of bodily violence. Jane writes, "Every nerve I had feared him, and every morsel of flesh on my bones shrank when he came near" (8). At this moment of crisis, the language of gothic tale, of romance, of fairy tale fail her—in fact, Bewick's *History of British Birds* is transformed into a missile to hurt her—and Jane must resort to alternate forms of expression.

Adventure tales and romances, which had once provided pleasurable or thrilling escape, now offer little succor. Jane, it turns out, has outgrown her reading materials. Where she had once "perused with delight" the charms of *Gulliver's Travels*, she now sees in the hero an incarnation of herself: "a most desolate wanderer in most dread and dangerous regions" (17). Likewise, the *Arabian Tales* no longer hold magic for her: "I sat down and endeavoured to read. I could make no sense of the subject; my own thoughts swam always between me and the page I had usually found fascinating" (32). And Mr. Brocklehurst's reading recommendation, the "Child's Guide," comes across as a penny dreadful disguised as a Christian morality tale: "[It is] an account of the awfully sudden death of Martha G—, a naughty child addicted to falsehood and deceit" (29). All these texts are "children's books," composed for the diversion or instruction of impressionable young minds. But fairy tales, religious tracts, and gothic novels no longer captivate or placate Jane; her own life exceeds the imaginative limits of such genres.

Even the Bible provides only partial relief. When Mr. Brocklehurst asks Jane if she is "fond" of the Bible, she responds, "I like Revelations, and the book of Daniel, and Genesis and Samuel, and a little bit of Exodus, and some parts of Kings and Chronicles, and Job and Jonah" (27). These books comprise the narrative portions of the Bible and share a common theme of oppression and resistance. The book of Revelation, with its lurid depiction of Judgment Day, suggests a moment of final reckoning, a millennial apocalypse. Daniel depicts the young man's escape from lions. Genesis includes the story of Cain and Abel and the sale of Joseph by his brothers, Samuel and Kings the history of the Israelites from the death of Moses to their exile, Chronicles the Babylonian Captivity, Exodus the flight from Egypt, Job the question of "why do the righteous suffer?" and Jonah the capture and escape from the whale. Each biblical selection deals explicitly with questions of injustice, endurance, exile, enslavement, and escape—in other words, the questions that figure most prominently in the life of the modern slave. As Lisa Sternlieb argues, "[Jane] finds precedence for her hatred of John Reed in the stories of Cain and Abel and Joseph and his brothers, and she finds hope in the tales of Exodus that the guilty will be punished, the oppressed rewarded."[40] By professing a fondness for these parts of the Bible, Jane declares her solidarity with the oppressed Israelites, much as she had declared her solidarity with Roman slaves.[41]

To some of *Jane Eyre*'s contemporary critics, the novel was less spiritual autobiography than "pre-eminently an anti-Christian composition,"[42] marked by a willingness to skewer Christian hypocrisy and advocate violent resistance. Elizabeth Rigby, in her famous 1849 review of the novel, denounces *Jane Eyre* as "the personification of an unregenerate and undisciplined spirit, the more dangerous to exhibit from that prestige of principle and self-control which is liable to dazzle the eye too much for it to observe the inefficient and unsound foundation on which it rests."[43] Jane is an unworthy heroine of fiction because she is "uninteresting, sententious, pedantic," and—worst of all—rebellious. Rigby continues, "We do not hesitate to say that the tone of mind and thought which has overthrown authority and violated every code human and divine abroad, and fostered Chartism and rebellion at home, is the same which has also written *Jane Eyre*."[44] Jane's greatest flaw, aside from her general unattractiveness, is her proclivity for violent, "anti-Christian" resistance.

Brontë seems to anticipate Rigby's reservations in her novel by placing many of her concerns in the mouth of Helen Burns. To Jane's vow that "I must resist those who punish me unjustly," Helen replies, "Heathens and savage tribes hold that doctrine, but Christians and civilized nations disown it. . . . It is not violence that best overcomes hate—not vengeance that most certainly heals injury" (49). For Helen, the true prescription is to "Read the New Testament, and observe what Christ says, and how he acts; make his word your rule, and his conduct your example. . . . Love your enemies; bless them that curse you; do good to them that hate you and despitefully use you" (49). Helen's advice is culled from the New Testament and espouses a pacifist ethics far removed from the vengeful wrath exhibited by the Old Testament God. But we have seen that, apart from the book of Revelation, Jane is an Old Testament devotee; she prefers to retaliate rather than turn the other cheek.[45] She abhors hypocritical Christianity above all: at Gateshead, she lashes out against John Reed and Mrs. Reed; at Lowood, she resists the sanctimonious Brocklehurst. She admits that she "could not comprehend [Helen's] doctrine of endurance," and though she respects Helen's ethical piety, she ultimately rejects Helen's doctrine for her own. Nonetheless, Helen does temper Jane's impulsiveness and imaginative excess. In the place of extravagant and self-defeating shows of insubordination, Jane learns to be more calculating and covert; she learns how to survive in a disciplinary society while maintaining her hatred for injustice.

Like other dissidents, be they Chartists, Christians, or slaves, Jane must reconcile ethical integrity with practical exigencies. To use an analogue from the abolitionist movement, Jane adopts a stance of Garrisonian non-violence. Her new position emerges most plainly after she is instructed by Mr. Brocklehurst to stand on a pedestal in the middle of the classroom:

> There was I, mounted aloft: I, who had said I could not bear the shame of standing on my natural feet in the middle of the room, was now exposed to general view on a pedestal of infamy. What my sensations were, no language can describe: but just as they all rose, stifling my breath and constricting my throat, a girl came up and passed me: in passing, she lifted her eyes. What a strange light inspired them! What an extraordinary sensation that ray sent through me! How the new feeling bore me up! It was as if a martyr, a hero, had passed a slave or victim, and imparted strength in the transit. I mastered the rising hysteria, lifted up my head, and took a firm stand on the stool. (57)

Jane, who had previously vowed to Helen that she "could not bear" such a disgrace and would even wrest the ruler from her teacher's hand should she be flogged, now submits to her punishment with no visible resistance. She neither lashes out physically, as she did with Master John, or verbally, as she did with Mrs. Reed. Instead, she arrives at a third, more subtle, form of resistance.

Borrowing Christian imagery, Jane likens Helen to a "martyr, a hero," while her self-characterization as "slave or victim" is somewhat more secular. The distinction is significant, for Jane channels Helen's "doctrine of endurance" and transmutes it into a form of resistance she can accept. Where previously she had attempted physical (and verbal) mastery over her opponents, here she demonstrates a mastery over her own self. Lifting herself from the degradation of her situation, Jane becomes a "heroic slave" (to borrow the title of Douglass's 1852 novella)—a slave in fact, but no longer a slave in spirit. And though Jane still feels "crushed and trodden on," wondering afterward, "Could I ever rise more?" she has made a critical choice. Jane is, in her own words, "no Helen Burns" (55), and she will continue to reject the Christian promise of afterlife for an earthly form of resurrection.

The scene of Jane's public humiliation invokes similar scenes of Christian persecution in Goldsmith's *History of Rome* and even John Foxe's *Book of Martyrs*. But it also brings to mind contemporaneous examples of physical exposure and torture. Jane is a "slave or victim," and her summoning to the "pedestal of infamy" serves as a warning to the other "slaves"—in this case, the pupils of Lowood School. Such an episode closes the first chapter of Douglass's *Narrative*, in which the young Douglass is first introduced to the horrors of slavery. Aunt Hester, having disobeyed her master, Colonel Lloyd, is stripped naked and prepared for a whipping. Douglass writes,

> [Colonel Lloyd] took her into the kitchen, and stripped her from neck to waist, leaving her neck, shoulders, and back, entirely naked. He then told her to cross her hands, calling her at the same time a d—d b—h. After crossing her hands, he tied them with a strong rope, and led her to a stool under a large hook in the joist, put in for the purpose. He made her get upon the stool, and tied her hands to the hook. She now stood fair for his infernal purpose. Her arms were stretched up at their full length, so that she stood upon the ends of her toes. He then said to her, "Now, you d—d b—h, I'll learn you how to disobey my orders!" and after rolling up his sleeves, he commenced to lay on the heavy cowskin. . . . I was so terrified and horror-stricken at the sight, that I hid myself in a closet, and dared not venture out till long after the bloody transaction was over. I expected it would be my turn next. It was all new to me. I had never seen any thing like it before. (26)

Before her own public humiliation, Jane had watched Helen "sent to stand in the middle of the large schoolroom," a punishment that "seemed to me in a high degree ignominious, especially for so great a girl—she looked thirteen or upwards" (43). She later witnesses Helen's whipping with a "bunch of twigs": "This ominous tool [Helen] presented to Miss Scratcherd with a respectful curtsy; then she quietly, without being told, unloosed her pinafore, and the teacher instantly and sharply inflicted on her neck a dozen strokes with the bunch of twigs" (45). Helen's disrobing and public flagellation moves Jane later to tell her, "'But then it seems disgraceful to be flogged, and to be sent to stand in the middle of a room full of people; and you are such a great girl: I am far younger than you, and I could not bear it" (47). Jane's emphasis on Helen's age underscores the sexually degrading aspect of her punishment. Helen is a "great girl"; her public disgrace is a breach of her womanly modesty. Although she is not stripped from "neck to waist" like Aunt Hester, she must partially undress to expose her body to the blows of the twigs. And though she is not called a "d—d b—h," she is deemed a "slattern" (45, 62), slovenly in person and, by implication, in morality. Jane experiences a similar bodily mortification when she is placed on the stool, and her situation is made worse by the presence of Brocklehurst, with his menacing masculinity.[46]

In the intensity of these moments, Jane again reaches for literary sustenance in the genre of slave narrative. She learns, however, to modulate her tone when communicating with others, to curb her more extravagant flights of fancy in the interest of credibility. Asked by Miss Temple to defend herself against Brocklehurst's accusations, Jane chooses her words with care:

> I resolved, in the depth of my heart, that I would be most moderate—most correct. . . .Exhausted by emotion, my language was more subdued than it generally was when it developed that sad theme; and mindful of Helen's warnings against the indulgence of resentment, I infused into the narrative far less of gall and wormwood than ordinary. Thus restrained and simplified, it sounded more credible: I felt as I went on that Miss Temple fully believed me (60).

Jane moves away from overheated rhetoric and generic ventriloquism, demonstrating her intellectual and epistemological maturation. In response, Miss Temple agrees to write to Mr. Lloyd for corroboration of Jane's story, assuring her that "if his reply agrees with your statement, you shall be publicly cleared from every imputation" (60). Mr. Lloyd's reappearance here reiterates the importance of rhetorical integrity. The first person to believe Jane's account of injustice at Gateshead, Mr. Lloyd had nonetheless scoffed at her initial complaint, "I was shut up in a room where there is a ghost till after dark" (19). "Ghost!" Mr. Lloyd cries, "What, you are a baby after all! You are afraid of ghosts!" (19). It is only after Jane rejects gothic convention that Mr. Lloyd finally believes her tale. As if mindful of this lesson, Jane refrains from narrative indulgence in recounting her story to Miss Temple, with the result that her character and veracity are upheld.[47]

The change in Jane's narrative method parallels her physical and intellectual maturation. Knowledge replaces brute force as the most tenable strategy of liberation. Jane now "had the means of an excellent education placed in my reach" (71) and learns of "nations and times past; of countries far away; of secrets of nature discovered. . .of books" (62). Education, and specifically literacy, empowers Jane within a power structure that enslaves her, eventually offering her the means of "escape" through her job as governess. It is at Lowood that Jane first learns how to conjugate the French verb, "être," a lesson whose significance is not so much grammatical as ontological: Jane learns how to speak, but she also learns how to be. From these humble beginnings, Jane scratches together the skills necessary to engineer her next escape, this time to the confines of Thornfield.

A New Servitude

Lowood had provided greater autonomy than Gateshead, and so Thornfield promises greater autonomy than Lowood. Still, the ultimate prize remains stubbornly out of reach:

> I desired liberty; for liberty I gasped; for liberty I uttered a prayer; it seemed scattered on the wind then faintly blowing. I abandoned it

and framed a humbler supplication; for chance, stimulus: that petition, too, seemed swept off into vague space: "Then," I cried, half desperate, "grant me at least a new servitude!" (72)

Jane craves the "delightful sounds" of "Liberty, Excitement, Enjoyment" (73), a motto that evokes the French revolutionary cry, "*Liberté, Egalité, Fraternité*" as well as the American promise of "Life, Liberty, and the Pursuit of Happiness." Yet she recognizes her need to compromise, to postpone full liberty to some distance future. Thus, governessing, though a means to escape the "rules and systems" of Lowood, becomes only an intermediary step in her pursuit of self-emancipation.

Where slavery had previous signified Jane's experience of childhood oppression, it now shifts to signify the "new servitude" that is governessing. Blanche Ingram compares governesses to "incubi" (150) and complains of their tendencies toward "mutiny and general blow-up" (153), dismissing "the whole tribe" as "a nuisance" (150). Her choice of language recalls Helen Burns's belief that "heathens and savage tribes hold that doctrine [of violent resistance]" (49) and links Jane's present, economic exploitation to her youthful insubordination. The use of the word "race" likewise ties the two experiences. As a child, Jane had described herself as "an interloper not of [Mrs. Reed's] race, and unconnected with her, after her husband's death, by any tie" (13); now she is figured as "one of the anathematised race" (151) of governesses. Mr. Rochester puts it most bluntly when he proposes marriage to Jane at Thornfield, announcing, "You will give up your governessing slavery at once" (230).

While the experience of slavery is encoded metaphorically in these passages, Brontë also acknowledges the existence of a larger, global network in which these metaphors circulate. In perhaps the most famous passage from the novel, Jane speaks of the universal restiveness of all "human beings":

> Millions are condemned to a stiller doom than mine, and millions are in silent revolt against their lot. Nobody knows how many rebellions besides political rebellions ferment in the masses of life which people earth. Women are supposed to be very calm generally: but women feel just as men feel; they need exercise for their faculties and a field for their efforts as much as their brothers do; they suffer from too rigid a restraint, too absolute a stagnation, precisely as men would suffer. (93)

Critics have noted the gender implications of the above passage, building upon Gilbert and Gubar's contention that "the distinction between male and female images of imprisonment is—and always has been—a distinction between, on the one hand, that which is both metaphysical and metaphorical, and on the other hand, that which is social and actual."[48] Yet Jane's stated solidarity with "millions" of other victims seems to transcend gender—and even racial—boundaries. She feels "just as men feel" and she suffers as much as her "brothers," a rhetorical plaint that resonates with the famous abolitionist plea, "Am I not a man and a brother?" Rochester too relies on the abolitionist motto to emphasize a common humanity that unites disparate groups. He tells Jane, "The Lowood constraint still clings to you somewhat, controlling your features, muffling your voice, and restricting your limbs; and you fear in the presence of a man and a brother—or father, or master, or what you will." (118). Human suffering is universal; it transforms relations of hierarchy (father to son, master to servant) to those of contiguity (brother to brother, human to human).

Slavery is the indexical marker of this global network. Jane alludes to those who are "condemned to a stiller doom than mine," a description that sets up a continuum of suffering that transcends history and geography. Her particular misery does not so much replace or diminish other forms of misery as point them out. In this community of governesses, slaves, men, women—the millions who are "in silent revolt against their lot"—race reveals itself metonymically, through a network of kinship and association. Rochester, for example, describes hiring a mistress as "the next worse thing to buying a slave: both are often by nature, and always by position, inferior: and to live familiarly with inferiors is degrading" (266). Meyer has argued that Brontë "use[s] race metaphorically in [her] fiction...[to] explore issues of gender,"[49] a strategy that risks suborning vehicle (race, slavery) for tenor (gender, governessing). But at this particular moment, slavery is also being used metonymically, as a fixed signifier on the continuum (or signifying chain) of injustice. Slavery becomes the benchmark of degradation, "the worst" thing against which all other relationships are compared.[50] Mere contact with slavery ("to live familiarly with inferiors") infects those around it.

Slavery's metonymic reach extends to its historical and economic role in Atlantic slavery. Everyone is implicated in this network, from the West Indian plantation owner to the English consumer of slave-produced goods. Within the narrative, Bertha Mason has generally been read as the most direct link to Atlantic slavery, a character whose West Indian background and contact with slaves conspire to racialize her character and render her slavelike. For Gayatri Spivak, she is "a figure produced by the axiomatics of imperialism,"[51] an ideological construct of British colonialism. For Susan Meyer, she evokes a history of slave rebellion and the postemancipatory decline of the British West Indian colonies. And for Gilbert and Gubar, her purpose is monitory and psychological: she is a "dark double" who "acts *like* Jane" and also "acts *for* Jane," serving as a repository for Jane's repressed desires.[52]

These readings are not incompatible once Jane's connection to Atlantic slavery, from her appropriation of the slave narrative to her description of a global humanitarian network, reveals itself. Despite her white Englishness, Jane is more accurately the literary and political ally, not the "antipodes," (265) of the West Indian Bertha Mason. Like Jane, Bertha is an outcast. Her behavior parallels Jane's, from her feral rage to her resistance to imprisonment. Both are violently cordoned to a chair, Jane by Bessie and Miss Abbott, Bertha by Grace Poole and Mr. Rochester; both are described as animals, Jane as a "mad cat," a "rat," and a "bad animal," Bertha as a "wild beast" (264), a "hyena" (25), and a "wild animal" (250).[53] If Bertha more broadly represents the vexed consequences of West Indian enslavement and emancipation—in other words, if she becomes an allegorical icon of what Wendell Phillips called "the West Indian experiment"[54]— she also becomes the political precedent by which all subsequent acts of emancipation within the novel are evaluated. Given the historical moment in which Brontë was writing and the political reverberations of West Indian abolition upon American slavery, the character of Jane suggests a sort of "American experiment" who sees in her West Indian analogue the pitfalls of slavery and its aftermath.[55]

In Bertha, Brontë offers a lurid projection of Jane's future. Yet Jane comes close to repeating Bertha's fate, and her straying from the path to emancipation is accompanied by repeated allusions to Eastern slavery. Rochester exclaims, "I would not exchange this one little English girl for the grand Turk's whole seraglio," which provokes Jane to respond, "I'll not stand you an inch in the stead of a seraglio [. . .] so don't consider me an equivalent of one; if you have a fancy for anything in that line, away with you, sir, to the bazaars of Stamboul without delay; and lay out in extensive slave-purchases some of that spare cash you seem at a loss to spend satisfactorily here" (229). Although Jane rejects Rochester's comparison, even vowing to "preach liberty to them that are enslaved" and to "stir up mutiny" (230) she ultimately submits to Rochester's loving "despotism" (234); the "one little English girl" finds herself residing on the same continuum as the seraglio, assessed as "so many tons of flesh and such an assortment of black eyes" (229). Her seduction takes on the weightiness of biblical transgression, as Jane compares herself to the Israelites who, having been led out of Egypt, waver in their quest for freedom: "My future husband was becoming to me my whole world; and more than the world: almost my hope of heaven. He stood between me and every thought of religion, as an eclipse intervenes between man and the broad sun. I could not, in those days, see God for his creature: of whom I had made an idol" (234).[56] Rochester "unworlds" Jane; he replaces the global, collective network in which she had previously situated herself with the egotism of the individual.

During her tenure at Thornfield, the larger world is relegated to the outer edges of Jane's consciousness. But it emerges forcefully in her dreams and artwork, channeled through her "spiritual eye" (107). The image of a turbulent sea and shipwreck is one such vision that repeatedly haunts Jane. It is a common Christian topos, foreshadowing Jane's spiritual foundering. Yet it also has historical resonance when set against the history of Atlantic slavery. One of Jane's watercolors particularly invites such a connection, depicting "clouds low and livid, rolling over a swollen sea":

All the distance was in eclipse; so, too, was the foreground; or, rather, the nearest billows, for there was no land. One gleam of light lifted into relief a half-submerged mast, on which sat a cormorant, dark and large, with wings flecked with foam: its beak held a gold bracelet. . .

sinking below the bird and mast, a drowned corpse glanced through the green water; a fair arm was the only limb clearly visible, whence the bracelet had been washed or torn. (107)

Jane's watercolor is clearly inspired by J. M. W. Turner's famous painting, *The Slave Ship*, or *Slavers Overthrowing the Dead and Dying — Typho[o]n Coming On*, exhibited at the Royal Academy in 1840 (see figure 1.2). Based on the Zong Massacre of 1781, when over a hundred slaves were thrown overboard so a British slaver could collect on its insurance policy, *The Slave Ship* was lauded by John Ruskin for its sublime depiction of the sea:

> Purple and blue, the lurid shadows of the hollow breakers are cast upon the mist of night, which gathers cold and low, advancing like the shallow of death upon the guilty ship as it labours amidst the lightning of the sea, its thin masts written upon the sky in lines of blood, girded with condemnation in that fearful hue which signs the sky with horror, and mixes its flaming flood with the sunlight, and, cast far along the desolate heave of the sepulchral waves, incarnadines the multitudinous sea.[57]

In the foreground of the painting is the shackled leg of a female slave, half-submerged in the roiling waters and incongruously graceful (see figure 1.3). Carrion birds circle the leg, which is in the process of being

Figure 1.2.   J. M. W. Turner, *The Slave Ship (Slavers Throwing Overboard the Dead and Dying, Typho[o]n Coming On)*, 1840. Reproduced with permission, Museum of Fine Arts, Boston.

Figure 1.3. [Detail] J. M. W. Turner, *The Slave Ship* (1840). Reproduced with permission, Museum of Fine Arts, Boston.

devoured by a swarm of sea-creatures. The broken end of the chain waves almost gaily in the air and accentuates the irony of the slave's end: she is free, but dead.

The Slave Ship inspired a great deal of controversy, not the least for its subject matter.[58] Its exhibition was timed to coincide with the first World Anti-Slavery Convention in London. Although England had abolished the slave trade in 1807, the painting was a sordid reminder of the nation's past history, as well as a call to arms for a new generation of abolitionists intent on eradicating American slavery. Abolitionists hoped that just as the actual Zong Massacre had been critical in mobilizing the early anti-slave-trade movement (it was Olaudah Equiano who first shared details of the massacre with the abolitionist Granville Sharp), Turner's rendering of the massacre would help mobilize a new wave of antislavery sentiment.

Jane's version of Turner's painting prefigures her own demise, replacing the leg of the "negress" with "a fair arm," the shackle with a "gold bracelet." As she falls under Rochester's sway, she dreams she is tossed on a buoyant but unquiet sea, where billows of trouble rolled under surges of joy. I thought sometimes I saw beyond its wild waters a shore, sweet as the hills of Beulah; and now and then a freshening gale wakened by hope, bore my spirit triumphantly towards the bourne; but I could not reach it, even in my fancy,—a counteracting breeze blew off land and continually drove me back. (129–30)

Jane catches glimpses of the promised land, yet her successful passage is repeatedly flouted. This dream foreshadows the spiritual upset that ends the second volume of the novel, when Jane discovers Rochester's secret. Falling into a troubled sleep, Jane

heard a flood loosened in remote mountains, and felt the torrent come: to rise I had no will, to flee I had no strength [. . .] it came: in full, heavy swing the torrent poured over [. . .] That bitter hour cannot be described: in truth, "the waters came into my soul; I sank in deep mire: I felt no standing; I came into deep waters; the floods overflowed me." (253)

Although she has escaped marriage to Rochester, Jane imagines her liberation as a form of death.

And yet, Jane does not die. According to Gilbert and Gubar, Jane is ultimately faced with three escape options: escape through flight, escape through starvation, or escape through madness. The first two options fit neatly within Orlando Patterson's paradigm of slavery, in which flight and physical death offer the only true respites from social death. The third option, escape through madness, appears less a true escape than simply another manifestation of social death. The insane person, like the slave, forfeits power, natality, and honor, but unlike the slave who is born into subjugation, the insane person—in this case, Bertha Mason—is what Patterson defines as "an insider who had fallen, one who ceased to belong and had been expelled from normal participation in the community because of a failure to meet certain minimal legal or socioeconomic norms of behavior."[59] Should Jane seek "escape" through insanity, she merely passes into another form of enslavement; already a slave, she will only make a lateral move to "a new servitude."

Jane had already rejected starvation and death as a viable escape option, first when she is imprisoned in the red-room, and subsequently at Lowood, when she declines to follow Helen Burns's doctrine of endurance and posthumous resurrection. She rejects death a third time during her desperate flight from Thornfield, collapsing on the road and crying, "And why cannot I reconcile myself to the prospect of death? Why do I struggle to retain a valueless life? [. . .] To die of want and cold, is a fate to which [my] nature cannot submit passively" (281). Though Jane speaks of her "physical inferiority" (5), her body is deceptively resilient. To Rochester's desperate overtures, she declares, "'I will *not* be yours. *I* care for myself.

The more solitary, the more friendless, the more unsustained I am, the more I will respect myself. I will keep the law given by God; sanctioned by man" (270). Jane's spiritual profession of faith also marks her recommitment to her cause—namely, her own liberation. Those energies that had been diverted to false idols and false escapes are now refocused upon herself, enabling her third, and final, escape. And though Jane is a reluctant fugitive, "pant[ing] to return" (274) to Thornfield, her flight is no expulsion from Paradise but an exodus from Egypt to some yet-unknown promised land.

Once Jane does escape Thornfield, the novel quickly reverts to the language of slave narrative and evokes once again parallel episodes in the American slave's journey to freedom. Remembering his own flight North, Douglass describes his "feelings of great insecurity and loneliness" (111) upon arriving in New York:

> There I was in the midst of thousands. . .of my own brethren—children of a common Father, and yet I dared not to unfold to any of them my sad condition. . . .It was a most painful situation; and, to understand it, one must needs experience it, or imagine himself in similar circumstances . . . I say, let him place himself in my situation—without home or friends—without money or credit—wanting shelter, and no one to give it,. . . and at the same time let him feel that he is pursued by merciless men-hunters, and in total darkness as to what to do, where to go, or where to stay,—perfectly helpless both as to the means of defence and means of escape,—in the midst of plenty, yet suffering the terrible gnawings of hunger,—in the midst of houses, yet having no home [. . .]. (111–112)

Jane is, in fact, placed in such a situation, "without home or friends— without money or credit," in constant fear of exposure as she makes her way not through New York but through Yorkshire. Jane avoids roads and takes to the heath, where she "had a vague dread that cattle might be near, or that some sportsman or poacher might discover me" (275). Just as Douglass is "afraid of speaking to any one for fear of speaking to the wrong one" (111), Jane frets that "strangers would wonder what I am doing, lingering here at the sign-post, evidently objectless and lost. I might be questioned: I could give no answer but that would sound incredible and excite suspicion" (275).

Jane's literalized enactment of the slave's flight extends to include the methods employed to recover her. "The country had been scoured far and wide," St. John later tells Jane, "[but] no vestige of information could be gathered respecting [Jane Eyre]. Yet that she should be found is become a matter of serious urgency: advertisements have been put in all the papers" (324). In eighteenth- and nineteenth-century England and America, it was not uncommon for governesses to run away from unhappy positions. Owners would publish notices in local papers, including a physical description of the woman and sometimes the promise of a monetary reward. Marcus Wood has shown how advertisements for runaway servants bore a striking resemblance to advertisements for runaway slaves—down to the printer's icon of a fleeing man or woman that headed such advertisements.[60] To avoid discovery, runaway slaves like Douglass changed their names, as much to avoid recapture as to symbolize their rebirth as free men.[61] Jane, for "fear [of] discovery" (297), adopts the name Jane Elliott.

It is impossible, of course, to claim Jane's plight ever truly approaches that of American slaves, who were fleeing brutal slave owners, not spurned lovers. But at this moment in the novel, Jane comes closest to approximating the experience of a true runaway slave. She is beset by feelings of "hunger, faintness, chill, and [a] sense of desolation" (281), and this despair exceeds even her childish misery at the hands of the Reeds and Brocklehurst. Having wandered briefly into a life of ignorance and ease, Jane must be reinitiated into the life of the dispossessed, and the slave narrative becomes the engine that propels a reluctant Jane forward, reigniting an emancipatory quest that had temporarily stalled.

Jane's Declaration of Independence

At the height of her enthrallment to Rochester, Jane almost casually identifies a solution to her plight:

> the more he [Rochester] bought me, the more my cheek burned with a sense of annoyance and degradation. . . .I remembered what in the hurry of events, dark and bright, I had wholly forgotten—the letter of my uncle, John Eyre, to Mrs. Reed: his intention to adopt me and make me his legatee. "It would, indeed, be a relief," I thought, "if I had ever so small an independency [. . .] I will write to Madeira the moment I get home, and tell my uncle John I am going to be married, and to whom: if I had but a prospect of one day bringing Mr. Rochester an accession of fortune, I could better endure to be kept by him now." (229)

Jane's words become a portent of the future for, unable to gain true freedom through education or marriage, she is faced with only one last, viable option: Jane must purchase her freedom.

Jane's life of servitude ends definitively on the fifth of November, or Guy Fawkes Day. As a child, Jane had been likened to "a sort of infantine Guy Fawkes," and her rebellion at Gateshead and her discovery of her uncle's legacy both occur around this date. Jane's association with Guy Fawkes underscores her rebellious nature, and like the famous perpetrator of the Gunpowder Plot, she is painted as a traitor and outcast by the Reeds. Yet Guy Fawkes Day is also Jane's Independence Day, the moment at which she finally achieves sovereignty over herself and her life. As such, the holiday invokes Jane's earlier longing for "Liberty, Excitement, Enjoyment" and the republican sentiments of France and America. Jane is a successful rebel, one who is not tortured, killed, and then burned in effigy but who definitively overthrows her oppressors.

Jane's independency gives her just that—independence. Upon learning that she is an heiress, Jane thinks, "It was a grand boon doubtless; and independence would be glorious—yes, I felt that—*that* thought swelled my heart" (326). Still more, the size of her inheritance allows her to purchase not just her own freedom, but the freedom of those she loves. About Mary, Diana, and St. John Rivers, she thinks, "They were under a yoke: I could free them: they were scattered,—I could reunite them—the independence, the affluence which was mine might be theirs too" (328–29). To be sure, Jane seeks to release her cousins from no less than governessing slavery and foreign exile. When St. John resists Jane's generosity, saying, "'Jane: I will be your brother—my sister will be more sisters—without stipulating for this sacrifice of your just rights,'" Jane retorts,

> "'Brother? Yes; at the distance of a thousand leagues! Sisters! Yes; slaving among strangers! I, wealthy—gorged with gold I never earned and do not merit! You, penniless! Famous equality and fraternisation! Close union! Intimate attachment!'" (330)

Jane's choice of words again reveals her indebtedness to French and American ideals of "equality," "fraterni[ty]," and "union." Moreover, her invocation of sister- and brotherhood reinforces Jane's sense of solidarity with those in similarly oppressive plights—the "millions" who are also "in silent revolt against their lot," who are her sisters and brothers in suffering.

Some may find it troubling that Jane's bequest from her uncle is linked to the Madeira wine trade and implicates her in the Atlantic slave economy. Yet slavery connects and contaminates all within its network, leaving no one, as it were, untouched. Others may find it troubling that Jane ultimately gains freedom through financial, rather than ideological, means, taking this as a sign of the novel's fundamentally conservative nature. Yet Jane's liberation is far more radical than it may initially appear. Her recognition of money's critical role in a woman's independence anticipates Virginia Woolf's "A Room of One's Own," but while Woolf argues that a "fixed income" is necessary for a woman to write, Brontë suggests that a woman can write in order to achieve a fixed income. To put it another way, Jane writes her way to freedom.

In her childhood skirmish with Master Reed, Jane learns that literacy, when placed in the hands of the oppressed, can be turned into a weapon of resistance. Master Reed physically injures Jane with Bewick's *History of British Birds*; Jane verbally injures Master Reed with Goldsmith's *History of Rome*. Through her reading of Goldsmith's *History* and the Old Testament Bible, she learns to articulate her own condition, to "[give] tongue," in the words of Frederick Douglass, "to interesting thoughts of my own soul, which had frequently flashed through my mind, and died away for want of utterance" (55). At Lowood, the transgressive nature of literacy is affirmed once again when Jane accidentally drops her slate and incurs Brocklehurst's wrath. She writes,

> [I had not] neglected precautions to secure my personal safety; which I thought would be effected, if I could only elude observation. To this end, I had sat well back on the form, and while seeming to be busy with my sum, had held my slate in such a manner as to conceal my face: I might have escaped notice, had not my treacherous slate somehow happened to slip from my hand and falling with an obtrusive crash, directly drawn every eye upon me; I knew it was all over now, and, as I stooped to pick up the two fragments of slate, I rallied my forces for the worst. (55)

Jane's desire to avoid detection hearkens back to her attempt to conceal herself, in "double retirement," in the window seat with Bewick's *History*. Whether writing or reading, Jane understands implicitly the danger of such activities; they must be done in secret or, at the every least, outside the master's gaze.

While the slate ultimately betrays Jane, it also—at least temporarily—protects her. Jane uses it as a makeshift shield to ensure her "personal safety," hiding behind it to avoid Brocklehurst's scrutiny and recognition. This episode may act as a biographical link to Brontë's own authorial situation, hiding, as she did, behind the pseudonym Currer Bell. But the slate here is described as "treacherous," an example of prosopopoeia that suggests that the slate is both a traitor to Jane *and* a tool of treachery in general. Yes, the slate, as if by its own volition, slips from Jane's hand, but its loud "crash" simply exposes Jane for what she is: a rebel and traitor. Even her subsequent public shaming is a traitor's sentence, apropos of this "infantine Guy Fawkes."

The process by which Jane learns to use literacy as an offensive as well as defensive tool parallels Jane's maturation in general. From her inauspicious beginning scratching out elementary sums on a broken slate, Jane progresses to French and drawing, to greater literary sophistication. This "excellent education" allows Jane to make her way in the world as a governess, and her education continues at Moor House under the tutelage of the Rivers: she "liked to read what they liked to read" and "devoured the books they lent to me" (298), picking up German and even Hindustanee. In her turn, Jane teaches the village schoolchildren how to "write [and] cipher" (306), passing on those skills that had been so hard-won.

It is at Moor House that Jane finally confronts and then exorcises the demons of her past—through writing, no less. The moment she reveals her true identity to St. John parallels the broken-slate episode at Lowood and transforms a moment of shame into one of redemption. As St. John admires Jane's portrait of Rosamond, he suddenly starts:

> What he suddenly saw on this blank paper it was impossible for me to tell: but something had caught his eye. He took it up with a snatch; he

looked at the edge; then shot a glance at me, inexpressibly peculiar and quite incomprehensible: a glance that seemed to take and make note of every point in my shape, face, and dress [. . .] I saw him dexterously tear a narrow slip from the margin. (320)

What Jane has traced "in Indian ink, in [her] own handwriting" are the words "'Jane Eyre'—the work doubtless of some moment of abstraction" (325). St. John's response, his sudden and focused attention, destroys Jane's attempt at anonymity. And yet Jane has unwittingly betrayed herself: in absentmindedly tracing her name, she has written her way to freedom. Scrawled in the margins of a piece of paper, her signature is, quite literally, a piece of "marginalized writing," reflective of Jane's position at the margins of society and the gendered space occupied by "scribbling women."[62] But despite its origin in "some moment of abstraction," Jane's signature is no meaningless or frivolous act. In writing her name, Jane writes herself from the margin to the center, from "Jane Eyre" to *Jane Eyre*.[63]

Though the attention she garners is nothing like the harsh censure of Brocklehurst, Jane has nonetheless exposed herself in a similar moment of carelessness. The "treacherous" slate slips from her hands; the piece of scrap paper scrawled in "some moment of abstraction" reveals her identity. Yet the latter episode proves a corrective to the former. The broken slate, which leads to Jane's public vilification as a "castaway," "interloper," "alien," and "liar" (in the midst of his diatribe, Brocklehurst never uses her real name) gives way to the torn scrap of paper, which reveals her true identity as "Jane Eyre," not "Jane Elliott." In both cases, Jane's person has been revealed by the tools of literacy, but the latter episode restores her to her rightful legacy whereas the former deprives her of dignity. The greater sophistication of the materials similarly reflects the evolution and redemption of Jane's character. Where Jane had once used a slate and chalk to solve sums, she now wields "ultramarine and lake and vermilion" to paint human portraits (325). Her signature in Indian ink becomes a claim to identity and also to authorship, a signal that Jane is ready to take ownership of her self and to acknowledge her previously unknown origins.

Jane's pursuit of true independence continues even after she comes into her inheritance and must stave off the "claims" of St. John. For though St. John wishes to place her under the "yoke" of marriage, Jane has already learned firsthand the impossibility of such a union: St. John offers her only the tepid, Christian alternative to Rochester's "Eastern" sexual enslavement. After her final rejection of St. John's marriage proposal, she writes, "It was *my* time to assume ascendancy. *My* powers were in play, and in force" (358). Spiritual and emotional autonomy follow financial autonomy as Jane's process of restoration continues. Only then can she return to Rochester as a completely "free" woman.

The difference between Jane's flight from Rochester and her return offers an instructive contrast. When she flees Thornfield, Jane's movements are furtive and desperate. She slips away at dawn and attempts to avoid suspicion on the road. Her actions and concerns are those of a fugitive, and her heightened sense of anxiety stems from a fear of recapture. If Thornfield had been her Egypt, Jane is a runaway slave, a latter-day Israelite destined to "drear flight and homeless wandering" (274), hunted like an animal and compelled to take an alias to conceal her identity. Moor House and her job as village schoolmistress offer her temporary but "safe asylum: it was plodding—but then, compared with that of a governess in a rich house, it was independent" (303).

Jane's return is considerably different. Having secured her freedom, she finds herself in a position of power and authority, no longer financially and emotionally dependent upon Rochester, but, in fact, her "own mistress" to his "master." To underscore the change in their relations, Brontë performs what Richard Chase considers a symbolic castration, depriving Rochester of his sight and his right hand. Certainly, Rochester is "unmanned," forced to rely on the woman he had previously treated as a harem girl. But Brontë more importantly deprives him of literacy—the ability to read and write. Jane becomes "his vision" and "his right hand" (384), taking pleasure in "reading to him" and in writing "letter[s] to his dictation" (384). Even when Rochester regains some vision, he still "cannot read or write much" (384).

Why does Brontë so abruptly strip Rochester of literacy even as she allows Jane to exploit its power to greater and greater effect? Feminist critics understandably read this as Jane's womanly empowerment and Rochester's emasculation. But setting aside gender readings, what does this say about power in general—and literary power, in particular?

Even more so than money, literacy provides access to spiritual and physical freedom. Rochester, after all, is still wealthy at the end of the novel, but the injuries to his eyes and hand have lasting epistemological as well as physical effects. Without the ability to read and write, Rochester's "proud independence" is subdued and his knowledge of the world critically circumscribed. According to Marcus Wood, Rochester is thus transformed into "the figure of the slave victim," subordinated to an ascendant Jane. Yet such a reading simply reinscribes a power paradigm from which Jane had been trying to escape. Instead, Brontë offers a new social dynamic based on mediation and reconciliation. Jane describes how

> [Rochester] saw nature—he saw books through me; and never did I weary of gazing for his behalf, and of putting into words the effect of field, tree, town, river, cloud, sunbeam—of the landscape before us; of the weather round us—and impressing by sound on his ear what light could no longer stamp on his eye. (386)

Jane becomes Rochester's epistemological filter, translating written words and visual images into spoken sounds. In other words, she becomes an author and narrator, and this passage becomes a *mise-en-abîme* in which Jane's relationship with the reader is paralleled to Jane's relationship with Rochester.[64] Like Rochester, we "see" books through Jane—and not just the book that is *Jane Eyre*, but Bewick's *History of British Birds*, Goldsmith's *History of Rome*, the Old Testament Bible.

Moreover, the authorial presence of Brontë hovers above the novel, adding a second layer of literary mediation. For in addition to the books we explicitly see through Jane, there are those books we implicitly see through Brontë. The novel's overarching emphasis on literacy and freedom, dispossession and exile, in conjunction with its potent combination of autobiography, history, and gothic fiction, gestures compellingly to the African American slave narrative. And in a final, serendipitous convergence of fact and fiction, *Jane Eyre*'s commercial and literary success ushered in a new period of financial independence for Charlotte Brontë herself. Joining the ranks of Frederick Douglass, William Wells Brown, and other bestselling authors of the 1840s, Brontë had made safe passage from "governessing slavery" to authorship and freedom.

2

Slaves and Brothers in *Pendennis*

On Christmas Eve of 1863, William Thackeray died suddenly of a stroke. In the months that followed, he was eulogized in the nation's newspapers and magazines, perhaps nowhere more extravagantly than in a tribute written by Henry Kingsley, published in *Macmillan's* in February of 1864. Acknowledging Thackeray's widespread appeal, Kingsley imagined how news of Thackeray's death would spread through America, which at that moment was consumed by the Civil War. Kingsley writes,

> [The news] will come first to New York, where they loved him as we did. And the flaneurs of Broadway, and even the busy men in Wall-street, will stay their politics, and remember him. They will say, "Poor Thackeray is dead." [. . .] And so the news will travel southward. Some lean, lithe, deer-eyed quadroon lad will sneak, run swiftly, pause to listen, and then hold steadily forward across the desolate war-wasted space, between the Federal lines and the smouldering watchfires of the Confederates, carrying the news brought by the last mail from Europe, and will come up to a knot of calm, clear-eyed, lean-faced Confederate officers (Oh! That such men should be wasted in such a quarrel, for the sin was not theirs after all); and one of these men will run his eye over the telegrams, and will say to the others, "Poor Thackeray is dead."[1]

One wonders how Thackeray would have responded to Kingsley's mawkish sentiment. "Poor Thackeray," indeed! For a man who had spent his life rejecting the fetishization of authorship and comparing his work to that of bootblack, Kingsley's accolade seems comically inflated.[2] And yet, in Kingsley's earnestness, we can see an unexpected outcome to Thackeray's *procurantism*,[3] his attitude of detachment and nonchalance toward controversial political, social, and literary topics. To be sure, Kingsley's choice of a "lean, lithe, deer-eyed quadroon lad" as agent of transmission can be read as one of the more unfortunate imaginative excesses of the passage, one that taps into romanticized notions of race. But the inclusion of this boy, who embodies the divisive fact of slavery but also delivers news that, for a moment, unites the two sides, emphasizes Thackeray's transcendence of ideological lines. To Kingsley's mind, English citizen, Broadway flaneur, Wall Street businessman, Confederate soldier, and even mulatto child could join in the universal lament raised upon Thackeray's death.

Unlike Dickens and Gaskell, Thackeray is not easily linked to a particular political ideology, and it is this coyness—some would say cowardice—that makes him a particularly difficult subject for the literary critic. As Peter Shillingsburg has noted, Thackeray lacks the moral clarity of a Dickens, and his novels offer no explicit agenda for reform. But in his willingness to satirize everyone, from gentleman to hack writer to servant, Thackeray exhibits not a misanthropic impulse but, more accurately, a *democratic* one. At least some of Thackeray's contemporaries recognized the liberalism concealed behind Thackeray's wit; Theodore Martin, in the April 1853 issue of the *Westminster Review*, writes, "[Thackeray] did not look down upon his fellowmen from those heights of contempt and scorn, which make satirists commonly the most hateful as well as the most profitless of writers. . . . He claimed no superiority, arrogated for himself no peculiar exemption from the vices and follies he satirized."[4]

This is not to say Thackeray was incapable of bigotry or intolerance, but it does suggest that by remaining resolutely apolitical (or "quietist," as he described himself), Thackeray was attempting to move beyond the merely partisan. A case in point is Thackeray's use of the famous abolitionist phrase, "Am I not a man and a brother?"—a phrase he parodied repeatedly over the course of his career. John Sutherland calls it a "professional catch-phrase" that first appeared in Thackeray's sketch, "On Some Political Snobs," published in *Punch* on 4 July 1846. Criticizing extravagant footmen liveries, his sardonic narrator writes, "We can't be men and brothers as long as that poor devil is made an antic before us in his present fashion . . . we have abolished negro slavery. John must be *emancipated from plush*."[5] In *Vanity Fair* (1847–48), Thackeray's narrator asks "leave as a man and a brother not only to introduce [the novel's characters], but occasionally to step down from the platform and talk about them,"[6] an acknowledgment of his flexible and even contradictory narrative role: he is one of us, yet he also judges us.[7]

The phrase most famously ends Thackeray's autobiographical novel *Pendennis*, as the narrator admonishes us to "give a hand of charity to Arthur Pendennis, with all his faults and shortcomings, who does not claim to be a hero, but only a man and a brother."[8] In contemporaneous reviews, critics dwell on the phrase, puzzling over Thackeray's meaning and sometimes accusing him of hypocrisy. An anonymous reviewer in the *Athenaeum*, writing in December of 1850, complains, "how are we to acquit [Thackeray] of being 'a man and a brother,' like every one of those whom he dissects; a creature of mixed motives, into whose authorship a certain professional causticity may have come to be kneaded, from its having been found on former occasions appetizing rather than unpleasant?"[9] (The reviewer complains of Thackeray's "mixed motives" but perhaps should be more concerned with his own mixed metaphors.) That same month, in the *Scotsman*, J. R. Findlay alludes to these same lines with considerably less antagonism: "It is one of [Thackeray's] best peculiarities that he remonstrates as a brother, rather than reproves as a judge, and speaks the bitterest home-truths in a tone generally as full of charity as of contempt."[10] Still another reviewer, David Masson, in the *North British Review* of May 1851, writes, "The last words of his *Pendennis* are a petition for the charity of [Thackeray's] readers in behalf of the principle personage of the story, on the ground that not having meant to represent him as a hero, but 'only a man and a brother,' has exposed his foibles rather too freely. So, also, in almost all his other characters his study seems to be to give the good and the bad together."[11]

What had been a politically charged plea for slave emancipation is emptied out and opened up, applied by Thackeray and his critics to the ethics of author- and readership. Let us be tolerant of Arthur Pendennis, Thackeray seems to argue, for his status as fictional character makes him no less human than the novelist who creates him and the reader who buys the serial of his life. Let us be tolerant too of William Thackeray, whose acerbic wit does not emerge from any imagined superiority but rather from his complicity as a "brother" in virtue and vice. Although Thackeray's use of the motto is at least partly ironic—the abolitionist phrase had by the mid-nineteenth century becomes a cliché—there is also a real earnestness in his plea for tolerance. In other words, even as Thackeray was depoliticizing a threadbare abolitionist catchphrase, he was simultaneously repoliticizing and reenergizing it, broadening its application to those who participated in the market for *literature*. It was precisely Thackeray's ability to see literature as a market commodity detached from aesthetic, political, or social ideology that ironically (and briefly) allowed him to become a model of Victorian liberalism. Everyone, Thackeray suggests, is a man and a brother, for everyone is equally implicated in capitalist getting and spending. As an expression of literary and economic pluralism, the phrase would become the byword of Thackeray's career—and would remain so even after Thackeray subsequently abandoned it in the latter half of his career.

This chapter departs from the more straightforward formal borrowings of the slave narrative demonstrated in other chapters, offering a broader contemplation of the problematics that come with the appropriation of antislavery discourse and its representative genres. In manipulating the abolitionist motto, Thackeray was simultaneously redefining what it meant to write a narrative of the slave experience. His objective in *Pendennis* is not to humanize slaves but to (satirically) dehumanize authors. Rather than depict a universal brotherhood, he depicts a universal chattelhood. Exploiting popular metaphors of slavery, Thackeray situates the hack writer in his own Atlantic labor economy, composing a slave narrative stripped of political ideology and racial specificity. By challenging what it meant to be a "slave narrator," however, Thackeray was simultaneously acknowledging the slave narrative's importance to mid-century print culture. His ironic use of abolitionist discourse, images, and genres underscores their cultural saturation and power. Within this literary economy, Thackeray demonstrates, there is room for both black slave and white author, for slave narrator and "slave" narrator.

Authorship and Slavery

Shillingsburg, Craig Howes, and Sutherland have dealt extensively with Thackeray's relationship to Grub Street and his pragmatic approach to literary production, an approach that led him to clash with Dickens over issues such as the international copyright. While Dickens railed furiously against American publishers and their rampant literary piracy, Thackeray responded with surprising equanimity. Shillingsburg writes, "Thackeray, acknowledging that half a loaf was better than no loaf, laughed and befriended the American publishers: James Fields in Boston, George Putnam in Philadelphia, and, in New York the Appletons and the Harper Brothers, who were the biggest pirates of them all."[12] This pragmatic response to exploitation does not imply Thackeray was writing for altruistic ends or that he undervalued his own work. Thackeray was acutely aware of his market value and, when underpaid, did not hesitate to demand full remuneration. In an 1854 letter to the editor of *Punch*, he calculates his fee with legalistic precision:

> A column of Punch contains 85 lines of 57 letters = 4,760 letters.
> A page = 9,520.
> A page of Newcomes contains 47 lines of 56 letters = 2,612 letters.
> 4 pages = 10,448.
> A page of Blackwood contains 60 lines of 56 letters = 3,360.
> A page of Punch = say 3 pages of Blackwood. 4 of Newcomes.
> 3 pages of Blackwood at 5 guineas is 35 per page of £28 per sheet.[13]

Thackeray's more yielding approach to American publishers can be attributed to his frank awareness that in the absence of an international copyright, he had no legal clout with which to make his claim. Moreover, Thackeray recognized the danger of alienating his American readers, as Dickens did with his voluble attack on literary piracy in the 1840s and 1850s. As part of a transatlantic publishing economy, Thackeray recognized where he wielded—and lacked—power.

Part of Thackeray's greater pliancy can be attributed to a fundamental difference in his conception of authorship. In his 1864 *Cornhill Magazine* memorial to Thackeray, Dickens admits, "We had our differences of opinion. I thought that he too much feigned a want of earnestness, and that he made a pretence of undervaluing his art, which was no good for the art that he held in trust."[14] While Dickens envisioned the writer as a Romantic man of letters, Thackeray, in Shillingsburg's words, "pictured the author in a natural world beset by natural evils, fighting the same fight that other tradesmen fought, and like them capable of self-reliance and economic competence, though perhaps occasionally in need of a hand when things got especially rough."[15] This emphatically practical attitude toward authorship emerged from Thackeray's long career as a "hack writer," or writer for hire. In *Pendennis*, Thackeray describes the hack writer as "Pegasus in harness," an image that yokes a mythic animal to the mundane machinery of Victorian publishing. The hack writer, despite his pretensions, is less Pegasus than humble workhorse.

Thackeray's image of writer as chattel exploited popular metaphors of slavery as a dehumanizing, degrading force. Marcus Wood describes how "the comparison of slaves with horses had become a staple of abolition propaganda" in the mid-nineteenth century, inspiring Thomas Carlyle's satirical conflation of black slave and horse in his "Occasional Discourse on the Negro Question" (1849) and *Latter Day Pamphlets* (1850).[16] Lamenting the postemancipatory decline of the West Indian sugar colonies, Carlyle derides the emancipated slave as having "excellent horse-jaws"[17] and mockingly anticipates the day that "in the progress of Emancipation," not just blacks but "all the Horses also are to be emancipated":

The Horse, poor dumb four-footed fellow, he too has his private feelings, his affections, gratitudes; and deserves good usage; no human master, without crime, shall treat him unjustly either, or recklessly lay on the whip where it is not needed. . . . "Am I not a horse, and half-brother?"—To remedy which, so far as remediable, fancy—the horses all "mancipated"; restored to their primeval right of property in the grass of this Globe.[18]

Pushing the metaphor to the point of absurdity, Carlyle skewers abolitionist sentiment by subverting its famous motto. Instead of a black slave pleading, "Am I not a man and a brother?" he depicts a horse whinnying, "Am I not a horse, and half-brother?" Carlyle suggests that in their eagerness to affirm the slave's humanity, abolitionists go too far: if the slave is treated like an animal, is not the animal treated, then, like a slave? Should we not, then, establish a "UNIVERSAL ABOLITION-OF-PAIN ASSOCIATION" that includes all who believe themselves dehumanized—including animals, themselves?

An admirer and friend of Carlyle, Thackeray seemed to share his impatience with those who hopped on the "emancipation" bandwagon. While Thackeray tapped into a long tradition of horse-slave metaphors in coining "Pegasus in harness," he also resisted the excessive degradation of authorship in the same way he resisted its excessive aggrandizement. He maintained a satiric distance to popular comparisons of authorship to slavery, which authors like Dickens seized upon to articulate their fractious relationship with American publishers. In 1847, *Punch* claimed, "An

English writer is treated by America as America treats her negroes: he is turned into ready money for the benefit of the smart dealer who robs him. His brains are taken to market, and knocked down to the highest bidder."[19] Such rhetoric, which inflamed already existing tensions between America and England, reduced American booksellers to money-hungry crooks, real-life "*Fagins* of letters."[20] The British author, meanwhile, became the hapless victim of the capitalist market, his wares (or brains) auctioned off without his permission, as a black slave was auctioned off to ruthless slave owners.[21] As Charles Reade acerbically observed, "A Briton's literary property is less safe than his house, hovel, haystack and dunghill."[22]

The problem with the slavery metaphor, however, was the plain fact that a British author *chose* to enter the literary profession and stood to gain financially from his product, despite the inevitable losses to unscrupulous American publishers. Likewise, the publisher chose which books to purchase and which to reject, turning the relationship into a mutually beneficial exchange between two willing parties. In *Pendennis*, the friction between these two points of view, one exploitative, the other reciprocal, is played out in the debate between Pendennis and Warrington. Adopting the indignant tone of *Punch*, Pendennis argues,

> "No man shall tell me that a man of genius, as [the author] Shandon is, ought to be driven by such a vulgar slave driver, as yonder Mr. Bungay, whom we have just left, who fattens on the profits of the other's brains, and enriches himself upon his journeyman's labour. It makes me indignant to see a gentleman the serf of such a creature as that, of a man who can't speak the language that he lives by, who is not fit to black Shandon's boots." (P I: 327)

According to Pen, the author, like the slave, is shamelessly exploited by his handlers, reduced from his gentlemanly, even heroic status to that of "serf" and servant. But according to Thackeray, the author's profession is no loftier than a bootblack's, lending amusing irony to Pen's overheated objections. Bungay may not be "fit to black Shandon's boots," but Shandon is quite fit to shine Bungay's.

Warrington, a seasoned veteran of the literary market, meanwhile scoffs at Pen's inflated opinion of authorship. "I am a prose labourer," he flatly admits, while "you, my boy, are a poet in a small way, and so, I suppose, consider you are authorized to be flighty. What is it you want? Do you want a body of capitalists that shall be forced to purchase the works of all authors, who may present themselves, manuscript in hand?" (P I: 328). In Pen's quixotic vision of literary authorship, the writer, or "man of genius," deserves to be treated as a gentleman and king, but is instead treated as a slave. In Warrington's more pragmatic eyes, the writer is neither genius nor slave but a hack writer (and bootblack), hired to perform a job and please his publisher and, ultimately, the consumer. Like all writers, Pendennis, true to his nickname, is merely a "pen"—a commodity for sale. Warrington explains, "capital is absolute, as times go, and is perforce the bargain-master. It has a right to deal with the literary inventor as with any other;—if I produce a novelty in the book trade, I must do the best I can with it; but I can no more force Mr. Murray to purchase my book of travels or sermons, than I can compel Mr. Tattersall to give me a hundred guineas for my horse. I may have my own ideas of the value of my Pegasus, and think him the most wonderful of animals; but the dealer has a right to his opinion, too, and may want a lady's horse, or a cob for a heavy timid rider, or a sound hack for the road, and my beast won't suit him." (P I: 328)

Warrington's expansion of the Pegasus metaphor is tongue-in-cheek, but he hesitates to leap, as Pen does, from horse selling to human selling. Instead, he maintains that the literary market is as prosaic as any other legitimate market for goods, where the ethics of capitalism prevail. In the place of the "vulgar slave driver" Bungay, we have the abstracted "bargain master," capital. Warrington's use of less inflammatory metaphors underscores his reluctance to romanticize the writing profession or to demonize the publisher—in other words, to personalize the professional.

Throughout the novel, Warrington continues to defuse incendiary rhetoric through such skilled manipulation of metaphors. His strategy is double-pronged—to undermine or to exaggerate in order to critique—and reveals his satiric sensibility. To Pen's sanctimonious indignation at Shandon's plight, Warrington responds by revealing the banality of literary work. Elsewhere, he willfully inflates the mundane to the point of absurdity. For example Pen, having rediscovered the manuscript for *Walter Lorraine*, his first novel, asks Warrington, "Shall we take him [*Walter Lorraine*] to the publishers, or make an *auto-da-fe* of him?" (P II: 26), to which Warrington responds, "You have much too great a value for him to hurt a hair of his head" (P II: 26). The personification of *Walter Lorraine* is complicated by the fact that *Walter Lorraine* is really the story of Pendennis, thinly veiled; by burning his novel, Pen would perform a metaphoric homicide-suicide. Yet Warrington turns a potentially grim metaphor into a satirical conceit:

"No, we won't burn him: we will carry him to the Egyptians, and sell him. We will exchange him for money, yea, for silver and gold, and for beef and for liquors, and for tobacco and for raiment. This youth will fetch some price in the market; for he is a comely lad, though not over strong; and we will sell him for a hundred piastres to Bacon or Bungay." (P II: 26–27)

Adopting Pen's metaphor of authorship as slavery, Warrington fabricates an absurd auction scene, one in which he and Pen become human traffickers. Yet Warrington's conceit is notable for the way it shifts the author's role from commercial victim to commercial participant. Pen, like Bacon and Bungay, stands to profit from the sale of *Walter Lorraine*, and his novel, despite its personification as a slave, is little more than a commodity or other fungible good.

Warrington's use of slavery metaphors is, above all, ironic. He seeks not to humanize injustice but to dehumanize commerce. In the same way he shuns the title of artist or poet for "prose-labourer," he harbors little romantic sentiment when it comes to the literary market. And though he talks of *Walter Lorraine*'s sale in extravagant terms, it is clear that this "comely young lad" is far from human and his sale far from ethically dubious. The looseness with which Thackeray deploys his metaphors of slavery suggests that, depending on the situation, every person cycles through the position of slave or slave driver, sometimes occupying the positions simultaneously. Captain Shandon, reading the *Pall-Mall Gazette*, remarks to his wife that

> Jack Finucane's hand was no longer visible in the leading articles, and that Mr. Warrington must be at work there again. "I know the crack of his whip in a hundred, and the cut which the fellow's thong leaves. There's Jack Bludyer, goes to work like a butcher, and mangles a subject. Mr. Warrington finishes a man, and lays his cuts neat and regular, straight down the back, and drawing blood every line;" at which dreadful metaphor, Mrs. Shandon said, "Law, Charles, how can you talk so!" (P II: 141)

In a humorous variation of the phrase "the pen is mightier than the sword," the pen here is likened to a less noble weapon, the whip. The author is figured not as a knight but as a slave driver, whose cuts are offensive and brutal. His victims? The "subject[s]" of his articles, whom the author skewers or mocks. Yet Mrs. Shandon's shock at her husband's "dreadful metaphor" does not prevent him from subsequently announcing that he will "go back into harness soon" (P II: 141). Figuratively linking the "Pegasus in harness" metaphor to that of the prose-labourer-cum-slave, Shandon acknowledges his mutual position as horse and driver, victim and administrator of the lash.

That one's writing style can be compared to the cut of a whip is an image that exploits common notions of authority and ownership. Whether the property is literary (a novel or article) or human (a slave), both are "marked" by the proprietor. Dickens, in the "Slavery" chapter of *American Notes*, describes how "American taskmasters . . . learn to write with pens of red-hot iron on the human face, rack their poetic fancies for liveries of mutilation which their slaves shall wear for life and carry to the grave,"[23] a statement that simultaneously evokes Dickens's fury at American appropriation of his own literary property.[24] And Frederick Douglass, in a speech to the British people that cites *American Notes*, describes how slaves are "branded with red-hot irons, the initials of their master's name burned into their flesh; and their masters advertise the fact of their being thus branded with their own signature."[25] In this way, Douglass declares, "the slave-dealer boldly publishes his infamous acts to the world."[26] Inscribed with his master's signature and circulated like a printed text, the slave becomes a literalized embodiment of a novel like *Walter Lorraine*.

Earlier, Pen had accused Warrington of "deal[ing] in metaphors" in his irreverent summation of the literary market. But metaphors are, in fact, authors' stock in trade (to use another metaphor). Shandon, Warrington, and even Pen traffic in *words*, and their proclivity for elaborate conceits are a form of market display that, like the slave dealer's initials on his slave, verge on advertising and even propaganda. But lest the reader err on the side of misplaced sympathy or outrage, the narrator informs us that though "Pegasus trots in harness, over the stony pavement, and pulls a cart or cab behind him" and often "does his work with panting sides and trembling knees, and not seldom gets a cut of the whip from his driver," we should not be "too prodigal of our pity upon Pegasus":

> There is no reason why this animal should be exempt from labour, or illness, or decay, any more than any of the other creatures of God's world. If he gets the whip, Pegasus often deserves it, and I for one am quite ready to protest with my friend, George Warrington, against the doctrine which some poetical sympathizers are inclined to put forward, viz., that men of letters, and what is called genius, are to be exempt from the prose duties of this daily, bread-wanting, tax-paying life, and are not to be made to work and pay like their neighbours. (P II: 353–354)

In an interesting reversal, the narrator initially expands upon the "Pegasus in harness" conceit but rather abruptly withdraws from metaphorization, making clear that Pegasus is no special victim but rather, a fellow citizen, subject to the same travails as his neighbors. If the hack writer is indeed a "man and a brother," he must partake in the burdens as well as privileges of such a position.

Here again, we see the influence of Carlyle in the depiction of a recalcitrant horse. In the same passage from *Latter Day Pamphlets* where he ironically calls for the emancipation of all horses, Carlyle attacks the ensuing breakdown of the labor economy, drawing a connection between this equine dystopia and the economic crisis in the West Indies and Ireland. Approaching an emancipated horse, "Farmer Hodge" pleads,

> Help me to plough this day, Black Dobbin: oats in full measure if thou wilt. "Hlunh, No—thank!" snorts Black Dobbin; he prefers glorious liberty and the grass. Bay Darby, wilt not thou perhaps? "Hlunh!"— Gray Joan, then, my beautiful broad-bottomed mare,—O Heaven, she too answers Hlunh! Not a quadruped of them will plough a stroke for me. Corn-crops are *ended* in this world! . . . Small kindness to Hodge's horses to emancipate them! The fate of all emancipated horses is, sooner or later, inevitable. To have in this habitable Earth no grass to eat,—in Black Jamaica gradually none, as in White Connemara already none.[27]

Carlyle allegorizes the failures of emancipation in "the lazy refusal to work" by "Black Dobbin," "Bay Darby," and "Gray Joan," equine stand-ins for the "Black West Indies" and "White Ireland."[28] Freedom, Carlyle argues, has become conflated with indolence. Horses—and former slaves—must be *made* to work.

"Pegasus in harness" might also demur from working, given the opportunity, but Thackeray cautions us against misguided sympathy. All animals—including hack writers—must be made to work, and if this fate is misrepresented as slavery, so be it. As Thomas L. Jeffers writes, "Thackeray finds nothing cruel about the cash nexus."[29] In *Pendennis*, the true tragedy lies in idleness, not toil. Pen's major flaw, at least at the beginning of the novel, is his laziness. Jeffers continues, "Spoiled by his mother and her small household, he escapes a life of idleness only by the grace of imminent poverty."[30] Pen ironically escapes a life of parasitism by his introduction into the Atlantic publishing economy. This economy is *not* a slave economy in the way Jamaica is figured by Carlyle as such, and Thackeray does not go so far as to suggest Pen risks becoming a domestic incarnation of the West Indies or Ireland. Yet Pen now enters a world that is not simply infiltrated by metaphors of slavery but also by the cultural production of American slaves. The flexibility and adaptability of this space, for white as well as black author, is the focus of the next section.

Slave Narratives and "Slave" Narratives

The ubiquity of slave metaphors in *Pendennis* leads Deborah Thomas to conclude that slavery, according to Thackeray, is a universal curse, one that victimizes the lowly and great alike. And certainly, Thackeray is almost promiscuous in his use of the figure, likening everything—from marriage to valetry to governessing—to slavery. "How many governesses are there in the world . . . how many ladies, whose necessities make them slaves and companions by profession!" (P II: 278), the narrator wonders, evoking a comparison made famous by Charlotte Brontë. Pen's relationship with women is described as a form of Eastern slavery, with himself as a "sultan" and "despot": "The women had spoiled him, as we like them and as they like to do. They had cloyed him with obedience, and surfeited him with sweet respect and submission, until he grew weary of the slaves who waited on him" (P II: 143). And Morgan, the manservant of Major Pendennis, chafes under his servitude, eventually rebelling with the cry, "I'll be your beast, and your brute, and your dog, no more" (P II: 296).

These instances of figurative slavery had become themselves as threadbare as the abolitionist phrase, "Am I not a man and a brother," but where Thackeray injects novelty is in his opportunistic attitude toward the business of human commerce, Morgan, for example, overthrows subjugation through economic means; having accumulated a good deal of wealth through speculative ventures, he purchases the very house in which the Major resides. Flush with his newfound power, he goes so far as to perpetuate the cycle of enslavement, subsequently tyrannizing a young housekeeper "who was known by the name of Betty to her mistress and of 'Slavey' to Mr. Morgan" (P II: 301) and Mrs. Brixam, a clergyman's widow whose lease he buys from under her. The narrator tersely notes, "Mrs. Brixam was Morgan's slave. He was his landlady's landlord. . . . She was his slave. The little black profiles of her son and daughter . . . [were] now Morgan's property" (P II: 294). The ease with which power relations are subverted testifies to the transformative effect of capital. From the position of subordinate or peer, Morgan now finds himself in the position of landlord and owner, blithely exploiting others in the way he had once been exploited.

It is an attitude to which Pen soon finds himself converted, as he demonstrates in his candid assessment of marriage as a business transaction. He asks Blanche Amory,

> If I offer myself to you because I think we have a fair chance of being happy together, and because by your help I may get for both of us a good place and a not undistinguished name, why ask me to feign raptures and counterfeit romance, in which neither of us believe? [. . .] Do you want me to make you verses as in the days when we were— when we were children? I will if you like, and sell them to Bacon and Bungay afterwards. (P II: 266)

Pen offers himself up for sale in the same way he offers his love poetry to publishers, and he is ruthlessly pragmatic about the economic benefits for both parties. Like his pretty verses, Pen is a commodity, as marketable (and banal) as the box of Fortnum and Mason bonbons "wrapped up in ready-made French verses, of the most tender kind" which he promises to send along with the poems "of his own manufacture" (P II: 267). Prefab sentiment replaces genuine affection; in fact, emerging as it does from commercial motives, prefab sentiment is perhaps *more* genuine than the potentially "feign[ed] raptures" and "counterfeit romance" of love. As if to stave off the disapproving reader, the narrator closes the chapter with the defense,

> And if, like many a worse and better man, Arthur Pendennis, the widow's son, was meditating an apostasy, and going to sell himself to—we all know whom,—at least the renegade did not pretend to be a believer in the creed to which he was ready to swear. And if every woman and man in this kingdom, who has sold her or himself for money or position, as Mr. Pendennis was about to do, would but purchase a copy of his memoirs, what tons of volumes Messrs. Bradbury and Evans would sell! (P II: 267)

In this homage to economic liberalism, every man and woman is implicated in the market for romantic, political, and literary goods. Those who sell themselves subsequently purchase the (literary) life of others, participating at both ends of the supply chain. And even Pen, who sells himself to Blanche Amory for "money or position," stands to benefit doubly through the sale of his memoirs, a copy of which presumably rests in the reader's hands.

This moment recalls Pen's sale of *Walter Lorraine*, another autobiography that stands as a metonym for a person. This time, though, Bradbury and Evans, Thackeray's actual publisher, is invoked, bringing the fictional events of the novel squarely into the realm of reality. The circulation numbers for *Pendennis* are, it is implied, practically limitless; if everyone who is a "slave" should buy Pen's "slave" memoirs, then Bradbury and Evans, Thackeray's own "Bacon and Bungay," stands to make a fortune. Thus, in a world in which everyone sells themselves in one way or another, the publishing industry offers an unexpected space of democratic potential. "We are all hacks," Warrington memorably tells Pen, and so Pen and Thackeray now tell us. "Like many a worse and better men," the eligible bachelor—or writer—sells himself in a mutually remunerative transaction. *Pendennis* becomes a "slave" narrative stripped of its political and racial specificity—emptied out in the way the abolitionist plea "Am I not a man and a brother?" is emptied out. What begins as a critique of the literary market's brutality becomes a celebration of its economic profitability and openness.

Possibly coded in this passage, which appeared in the October 1850 number, is the popular success of actual slave narratives. Considered as a publishing phenomenon separate from its propagandistic role, the slave narrative benefited from the literary market's conviction that "capital is absolute [. . .] and is perforce the bargain-master" (P I: 328). In the realm of book publishing, the slave could attain some certain authority; and indeed, aspects of the market that aggravated authors like Dickens could be turned to the slave author's advantage. Meredith McGill, in her study of reprinting in the nineteenth century, argues:

> the popular circulation of uncopyrighted texts helped to give certain kinds of writing by socially marginal authors a powerful cultural presence. For instance, both women and African-American authors gained broad readerships through the evangelical press, which depended on a combination of market mechanisms and charitable contributions to distribute uncopyrighted tracts and periodicals.[31]

Circulation—the free movement of bodies as well as texts—is figured as eminently desirable, a way to alleviate the curse of literary or physical servitude.

Of course, this attitude stood counter to Dickens's ardent support for an international copyright. In McGill's words, "Dickens expresses astonishment and revulsion at the violence done to his texts, and by extension, to himself, when his writing is circulated in newspapers."[32] The text becomes a synecdoche for the author, both of whom are whipped (recalling Thackeray's "Pegasus in harness") and circulated against their will.

Yet Dickens differs from the slave narrator—and, by extension, Pendennis and Thackeray—in his lofty and idiosyncratic position within the literary market's hierarchy. Dickens's adoption of the slave metaphor emphasizes his supposed degradation and disempowerment at the hands of unscrupulous publishers—the Inimitable Boz reduced to the Reprintable Boz. But for those writers who dwelt within the lowly depths of literary hackdom, reprinting could empower as well as enslave. Writing *already* from a position of subjugation—to publishers, to readers, to the market—the hack writer could climb his way into solvency and even prosperity. He could therefore be forgiven for tolerating lesser injustices in favor of greater gains. Sutherland writes, "the whole question of an author's independence was bound up with how much he earned. . . . Some writers, like Dickens and George Eliot, achieved artistic autonomy early and kept it. For others, like Thackeray and Trollope, it was harder to come by and to hold on to."[33]

If publishing and selling one's "life" could be interpreted as a form of voluntary human trafficking, then Dickens's indignation at his wronging seems misguided and even redundant. Of course Dickens is treated as a slave—but so, too, is every writer, every man and woman. Purged of its political ramifications, literary slavery becomes, ironically, a democratic institution, one in which the illustrious Dickens is exploited with the same ruthlessness as his less well-known literary brothers. Thus, when Thackeray ends his novel with his famous plea, "Let us give a hand of charity to Arthur Pendennis, with all his faults and shortcomings, who does not claim to be a hero, but only a man and a brother" (P II: 372), his invocation of the abolitionist motto is less an attempt to elevate a "degraded" protagonist than to humble an overly inflated one. Deborah Thomas suggests that Pen has become "'a man and a brother,' i.e., a slave, in the relatively positive sense that he has outgrown his self-centered dandyism and accepted his bondage to the responsibilities of adult life."[34] This movement, she argues, parallels the Wordsworthian journey from child- to adulthood—or, in Franco Moretti's terms, demonstrates the bildungsroman's impetus toward socialization.[35] Read this way, *Pendennis* seems to invert the traditional trajectory of the slave narrative; rather than opening with the image and motto of a slave in chains (as many abolitionists pamphlets and slave narratives did), *Pendennis* ends with this image. *The History of Pendennis*, it seems, is the history of a gentleman's descent into prose labour and servitude.

And yet, such a précis of the plot is untrue to the novel's spirit, for throughout, Thackeray makes clear that slavery warrants as irreverent treatment as any other topic of false morality. Indeed, Thackeray humorously inserts himself into the discourse with his illustrated capital to part II, chapter XV, "Convalescence," written as he himself was recovering from a near fatal bout of cholera.[36] Earlier in the novel, Warrington had asserted, "There is no reason why [Pegasus in harness] should be exempt from labour, or illness, or decay, any more than any of the other creatures of God's world," and so Pendennis, paralleling Thackeray, rouses himself from his sickbed:

> Having gone to bed ill with fever, and suffering to a certain degree under the passion of love, after he had gone through his physical malady, and had been bled and had been blistered, and had had his head shaved, and had been treated and medicamented as the doctor ordained:—it is a fact, that, when he rallied up from his bodily ailment, his mental malady had likewise quitted him, and he was no more in love with Fanny Bolton than you or I. (P II: 39)

Pen recuperates his physical strength and, more important, his boundless optimism. The capital, meanwhile, takes on a seemingly darker cast, depicting a kneeling Thackeray (easily distinguished by his curly hair and round glasses) pleading for mercy at the feet of two masked highway robbers (see figure 2.1).[37]

Catherine Peters captions this scene "The author in difficulties,"[38] a nod to Thackeray's recent illness, but a better descriptor would be the ubiquitous slogan, "Am I not a man and a brother?" Given Pen's previous description of Bungay as a "vulgar slave-driver" and the writer as a "serf" and slave, the illustration is evidently a caricature of the famous Wedgewood design of a kneeling, shackled slave. "At the time of the publication of *Pendennis*," Thomas writes, "the picture of the bound and kneeling black man, along with the associated motto, had been commonly used in antislavery material for over half a century and had become a familiar part of the early and mid-Victorian scene[39] (see figure 2.2).

Perhaps one robber is Bacon and the other Bungay, or one Bradbury and the other Evans, but the victim is, without a doubt, Thackeray himself. Yet the participants' gentlemanly garb—indeed, the very theatricality of the tableau, with the robbers clasping masks in their hands—turns the scene into one of playacting rather than real torture. Portly and well dressed, Thackeray bears little resemblance (apart from his posture) to his counterpart in popular slave narrative illustrations, where the slave-victim is both gaunt and half-naked. Moreover, Thackeray lacks the iron chains that fetter the real-life slave; for him, such chains are strictly metaphorical. A comparison of the victimizers yields similar results. Compare the image of Bacon and Bungay (or Bradbury and Evans) to that of the slave drivers in similar illustrations found in the narratives of Henry Bibb (1849, see figure 2.3) and Solomon Northup (1853, see figure 2.4). While the victimizers' garb is more or less similar—waistcoat, jacket, hat—Thackeray replaces the whip with the club and pistol, in keeping with the scene's displacement from Southern plantation to English highway. Stripped of more troubling racial and even ethical implications, the confrontation between Thackeray and his publishers is reduced to its economic essence: the struggle for capital. The robber-publishers demand Thackeray's purse—the fruits of his literary labor—under threat of retribution.

Figure 2.1. W. M. Thackeray, illustrated capital from Vol. II, Chapter XV of *The History of Pendennis*.

Thackeray's illustrated capital also bears a striking resemblance to a wood engraving in Mary Leatheley's *Large Pictures with Little Stories*, a piece of abolition children's literature that follows the life of Sambo, an African slave who is sold into American slavery and separated from his family. In the engraving (see figure 2.5), we see Sambo being whipped by his master for "*neglecting his work*" by tending to a "little lamb" that "reminded him of his own little lost baby."[40] The caption reads, "Sambo severely thrashed for thinking of a dumb animal." Like Stowe's Uncle Tom, Sambo is depicted as a maternal and Christlike figure, but he is

Figure 2.2. Josiah Wedgewood, "Am I Not a Man and a Brother?" woodcut, from John Greenleaf Whittier, "Our Countrymen in Chains" (New York: American Antislavery Society, 1837). Library of Congress.

also conflated with the lamb as chattel, struck by his master's riding whip. The master, in his top hat, waistcoat, and tartan trews, evokes Thackeray's highway robbers. And even the lamb, lapping from a dish, evokes the animal seen running off in the distance behind the kneeling Thackeray. But where the abolitionist illustration and Thackeray's capital diverge is in their treatment of coerced labor. Sambo is wrongfully accused of laziness, and his innocence is equated to that of the unsuspecting lamb. For Thackeray, however, any conflation of authorship and chattelhood brings him back to the image of "Pegasus in harness," who

Can a mother forget her suckling child?

The tender mercies of the wicked are cruel.

Figure 2.3. [Unknown artist], illustration from Henry Bibb, *Narrative of the Life and Adventures of Henry Bibb* (New York: MacDonald and Lee, 1849). Reproduced with permission, the University Library, University of North Carolina, Chapel Hill. Note that in the top image, the slave driver "robs" the slave mother of her child.

SCENE IN THE SLAVE PEN AT WASHINGTON.

Figure 2.4. [Unknown artist], illustration from Solomon Northup, *Twelve Years a Slave: Narrative of Solomon Northup* (London: Sampson Low, Son & Company, 1853). Reproduced with permission, the University Library, University of North Carolina, Chapel Hill.

may benefit from the occasional cut of the whip and who "should [not] be exempt from labour, or illness, or decay, any more than any of the other creatures of God's world" (P II: 353–54). The recently ill Thackeray places himself in the position of the whipped slave or animal, but he does not wallow in the comparison; instead, like the animal seen bounding behind him in the capital, he eventually resumes the serialized labor of *Pendennis*.

SAMBO SEVERELY THRASHED FOR THINKING OF A DUMB ANIMAL.

Figure 2.5. Anon., "Sambo and the Lamb" (hand-coloured wood engraving, c. 1855). From Mary Leatheley, *Large Pictures with Little Stories*. Reproduced with permission, Opie Collection, Bodleian Library, Oxford.

Men and Brothers?

The liberty with which Thackeray riffs upon a familiar abolitionist illustration and motto attests to the ubiquity and flexibility of visual and textual representations of slavery. It also reveals Thackeray's almost chilling ability to detach form from political content, to treat with levity even the most morbid subjects. Sutherland has argued that "in an oblique way, by using Wedgewood's plea to claim freedom for the author, Thackeray makes a collateral plea for the negro,"[41] but this is perhaps too generous a claim. As Thackeray himself would have admitted, he was more concerned with his own plight than that of the slave. Until 1852, when he first toured the United States, Thackeray's knowledge of the institution was derived from books and pamphlets, antislavery propaganda, newspapers, and the proselytizings of his mother, Mrs. Carmichael-Smyth, a devout Evangelical Anglican with antislavery sympathies.[42] In his early novels he refers flippantly to West Indian, Eastern, and even American slavery, but like Warrington, he prefers to deal in metaphors rather than realities. In a typical "throwaway" allusion from *Pendennis* Thackeray's narrator observes,

A man may be famous in the Honour-lists and entirely unknown to the undergraduates: who elect kings and chieftains of their own, whom they admire and obey, as negro-gangs have private black sovereigns in their own body, to whom they pay an occult obedience, besides that which they publicly profess for their owners and drivers. Among the young ones Pen became famous and popular. (P I: 179)

Thackeray here compares Pen's collegiate success to that of a slave leader in a "negro-gang," a tenuous analogy founded on the unofficial status of both men's power. As we have seen, Pen later complains of authorial enslavement at the hand of unscrupulous publishers, so perhaps Thackeray wishes to prefigure Pen's lifelong position as underdog. Yet Thackeray, in Warringtonian fashion, evokes and then sidesteps the darker political implications of such an image. The allusion to "private black sovereigns" to whom slaves pay "occult obedience" brings to mind Nat Turner, whose failed slave rebellion of 1831 horrified men and women on both sides of the Atlantic. Known to his fellow slaves as "The Prophet" for his visionary experiences, Turner channeled his private "popularity" into a bloody rebellion against white slaveowners.[43] Pen, on the other hand, channels his provincial fame into a life of dilettantism and drunkenness.

Thomas has argued that after Thackeray's trips to America in 1852–53 and 1855–56, "slavery waned in creative power in his fiction,"[44] as if witnessing the institution firsthand prevented him from further mining its imaginative potential.[45] In *The Virginians* (1857–59), Thackeray does portray American slavery, a feat facilitated by the novel's setting in colonial America, but his depiction of master-slave interactions is, like the novel as a whole, superficial and disorganized, calculated to add color rather than make any larger political point. Despite such literal representations of slavery, the phrase "Am I not a man and a brother?" drops out almost entirely in Thackeray's later fiction, reappearing only briefly in *Philip* (1861–62) when the mulatto Grenville Woolcomb is perceived as a "man and a brother" by his English compatriots, whereas "in some of the Southern States of America he would be likely to meet with rudeness in a railway car."[46] This example of British tolerance is itself suspect, based upon English society's mercenary interest in Woolcomb's wealth (a version of which we see in *Vanity Fair*, in society's sycophantic treatment of the mulatta Kittitian heiress Miss Schwarz).

It was during Thackeray's trip to America that he began to distance himself from the phrase that had become the shibboleth of his career. In a letter to his mother, he insists, "I dont believe Blacky *is* my man & my brother, though God forbid I should own him or flog him, or part him from his wife and children."[47] The declaration of interracial brotherhood, so easily burlesqued in his novels, now filled Thackeray with intense discomfort. In the same letter, Thackeray explains, "There was scarce any sensation of novelty until now when the slaves come on to the scene; and straightway the country assumes an aspect of queerest interest; I don't know whether it's terror, pity, or laughter that is predominant." A month later, Thackeray's feelings had not changed, and in another letter to his mother, he protests: "They are not my men & brethren, these strange people with retreating foreheads, with great obtruding lips & jaws: with capacities for thought, pleasure, endurance quite different to mine [. . .] Sambo is not my man & my brother; the very aspect of his face is grotesque & inferior."[48] Thackeray's levity gives way to a virulent negrophobia, his detachment to disgust.

If Thackeray was repulsed by the physical appearance of the American slave—and quick to deny any brotherhood, figurative or otherwise—he was likewise fascinated, calling the "nigger children" the "queerest grotesque little imps"[49] and spending his time "draw[ing] pictures of niggers"[50] for his daughters. His letters are covered with caricatures of slaves, anticipating his illustrations of the slave Gumbo in *The Virginians*. Thackeray's disdainful response to American slaves was undoubtedly encouraged by his Southern hosts, who took pains to defend the institution to their English visitor. In a letter to Mrs. Bryan Waller Procter dated 4 April 1853, Thackeray writes, "I have a hundred invitations to go to plantations . . . the Southern gentry are as a body the most generous and kind people. The negro flourishes and increases here enormously." And in another letter to his mother, Thackeray insists that "[the slaves] are not suffering as you are impassioning yourself for their wrongs as you read [in] Mrs. Stowe they are grinning & joking in the sun; roaring with laughter as they stand about the streets in squads; very civil, kind & gentle."[51] Harriet Beecher Stowe's *Uncle Tom's Cabin* had just been published to great acclaim, and though it is unclear whether Thackeray actually read the novel (after meeting Stowe in June 1853, he vowed to "buckle to Uncle Tom and really try to read it"[52]) he was certainly aware of its plot and reformist impulse, and in several letters to his mother—who, it was clear, read and sympathized deeply with the novel— expressed skepticism of Stowe's "philosophy."[53] Thackeray concedes that "individual instances of cruelty" against slaves may have occurred, as recounted in Stowe's novel, but on the whole he seems skeptical of widespread abuse or even injustice.[54]

One wonders how and if Thackeray sought to reconcile his private conviction that "Blacky *is* [not] my man & my brother" with his public avowals of magnanimity and kinship. In a letter to his mother, he attempts to parse the difference:

> But [the slaves] don't seem to me to be the same as white men any more than asses are the same animals as horses; I don't mean this disrespectfully, but simply that there is such a difference of colour, habits, conformation of brains, that we must acknowledge it, & can't by any rhetorical phrase get it over.[55]

In what could be read as an indictment of his own rhetorical glibness, Thackeray cannot subscribe to the very ethical philosophy he vaunts. Even his distinction between asses and horses seems a tacit contradiction of the supposed democracy of the publishing world, where the hack writer and his product are all, at least, of the same species: one may sell a "lady's horse," another a "cob" or "sound hack"—but never an ass.

America cured Thackeray of his rhetorical infatuation with the abolitionist motto and his easy manipulation of antislavery genres by demonstrating that they still possessed signification. What Thackeray had perceived as clichés, available for appropriation and revision, were not yet entirely free of their political associations and relevance. And true to his "quietist" stance, Thackeray chose to withdraw and remain silent rather than promote, even obliquely, a brand of egalitarianism in which he no longer believed. "I shant speak about [slavery], till I know it, or till its my business, or I think I can do good," he promised his mother, and publicly he kept his vow, offering less and less insight into literal or metaphoric slavery in his later novels.[56] In his letters he continued to express sympathy for the South and to question the brutality of slavery right up to the Civil War, but so successful was his public persona that on his death he remained indelibly associated with his earlier expressions of charity and acceptance. Thus the elegiac refrain of Kingsley's tribute, "Poor Thackeray is dead," becomes a public profession of forgiveness for a man who, despite his faults and shortcomings, did not claim to be a hero, but only a man and a brother.

3

Female Slave Narratives
"The Grey Woman" and *My Lady Ludlow*

While Elizabeth Gaskell never visited America during her lifetime, her fiction is animated by events across the Atlantic, from the Salem Witch Trials that form the inspiration for her 1859 novella, *Lois the Witch*, to the "American war" that frames the turn-of-the-century impressment scandal of *Sylvia's Lovers* (1863). In a letter to Charles Eliot Norton from June 10, 1861, she writes of her longing to visit the country: "Meta and I were having a long *yearning* talk about America, and our dear friends there. I am not sure that we did not shake hands upon a resolution that if we lived we *would* go over to America."[1] In other letters, she clamors for news about the American political situation and thanks Norton for some photographs of the American landscape that he had forwarded to her, expressing some disappointment that "Altogether I thought America would have been odder and more original; the underwood & tangle is just like England."[2] In Gaskell's mind, America should have looked more like a painting done by Barbara Leigh Smith, who went for her "honey-*year*" to "some wild luxuriant terrific part of Virginia? In a gorge full of rich rank tropical vegetation. . . . Well! That picture *did* look like my idea of America."[3]

Gaskell's romanticizing of America, her ardent desire that America be "odder and more original" and *not* "just like England," contrasts with her fundamental conviction that England and America shared much in common, from language to religion to commercial interests. In *Lois the Witch*, she chastises those English readers who would scoff at the superstition and hysteria of the Puritans, writing:

> We can afford to smile at them now; but our English ancestors entertained superstitions of much the same character at the same period, and with less excuse, as the circumstances surrounding them were better known, and consequently more explicable by common sense, than the real mysteries of the deep, untrodden forests of New England.[4]

Gaskell's familiar narrative voice comes through in her gentle insistence that differences in history, geography, and nationality cannot erode the commonality of human experience.

In the 1850s and 1860s, when Gaskell wrote most of her fiction, the conflict over American slavery would reach its zenith. Writing to Norton in December of 1857, she mentions an awkward meeting with the noted abolitionist Charles Sumner: "He talked Anti-Slavery,—of the ins & outs of which I know nothing,—so all I could say was that Slavery was a very bad thing, & the sooner it was done away with, & the better."[5] Despite her claims of ignorance, Gaskell, like most everyone in England, had read *Uncle Tom's Cabin* and had even begun a correspondence and friendship with Harriet Beecher Stowe, whom she described as "short and American in her manner, but very true & simple & thoroughly unspoiled & unspoilable."[6] Through Stowe, Gaskell would learn about Sojourner Truth, the runaway slave turned abolitionist and women's rights activist.[7] Norton himself was an avowed abolitionist, along with another of Gaskell's American correspondents, the author and Unitarian clergyman Edward Everett Hale. To them Gaskell directed many earnest questions about slavery and its role, official or otherwise, in the outbreak of the American Civil War.

At home, Gaskell had an even closer connection to the antislavery movement in her brother-in-law, William Robson, an English abolitionist and friend of William Lloyd Garrison. In February 1859, Gaskell wrote a letter to William's wife Anne ("Nancy") Robson (née Gaskell), begging off of a proposed visit by the abolitionist speaker Sarah Parker Remond.[8] While Gaskell professed "the greatest possible respect for *her* herself, (*from all your accounts of her*)," she "disapprove[d] of her object in coming to England":

> All the Anti Slavery people will attend her lectures to *be* convinced of what they are already convinced, & to have their feelings stirred up without the natural & right outlet of stirred feelings, the power of simple & energetic *actions*,—I know they can use any amount of *words* in reprobation of the conduct of American slave holders, but I don't call the use of words *action*: unless there is some definite, distinct, practical *course of action* logically proposed by those words.[9]

Although Gaskell would maintain antislavery sympathies throughout her lifetime, she would remain suspicious of any belief system prone to radicalism or extremism—including the abolitionist cause. Introduced to zealous "Anti Slavery people" like Charles Sumner and Mary Weston Chapman (whom she hosted in Manchester in 1856), Gaskell found herself simultaneously compelled and discomforted by their vivid stories of oppression and impassioned pleas for justice. In a letter to Mary Green, Gaskell writes:

> I am *very* fond of her [Chapman], tho' I know nothing about abolition, & that great interest of hers. . .we had a sort of Anti Slavery conference

in our drawing-room, & they sighed over my apathy, but I can not get up an interest in the *measures* adopted by people so far away across the Atlantic.[10]

Gaskell confesses great sympathy for the abolitionist cause, yet she consistently waffles between "apathy" and anxiety about how best to channel such passions into constructive and peaceable solutions.

Gaskell may not have witnessed American slavery for herself, and she may not have known all of its "ins & outs," but she repeatedly mined the slave narrative for literary inspiration, recognizing its potency as a genre of social protest. In the next two chapters, I will investigate three of Gaskell's fictions: a gothic short story, "The Grey Woman" (1861), a provincial novella, *My Lady Ludlow* (1859), and an industrial novel, *North and South* (1855). Spanning disparate modes, genres, and narrative methods, these works each borrow aspects of the slave narrative to draw larger conclusions about gender, class, and nationhood. In "The Grey Woman," Gaskell deploys the trope of racial "passing" and concomitant fears of miscegenation to comment on female subjugation and the instability of gender identity. In *My Lady Ludlow*, she depicts turn-of-the-century anxieties regarding working-class literacy while evoking mid-century fears over American slave literacy and British working-class reform. And in *North and South*, she reveals her fullest, most subtle use of the slave narrative in exposing the transatlantic network of the British textile industry. By importing the plot devices and narrative tropes of the slave narrative, Gaskell comments on both contemporary and historical events and draws ever closer the bond between England and America.

"The Grey Woman"

Published in January 1861 in *All the Year Round*, "The Grey Woman" is part fairy tale, part gothic horror story, part epistolary narrative, and part historical fiction. It appeared concurrently in the magazine with Dickens's *Great Expectations* and several articles detailing slavery in the American South. The story is framed by an anonymous English narrator's account of her visit to a German mill, where she goes to have coffee with friends sometime in the 1840s. The group is invited inside, where the narrator is struck by a painting of "a young girl of extreme beauty" dating from "the latter half of the last century."[11] The portrait is of Anna Scherer, the miller's great-aunt, who was also known as the Grey Woman because she "lost her colour so entirely through fright" (GW, 289). Eager to learn more of the story, the narrator is given a yellowed manuscript of a letter Anna Scherer had written to her daughter, Ursula. The rest of the story is relayed through the letter, which the narrator translates from the German.

Anna's letter is an apology and explanation for ending Ursula's engagement to a young French artist. Anna describes how as a young girl, she meets a handsome Frenchman named Monsieur de la Tourelle, to whom she hastily becomes engaged. After their marriage, M. de la Tourelle takes Anna with him to his chateau in Vosges, where Anna is forbidden to enter certain rooms and almost completely isolated from the outside world. Her only friend is her maid, a Norman woman named Amante. Anna becomes pregnant and is increasingly homesick for her former life. She slips into her husband's chambers to retrieve a letter from home and unexpectedly discovers that her husband is a member of a band of brigands known as the Chauffeurs. She learns that he has murdered a neighboring gentleman, the Sieur de Poissy, and also his first wife, Victorine.

Anna flees the chateau with Amante, and the two travel under the guise of a tailor and his wife. M. de la Tourelle zealously pursues the "wicked fugitives" (GW, 327) and despite several close calls, Anna and Amante are saved by their disguises. They escape to Frankfort, where Anna gives birth to Ursula. Amante is recognized and stabbed to death, and Anna is taken in by a kind doctor, whom she later marries. She once catches sight of M. de la Tourelle outside her home, but he does not recognize her because terror had turned her hair gray and drained her face of color. Anna eventually learns M. de la Tourelle has died, but she is still haunted by the past in the form of Ursula's suitor who, Anna now divulges, is the son of Sieur de Poissy.

"The Grey Woman" is both a retelling of the Bluebeard fairy tale and an allegory of the French Revolution, with its account of Anna's personal "Reign of Terror." Diana Wallace notes that "its framing devices of portrait and yellowing manuscripts are typically Gothic but its precise historical and geographical location on the French–German border in 1789, the year of the French Revolution (and of political 'terror'), emphasise its cultural and social realism."[12] In bringing together the gothic and the historic, Gaskell doubly emphasizes the durability of the past. Just as the story rehearses the gothic trope that "the sins of the fathers are visited on their children" (GW, 290), so too does it suggest that history is destined to repeat itself. Gaskell's narrator refers to the late-eighteenth century as "that unruly time that was overspreading all Europe, overturning all law, and all the protection which law gives" (GW, 324), a description that recalls the extradiagetic moment of "184-", when revolutions in France, led by a second "Napoleon," were again upsetting the social order. Moreover, Ursula, like her mother, falls in love with a French nobleman (albeit one who has changed his name to the more proletarian LeBrun after the Revolution), threatening to resurrect and then repeat her mother's cursed marital history.

"The Grey Woman" also recalls the political upheaval of mid-century America by borrowing sensational plot lines from two contemporaneous American slave narratives, Harriet Jacobs's *Incidents in the Life of a Slave Girl* (1861) and William and Ellen Crafts's *Running a Thousand Miles to Freedom* (1860). Both slave narratives detail the unique problems faced by female slaves, from sexually predatory masters to jealous mistresses to broken families. Each also addresses the issues of miscegenation and racial passing, as light-complected slaves often bore a phenotypic resemblance to their masters—and also to their white half-brothers and sisters.

In fashioning her story of sexual terror and oppression in eighteenth-century France, Gaskell looks to the plight of the American female slave in nineteenth-century America. She invokes the racial hysteria of the ante-bellum American South in the class hysteria of Revolutionary France, revising Jacobs's and the Crafts's narrative to compose a gothic tale of gender and class-passing.

Gaskell may have met Harriet Jacobs or read a manuscript of her book in 1859, when Jacobs was in England attempting to find a publisher for her full-length narrative. As early as 1853, Jacobs had anonymously published bits of her autobiography in a series of letters to the New York *Tribune*, describing the sexual commodification and abuse of slave women. By 1857, Jacobs had completed a full draft of her narrative and, having witnessed the transatlantic publishing success of slave narrators such as Moses Roper and Frederick Douglass, hoped to find a British publisher for her work. Jacobs had visited England earlier, in 1845, employed as a baby-nurse to Mary Stace Willis, and she fondly recollected her time there. "For the first time in my life," she writes in *Incidents in the Life of a Slave Girl*, "I was in a place where I was treated according to my deportment, without reference to my complexion."[13] Her visit overlapped with that of Frederick Douglass, who had fled America upon the publication of his narrative and was then touring Britain on an antislavery lecture tour.[14]

Despite Jacobs's hopes, her second trip to England ended without a British publishing agreement. She did, however, meet many members of the transatlantic antislavery community and may have crossed paths with Gaskell, herself, at Stafford House, the London home of the Duchess of Sutherland and a popular meeting place for British reformers. The Duchess of Sutherland was a prominent antislavery advocate who had helped to organize the Stafford House Address, an antislavery petition also known as "An Affectionate and Christian Address of Many Thousands of the Women of England to their Sisters, the Women of the United States of America."[15] With letters of introduction from abolitionist Mary Weston Chapman, Jacobs was warmly welcomed to England by Richard David Webb, the editor of the *Anti-Slavery Advocate*, and his wife, Hannah Waring Webb, both of whom were staying at Stafford House at the time of Jacobs's arrival. Soon, Jacobs, too, was invited to stay at Stafford House as a guest of the Duchess. Jean Fagan Yellin describes how over the course of the next few weeks, Jacobs interacted with members of the Duchess's house party, and "one member of the group (Garrisonians all) even read through her manuscript and judged Jacobs 'one of the truest heroines we have ever met with.'"[16] These weeks likely overlapped with a visit by Gaskell, who had asked to see the Duchess while she was in London during this same period of time.[17] In a letter dated June 18 [?1859], Gaskell thanks the Duchess for "the permission you so kindly sent me to see Stafford House" and looks forward to "the pleasure we expect to receive through your kind courtesy."[18]

Yellin speculates that Jacobs initial attempts to find a British publisher may have failed because "British abolitionists advised her to publish the book first in America because they feared British prudery. Certainly her story of a liaison with Sawyer [Mr. Sands in the narrative] challenged Victorian sexual practices."[19] Back in America, Jacobs sought the sponsorship of Lydia Maria Child, who helped edit her narrative and wrote one of its prefaces. Using the pseudonym Linda Brent, Jacobs eventually published *Incidents in the Life of a Slave Girl* in Boston in 1861, and it was enthusiastically promoted by the American antislavery press. The London *Anti-Slavery Advocate* also published a positive review, most likely written by Richard David Webb. Yellin writes, "[The reviewer]. . .wrote of having met Jacobs during her visit to England and testified that her published book was 'substantially the same' as the manuscript she had brought with her."[20] A year later, Jacobs's narrative was published in London by William Tweedie (who had earlier published William and Ellen Crafts's narrative) under the name *The Deeper Wrong; or, Incidents in the Life of a Slave Girl, Written by Herself*. Reviewers on both sides of the Atlantic commented on the narrative's depictions of sexual perversion and lamented the vulnerability of the American slave woman. William C. Nell, in a letter to the *Liberator*, touched upon the narrative's appeal to a female readership: "[From reading *Incidents*], especially mothers and daughters, may learn yet more of the barbarism of American slavery and the character of its victims (see figure 3.1)."[21]

In "The Grey Woman," Gaskell borrows several elements of Jacobs's narrative, from the experience of sexual victimization and rabid pursuit by a male "master," to the dangerous escape and subsequent concealment in garrets and lofts, to the lingering legacy of the fugitive experience. Gaskell's villainous M. de la Tourelle finds his antecedent in Jacobs's Dr. Flint. The latter is the owner of a "fine residence in town, several farms, and about fifty slaves" (HJ, 15); the former the "propriétaire" of "a small chateau on the Vosges mountains," the surrounding land, and a staff of servants (GW, 296). Dr. Flint is "wilful and arbitrary" (HJ, 37) and morbidly jealous of Jacobs's liaison with another man; he builds a "lonely cottage" (HJ, 55) in which to keep Jacobs as his mistress, and he is violent and tyrannical with his slaves. M. de la Tourelle is "jealous," "suspicious," and prone to "outbursts of passion" (GW, 302); he strictly limits his wife's access to certain parts of the chateau, and his treatment of his servants "was often severe even to cruelty" (GW, 304). The two men begin to blur further after their female victims escape. Dr. Flint "rave[s] and storm[s] at a furious rate" and accuses Jacobs of "[running] off without the least provocation" even though she had been "treated. . .very kindly" (HJ, 97). M. de la Tourelle uses similar rhetoric, describing how he had been "deserted and betrayed" by a wife "on whom I lavished all my love, but who has abused my confidence" (GW, 327).

The parallels between *Incidents in the Life of a Slave Girl* and "The Grey Woman" become more striking when Jacobs's escape is juxtaposed with Anna Scherer's. In Jacobs's case, she is first concealed in "a small room over [a sympathetic neighbor's] own sleeping apartment," a space that doubles as "a room to store away things that are out of use" (HJ, 100).

Figure 3.1. Harriet Jacobs in 1894. Cabinet photograph by Gilbert
Studios, Washington, D.C. Gold-toned albumin print. By permission
of Jean Fagan Yellin.

While hidden in this "retreat above stairs" (HJ, 103), Jacobs overhears Dr. Flint in the house, and she is immediately seized with terror at his close proximity. In Anna's case, she and Amante first find refuge at an old mill, where an old woman secretes them in "a kind of loft, which went halfway over the lofty mill-kitchen" (GW, 320). The loft doubles as "the store-room or garret for the household" and is filled with "bedding piled up, boxes and chests, mill sacks, the winter store of apples and nuts, bundles of old clothes, broken furniture, and many other things" (GW, 321). Through "the crevices between the boards that formed the flooring into the kitchen below," they experience their own close call, when one of M. de la Tourelle's servants, Lefebvre, enters the kitchen and asks the miller "sly questions" with "the hidden purpose" of discovering Anna and Amante's whereabouts (GW, 321).

As a result of their respective near discoveries, both Jacobs and Anna Scherer subsequently rely on disguises to flee to their next hiding place. Jacobs is given a suit of sailor's clothes, including "jacket, trousers, and tarpaulin hat" (HJ, 111), blackens her face with charcoal, and is instructed to "put [her] hands in [her] pockets, and walk ricketty, like de sailors" (HJ, 112). She is spirited to her grandmother's house, where she is hidden in "a very small garret" only "nine feet long and seven wide" (HJ, 114), pinned just below the roof and above some boards. Desperate for air and access to the outside world, she bores holes into the wall of her cell in order to catch sight of her children—though the first person she spies is Dr. Flint. As for Anna Scherer, she too is forced to take on a disguise when fleeing to the next safe house. With the help of Amante, she darkens her "fair hair and complexion" with walnut shells, blackens her teeth, and breaks her front tooth. Digging through the boxes and chests in the mill's storeroom, Amante discovers "an old suit of man's clothes, which had probably belonged to the miller's absent son" (GW, 323) and dons it to masquerade as an itinerant tailor. The two women seek shelter at an inn, where they bargain for "a small bedroom across the court, and over the stables" (GW, 329). In the middle of the night, they are awakened by M. de la Tourelle's voice below, as he arrives to stable his horse: "For five minutes or so he went on giving directions. Then he left the stable, and, softly stealing to our window, we saw him cross the court and re-enter the inn" (GW, 330).

Jacobs and Anna Scherer must subsequently endure the constant terror and uncertainty of fugitive life, an experience that leaves lasting physical scars. From years of being pent up in such a small space, Jacobs suffers from swollen limbs and diminished health. The intensity of Anna's terror turns her into an invalid and recluse. Yet although both women manage to escape their sexual oppressors, neither is able to escape fully the legacy of their past suffering. In both stories, the gothic trope that "the sins of the fathers are visited on their children" is terribly literalized. For Jacobs, the sexual sins of the slave master are revealed in the complexion of his illegitimate children. Jacobs describes an uncle who is "nearly white" for "he inherited the complexion my grandmother had derived from her [male] Anglo-Saxon ancestors" (HJ, 6). She describes a typical slave master who is "the father of many little slaves" and the slave mistress who watches as "children of every shade of complexion play with her own fair babies, and too well she knows they are born unto him of his own household" (HJ, 36). Indeed, Jacobs's own children bear the racial imprint of Mr. Sands, their white father. For Anna Scherer, her daughter Ursula carries within her the blood of M. de la Tourelle, a genetic legacy that both reminds Anna of her past sexual oppression and taints Ursula's eventual marriage prospects.

With their parallel accounts of sexual victimization and its legacy, *Incidents in the Life of a Slave Girl* and "The Grey Woman" allegorically reflect the social and political turmoil of their era. Nat Turner's Rebellion (1831) acts as the backdrop for Jacobs's narrative, embodying the racial hysteria of the mid-nineteenth-century South. Turner was a Virginian slave who, inspired by mystical visions, led a massive slave insurrection that claimed the lives of at least fifty-five white people. In the aftermath of the rebellion, close to two hundred black people were killed by white mobs, and Turner himself was hanged and skinned. Jacobs mentions this gruesome uprising's effect on her small town: "The news threw our town into a great commotion" (HJ, 63) and white mobs began to search and pillage black households. Racial paranoia reaches its apogee, as innocent slaves are whipped, jailed, and otherwise tortured. For Jacobs, Turner's rebellion confirms the volatile racial climate of the American South and the uneasy relations between masters and slaves. So terrified are slaveholders of future insurrection that "after the alarm caused by Nat Turner's insurrection had subsided, [they] came to the conclusion that it would be well to give the slaves enough of religious instruction to keep them from murdering their masters" (HJ, 68).

For Gaskell, it is the French Revolution that confirms the volatile social climate of Europe and the uneasy relations between the classes. "The Grey Woman" is not simply an allegory of M. de la Tourelle's marital "Reign of Terror," but a larger disquisition on how class complicates all social relations, from that between husband and wife to that between mistress and servant. Anna is a miller's daughter, whose "country breeding" (GW, 294) leaves her unprepared for the "court manners, or French fashions" (GW, 294) of life with M. de la Tourelle. Alienated from her husband, Anna transgresses class boundaries again by becoming "too familiar" with Amante. This friendship between the "lady of the castle" and the "Norman waiting-maid" eclipses the marriage between Anna and M. de la Tourelle as the central relationship of the story. It also further reveals Gaskell's debt to the slave narrative, in this case to William and Ellen Craft's *Running a Thousand Miles to Freedom*.

Most readers would agree that the most striking feature of "The Grey Woman" is the cross-dressing plot. In order for the two women to escape detection, Amante steals an old man's suit, cuts her hair "to the shortness of a man's," clips her eyebrows, stuffs a hump on her back, and fills her cheeks with cork to alter her voice and appearance (GW, 323). She dyes Anna's hair, darkens her skin, blackens and chips her teeth, and thickens her figure.[22] As husband and wife, Amante and Anna transgress traditional class and gender roles, a fact suggested by Amante's name, the French word for "lover." The woman "passes" for a man, the servant for a master. Even prior to the escape from the chateau, Amante is described as masculine in appearance and manner. She is "tall and handsome" and "somewhat gaunt" (GW, 302); she "fear[s] no one" and would "quietly beard" (GW, 303) the other servants. Her comportment contrasts markedly with the effeminacy of M. de la Tourelle, whose features are "as delicate as a girl's" and whose speech is characterized by an "affected softness" (GW, 295).

The relationship between Amante and Anna recalls the homosocial bonds of *Cranford*'s community of "Amazons," yet it also points to an actual historical episode—the cross-dressing escape plot of the American fugitive slaves William and Ellen Craft.[23] According to R. J. M. Blackett, "no other escape, with the exception of Frederick Douglass' and Josiah Henson's, created such a stir in antebellum America as did the Crafts' ".[24] In 1848, the Crafts fled from Macon, Georgia to Philadelphia. Ellen Craft, who was so fair-skinned she could pass for white, disguised herself as an invalid slave owner, donning men's clothes her husband had purchased "piece by piece," cutting her hair, and binding her head in a poultice to conceal her "beardless chin"[25] (see figure 3.2). Traveling as master and slave, Ellen and William Craft endured several close calls, once crossing paths with William's employer, another time with a friend of Ellen's master. Both times, Ellen's disguise saved them from recognition. Upon reaching Pennsylvania, the Crafts were taken under the wing of William Wells Brown, who "immediately ushered them into the inner clique of slave lecturers"[26] and organized a group lecture tour throughout New England and the British Isles.

In January 1851, William and Ellen Craft arrived in Liverpool, where their thrilling tale was widely recounted in British newspapers and magazines, including the Liverpool *Mercury*, the *Athenaeum*, and the *Scottish Press*.[27] Blackett writes, "British audiences knew about daring escapes from slavery—among them Douglass's, Roper's, and Henson's—but this tale involved unheard-of boldness and romance. And in a century still awed by the romance of the American frontier, this was strong stuff."[28] Particularly shocking to British audiences was Ellen Craft's appearance. The Leeds *Mercury* described her as being as "fair as British girls, and as intelligent,"[29] and to witness such a creature subjected to slavery emphasized the inhumanity and irrationality of the institution (see figure 3.3). Over the next decade, William and Ellen Craft continued their antislavery work, and with the sponsorship of British abolitionists, enrolled at the Ockham Agricultural School in Surrey, where they eventually became superintendent and matron, respectively. In 1860, inspired by the fact that "no major slave narrative had been issued in Britain since the early 1850s [and] none had appeared since *Uncle Tom's Cabin*,"[30] the Crafts decided to write a narrative of their escape, entitled *Running a Thousand Miles to Freedom*. Published by William Tweedie, printer of the London *Anti-Slavery Advocate*, the narrative went through two editions and "was generally well received by contemporary readers."[31]

Figure 3.2. [Unknown artist], frontispiece of a disguised Ellen Craft
from William Craft, *Running a Thousand Miles to Freedom; or, the Escape
of William and Ellen Craft from Slavery* (London: William Tweedie, 1860).
Reproduced with permission, the University Library, University of North
Carolina, Chapel Hill.

Figure 3.3. [Unknown artist], illustrations of William and Ellen Craft from William Still, *The Underground Railroad* (Philadelphia: Porter and Coates, 1872). Reproduced with permission, New York Public Library.

Running a Thousand Miles to Freedom reveals how William and Ellen Craft cross barriers of race, class, gender, and even geography in their escape from slavery. To draw the predominantly white readership further into the tale, William Craft devotes the first few pages of the narrative to tales of wrongful *white* enslavement, as much to remind the reader that "slavery in America is not at all confined to persons of a particular complexion" (Craft, 4) as to accentuate that "passing" goes both ways: just as Ellen Craft could be mistaken for white, so a white person could be mistaken for black. As an example, William describes the story of Salomé Muller, a German emigrant from Alsace, who arrives with her family in New Orleans in 1818 to work on the plantations and is enslaved for twenty-five years, only to be liberated when a German woman recognizes her working in a wine-shop. Years of laboring on cotton and sugar fields have turned her complexion "as dark as that of the darkest brunette," though her "long, straight, black hair, hazel eyes, thin lips, and [ ] Roman nose" betray "no trace of African descent" (Craft, 5).[32] According to Marjorie Garber, such a story serves as a powerful rhetorical strategy, placing the white reader "in a condition of imagined jeopardy, voiceless and placeless, caught in the same double bind as the Crafts themselves."[33]

In "The Grey Woman," Gaskell brings together the story of William and Ellen Craft and the story of Salomé Muller, relocating the dangers of racial passing onto the dangers of gender and class passing. Anna Scherer is born in the borderlands of France and Germany, in roughly the same region as Salomé Muller, whose name itself is a French-German hybrid.[34] Her problems begin when her friends and family push her into an advantageous marriage, one that elevates her to a "great lady, a lady of a castle" (GW, 303). Despite her new social position, Anna gravitates toward the company of Amante, who comes from a similarly humble background: "By birth," Gaskell writes, "we were not very far apart in rank: Amante was the daughter of a Norman farmer, I of a German miller" (GW, 303). Against the class warfare of the French Revolution, Anna is accused by her husband of being "too familiar" with Amante, of transgressing social boundaries, and it is this crime that later comes back to haunt her when she discovers that her daughter's suitor, Le Brun, is himself "passing" as a member of the Third Estate, having dropped his real name "because the blood-thirsty republicans might consider it too aristocratic" (GW, 340). Whether masquerading as a "great lady" or a tailor's wife, Anna must navigate the precariousness of class identity.

As she did with Harriet Jacobs's *Incidents in the Life of a Slave Girl*, Gaskell borrows sensational plot devices from the Crafts' slave narrative, one a moment of near-discovery and another a moment of mistaken identity. In *Running a Thousand Miles*, William Craft describes how he and his wife boarded a train for Savannah when they spy William's former employer, a cabinet-maker, on the platform. William writes, "Full believing that we were caught, I shrank into a corner, turned my face from the door, and expected in a moment to be dragged out. The cabinet-maker looked into my master's carriage, but did not know him in his new attire, and, as

God would have it, before he reached mine the bell rang, and the train moved off" (Craft, 22–23). Once the train had safely left the platform, however, Ellen "looked round in the carriage, and was terror-stricken to find a Mr. Cray—an old friend of my wife's master. . .sitting on the same seat" (Craft, 23). Mr. Cray attempts to make conversation with Ellen, who, terrified that he might recognize her voice, pretends to be deaf. To Ellen's relief, Mr. Cray's suspicions are not awakened, and he soon departs the carriage. In "The Grey Woman," the moment of near-discovery occurs at a blacksmith's house, where the disguised Amante and Anna have been hired to mend some clothes. M. de la Tourelle stops at the same blacksmith's house to have his horse reshod, and he joins Anna and Amante around the stove. Anna and Amante sit "in dusk shadow, pretending to stitch away, but scarcely able to see" (GW, 326). To avoid conversation, Amante whistles. They overhear M. de la Tourelle curse the two of them before he rides away.

Gaskell's second borrowing is significantly more disturbing, imaginatively extending a moment of misrecognition to its tragic end. As William and Ellen Craft make their way North, they encounter a "stout elderly lady" in Richmond who, stepping into the carriage, mistakes William for her own runaway slave. William writes:

Seeing me passing quickly along the platform, she sprang up as if taken by a fit, and exclaimed, "Bless my soul! there goes my nigger, Ned!"
My master [Ellen] said, "No; that is my boy."
The lady paid no attention to this; she poked her head out of the window, and bawled to me, "You Ned, come to me, sir, you runaway rascal!"
On my looking round she drew her head in, and said to my master, "I beg your pardon, sir, I was sure it was my nigger; I never in my life saw two black pigs more alike than your boy and my Ned." (Craft, 31)

The lady's bitterness at her slave's escape anticipates M. de la Tourelle's bitterness at his wife's. "Oh!" she cries to the disguised Ellen, "I hope, sir, your boy will not turn out to be so worthless as my Ned has. Oh! I was as kind to him as if he had been my own son. Oh! sir, it grieves me very much to think that after all I did for him he should go off without having any cause whatever" (Craft, 31). M. de la Tourelle likewise contrasts his own devotion to his wife's infidelity, his own innocence to her "corruption" (GW, 327).

The monomaniacal pursuit of a runaway "boy" or wife leads Southern slave mistress and French propriétaire to see their quarry everywhere, to populate their worlds with doppelgangers who act as constant, taunting reminders of their loss. The misidentification of William Craft leads the Southern lady to rehearse and relive her own history of slave ownership. For M. de la Tourelle, the moment of mistaken identification has even deadlier consequences. Anna's doppelganger is the Baroness de Roeder, a young lady with hair "exactly the colour of [Anna's]," who speaks German French and is attended by an elderly French maid. The two women check into the same inn as the disguised Anna and Amante, and in the middle of the night, M. de la Tourelle stabs the Baroness to death, believing her to be his wife. Ned and William Craft are tragically linked by race, Anna and the Baroness by class and gender.

While race appears elided in "The Grey Woman," the story's title does draw attention to the signifying power of Anna's complexion and offers a final clue to the influence of the slave narrative in the story. It is Anna's portrait that first catches the narrator's interest and leads to the tale of how "this pretty girl, with her complexion of lilies and roses, lost her colour so entirely through fright" (GW, 289). Terror has drained Anna of her physical vitality and made her literally unrecognizable to her husband and family. Catching sight of M. de la Tourelle years after her escape, Anna cries, "he saw me, an old grey woman, and he did not recognize me! Yet it was not three years since we had parted" (GW, 339). And reuniting with her brother some years later, Anna must point out the similarities in her features and that of her portrait in order to convince him of her identity. This dramatic change in her complexion can be linked to the years of "passing" as a tailor's wife, when she must dye her hair and darken her skin to escape exposure. Anna does not "pass" for black, as Salomé Muller had, yet her complexion and hair are permanently discolored by the experience. Her second husband urges her not to "renew" the dye once "it has passed away from [her] face" (GW, 339), but for Anna there is "no need": "my yellow hair was grey, my complexion was ashen-coloured, no creature would have recognized the fresh-coloured, bright-haired young woman of eighteen months before" (GW, 339). She is no longer fair, nor is she dark. Rather, she takes on an ambiguous, mixed complexion: not-black, not-white, but grey. The terror of gender and class transgression manifests itself in Anna Scherer's face, bringing the story back to its origins in tales of racial passing and escape.

My Lady Ludlow

First published in *Household Words* in 1858 and later packaged with several other short stories in a collection called *Round the Sofa* (1859), Gaskell's *My Lady Ludlow* is now rarely read and has received only scant critical attention. J. R. Watson, in one of the few critical essays on the novella, reads the work as a humorous contemplation of the problems of "dangerous writing," which Gaskell had "treated with such seriousness in the *Life [of Charlotte Brontë]* and which had caused her so much anguish in her own career."[35] Like "The Grey Woman," *My Lady Ludlow* has a highly mediated structure, narrated by a former ward of Lady Ludlow's named Mrs. Dawson and featuring an unwieldy *mise en abîme* narrated by Lady Ludlow. As repackaged in *Round the Sofa*, *My Lady Ludlow* is further framed by the conceit, narrated by a Miss Greatorex, that Mrs.

Dawson and several friends have gathered "round the sofa" to recount stories. Mrs. Dawson recounts the furor surrounding the attempts of a new clergyman, Mr. Gray, to establish a Sunday school in the village for the purpose of educating local working-class children. His scheme is received with horror by Lady Ludlow, who links literacy to insubordination and recounts, in rambling detail, an episode from the French Revolution to support her stance. When Mrs. Dawson eventually resumes her narrative, we learn that after some initial resistance, Lady Ludlow relents and allows the Sunday school to continue. The horrors of the French Revolution do not come to pass in provincial England and the working class is happily educated.

My Lady Ludlow taps into entrenched fears of working-class literacy that unite the novella's three diagetic planes: the extradiagetic, in which Mrs. Dawson gathers "round the sofa" with her friends; the diagetic, in which Mrs. Dawson recounts her past life with Lady Ludlow; and the metadiagetic, in which Lady Ludlow recalls the revolution in France. Lawrence Stone, in his study of English literature and education, describes early resistance to working-class education:

> A common opinion in eighteenth-century England was that education merely encouraged the poor "to imagine themselves to be judges of what they do not understand, and to despise the advice of their teachers. By reading seditious pamphlets and occasional papers, they also become factious, and, forgetting their proper business, their knowledge serves only to render them more troublesome members of society."[36]

The English Civil War and French Revolution only augmented suspicion of working-class education, and "between 1660 and 1790 most men were convinced that a little learning for the poor is a dangerous thing, since it encourages them to aspire beyond their station, and so threatens social stability and the domination of the elite."[37] Even as working-class education became more accessible by the mid-nineteenth century, middle-class anxiety did not cease.[38] Again, historical events exacerbated fears of the English "common reader,"[39] as Chartist demands for suffrage and the 1848 revolutions in Europe resurrected memories of class warfare and "the bogeyman of Victorian England—the French Revolution."[40]

The novella triggers a chain of retrospection that links the mid-century reader to the events of turn-of-the-century England and from there, to the events of the French Revolution. It simultaneously evokes mid-century anxieties over *slave* literacy. Stone notes the similar ideological barriers to both working-class and slave literacy, confirming that "in America in the eighteenth and early nineteenth centuries, slaves were kept illiterate by law on the grounds that 'teaching slaves to read and write tends to dissatisfaction in their minds, and to produce insurrection and rebellion.'"[41] Gaskell borrows liberally from slave narrative tropes throughout the novella, most evidently in her composition of Lady Ludlow's antieducation speeches but also in her rendering of the working-class "imp," Harry Gregson. In the process, she both perpetuates popular comparisons of worker and slave and updates her tale to resonate with the ongoing race conflict in America. Whether Gaskell wished her audience to read *My Lady Ludlow* through the lens of working-class reform, slavery reform—or both—her reliance on the slave narrative demonstrates its enormous cultural saturation and ability to cross generic boundaries. For a middle-class author like Gaskell, the "imagined" working class in her novella is constructed as much from the "real" narratives of American slaves as the autobiographical accounts of British workers.

Lady Ludlow, the novella's primary source of antiliteracy rhetoric, expresses deep apprehension at the prospect of an educated working class, dismissing working-class education as "levelling and revolutionary,"[42] and subscribing to "an all but inviolable rule" (LL, 14) to hire only illiterate servants. Her ire is first piqued by Mr. Gray, who proposes a "Sabbath-school" for the religious education of local workers, whom he hopes will use their new-found literacy to read their Bibles and save their souls. Mrs. Dawson recalls, "Mr. Gray was full of new things, and. . .what he first did was attack all our established institutions, both in the village and the parish, and also in the nation" (LL, 183). His reformist zeal extends to other humanitarian causes, including, most notably, the antislavery cause. Miss Galindo, a local gossip, reports,

> "And what's the next thing our young parson does? Why he tries to make us all feel pitiful for the black slaves, and leaves little pictures of negroes about, with the question printed below, 'Am I not a man and a brother?' just as if I was to be hail-fellow-well-met with every negro footman. They do say he takes no sugar in his tea, because he thinks he sees spots of blood in it. Now I call that superstition." (LL, 184)

Mr. Gray's boycott of West-Indian slave sugar and his distribution of abolitionist propaganda are met with the same incredulity that meets his calls for educational reform. To the mid-century reader, of course, Mr. Gray's activities are not so quixotic, given the eventual abolition of the slave trade in 1807 and the abolition of slavery in 1834. In fact, Mr. Gray's two pet causes, working-class literacy and antislavery, can be seen as earlier manifestations of the mid-century debate over abolition and slave literacy in the United States.

Also eager to educate local workers, albeit from a secular perspective, is Lady Ludlow's steward, Mr. Horner, who "hope[s] for a day school at some future time, to train up intelligent labourers for working on the estate" (LL, 58). Despite his lady's disapproval, Horner secretly teaches the "brightest and sharpest, although by far the raggediest and dirtiest" farm-lad, Harry Gregson, to read and write, "with a view of making use of him as a kind of foreman in process of time" (LL, 59). Harry Gregson's illicit education comes to Lady Ludlow's attention in comic fashion. Entrusted by Horner with a note to Lady Ludlow, Harry appears at Lady Ludlow's doorstep having lost the note but proudly announcing he can "say it off by heart" (LL, 65). He explains to Lady Ludlow, "Mr. Horner, my lady, has taught me to read, write, and cast accounts, my lady. And he was in a hurry, and he folded his paper up, but he did not seal it; and I read it, my lady" (LL, 65–66). The ensuing scene is broadly humorous, with Harry blithely unaware of his transgression and bewildered by Lady Ludlow's disapproving lecture. To Lady Ludlow's injunction that "you must not read letters that are not intended for you," Harry responds, "Please, my lady, I thought it were good for practice, all as one as a book" (LL, 67). And to her follow-up query, "you would not listen, I am sure. . .to anything you were not intended to hear?" Harry cheekily answers, "Please, my lady, I always hearken when I hear folk talking secrets; but I mean no harm" (LL 67–68).

This scene's humor partly derives from the racialization of Harry Gregson, who though a British "farm-lad" exhibits the mannerisms of an American pickaninny. When we are first introduced to Harry, he is described as a "lithe, wiry lad, with a thick head of hair, standing out in every direction, as if stirred by some electrical current" (LL, 64). He has a "short, brown face," a "resolute mouth," and "bright, deep-set eyes, which glanced keenly and rapidly round the room, as if taking in everything (and all was new and strange), to be thought and puzzled over at some future time" (LL, 64). Harry's disheveled hair, his caricatured features, and his darting glances evoke the slave-child Topsy from Stowe's *Uncle Tom's Cabin*, first published in England in 1852. Purchased by Augustine St. Clare for his sister Ophelia, Topsy is described as having "wooly hair [that] was braided in sundry little tails, which stuck out in every direction," "round, shining eyes, glittering as glass beads, [that] moved with quick and restless glances over everything in the room," and a mouth "half open with astonishment at the wonders of the new Mas'r's parlor, display[ing] a white and brilliant set of teeth."[43] Upon seeing Topsy for the first time, Aunt Ophelia exclaims, "What on earth did you want to bring [Topsy] here for?" and Augustine answers, "For you to educate—didn't I tell you? You're always preaching about education. I thought I would make you a present of a fresh-caught specimen, and let you try your hand on her, and bring her up in the way she should go" (Stowe, 207–8). A New England spinster with her own quixotic beliefs in slave education, Ophelia is immediately tested when Topsy filches a ribbon and gloves, denies the theft, eventually confesses, but then claims responsibility for thefts she has not committed. Later, when Eva informs her mother that "Miss Ophelia has taught Topsy to read," her mother responds, "Yes, and you see how much good it does. Topsy is the worst creature I ever saw!" (Stowe, 229).

By modeling Harry Gregson on Topsy, Gaskell extends a metaphorical connection between British worker and American slave that Stowe herself had explored in her novel. Augustine, quoting his twin brother Alfred, tells Ophelia that "the American planter is 'only doing, in another form, what the English aristocracy and capitalists are doing by the lower classes;' that is, I take it, *appropriating* them, body and bone, soul and spirit, to their use and convenience" (Stowe, 199), to which Ophelia protests, "'How in the world can the two things be compared? [. . .] The English worker is not sold, traded, parted from his family, whipped'" (Stowe, 200). Augustine's response is characteristic of working-class reformers like Wheeler: "Well, I've traveled in England some, and I've looked over a good many documents as to the state of their lower classes; and I really think there is no denying Alfred when he says that his slaves are better off than a large class of the population of England" (Stowe, 200). Augustine then makes explicit the parallel project of educating workers and slaves:

> "The fact is, that a mind stupefied and animalized by every bad influence from the hour of birth, spending the whole of every week-day in unreflecting toil, cannot be done much with by a few hours on Sunday. The teachers of Sunday-schools among the manufacturing population of England, and among the plantation-hands in our country, could perhaps testify to the same result, *there and here*." (Stowe, 200)

As the beneficiaries of education, Topsy and Harry Gregson initially appear botched experiments, proof that slaves and the lower classes are incorrigible. Topsy steals, Harry Gregson eavesdrops, yet both are insensible to their misdeeds.[44]

Gaskell subsequently models Lady Ludlow's turn-of-the-century fear of working-class literacy on mid-century ideological arguments against slave literacy. Here, she borrows directly from the slave narrative, a primary source of *Uncle Tom's Cabin* as well as *My Lady Ludlow*.[45] Education, to Lady Ludlow, "is a bad thing, if given indiscriminately": "It unfits the lower orders for their duties, the duties to which they are called by God; of submission to those placed in authority over them; of contentment with that state of life to which it has pleased God to call them, and of ordering themselves lowly and reverently to all their betters" (LL 191–92). Once a boy like Harry Gregson is taught to read and write, "his duties become complicated, and his temptations much greater, while, at the same time, he has no hereditary principles and honourable training to serve as safeguards" (LL 192). She repeatedly characterizes reading and writing as "edge-tools" that, if given to the "lower orders," will lead to "the terrible scenes of the French Revolution acted over again in England" (LL, 68). A similar logic informs the resistance to slave literacy, which likewise "spoils" the slave for a life of servitude and makes him dissatisfied with his lot. Frederick Douglass recounts his master's belief that "'if you teach that nigger (speaking of myself) how to read, there would be no keeping him. It would forever unfit him to be a slave. He would at once become unmanageable, and of no value to his master. . . .It would make him discontented and unhappy."[46] Subscribing to the belief that "if you give a nigger an inch, he will take an ell," Douglass's master cautions his wife that "If you learn [a slave] now to read, he'll want to know how to write; and, this accomplished, he'll be running away with himself."[47]

Lady Ludlow is nonetheless depicted with a great deal more sympathy and gentle humor than the irascible American slave owner. Although her fear of working-class literacy is genuine, her comparison of Harry Gregson's indiscretion to the events of the French Revolution seems ludicrous, not the least because the scene of Harry's indiscretion is rendered in largely comical terms, as opposed to the baroque tragedy of the Revolutionary tale.[48] Moreover, Lady Ludlow's antipathy toward working-class education is gradually overcome over the course of the novella. She withdraws her opposition to Mr. Gray's Sunday school, and ultimately allows that it is "right for [Harry Gregson] to be educated" (LL, 235).[49] Lady Ludlow's relenting attitude reflects her evolution from a staunch traditionalist to reluctant progressive. Although she longs for a return to a more "primitive" (LL, 58) feudal system, she eventually submits to the modernization of her estate. She watches as her new agent, a "good, orthodox, aristocratic, and agricultural Hanbury," marries the daughter of a Dissenter, tradesman, and Birmingham democrat. And though she cannot "endure any mention of illegitimate children" and believes that "society ought to ignore them" (LL, 252–53), she eventually receives the illegitimate Miss Bessy at the great Hall and blesses her marriage to Mr. Gray. In the face of considerable social, economic, and political change, Lady Ludlow clings to the old ways but eventually adapts to the new.

Mrs. Dawson's wistful tone further softens the portrayal of Lady Ludlow. As an old woman, herself, she can sympathize with her mistress's innate conservatism and nostalgia for the past. She begins her recollection with the statement, "I am an old woman now, and things are very different to what they were in my youth" (LL, 1). She laments the fast pace of modern life, from the "whizz" and "flash" of the train to the appalling frequency of the post (LL, 1). For Mrs. Dawson, Lady Ludlow is an icon of a simpler, more genteel time, and though her opinions regarding literacy may now seem quaint, they add rather than detract from her charm. Yet she can also recognize how Lady Ludlow's fears may appear overblown or foolish to her younger audience. Mr. Gray's and Mr. Horner's "new-fangled notions" would seem "sadly behind" to "folk at the present day" (LL, 57), but at the time of their introduction, they are understandably disquieting.

Gaskell's humorous and sympathetic portrayal of Lady Ludlow, her use of slave narrative conventions, and her reliance on a peculiar narrative structure necessarily complicate any straightforward reading of the novella as a reformist document. If we read the story through the lens of mid-century fears of popular literacy, Gaskell seems to suggest that the nervous middle-class reader is simply a latter-day Lady Ludlow: resistant to change, prone to alarmism, but fundamentally well-meaning. The brouhaha over popular literacy, like that over Mr. Gray's Sunday school and Mr. Horner's tutelage of Harry Gregson, will ultimately blow over. If we read the story through the lens of mid-century fears of slave literacy, the novella appears an indictment of American slave-holding society. By transforming Harry Gregson into a British Topsy and Lady Ludlow into an anxious slave owner, Gaskell reenacts American attitudes toward slave literacy in order to undermine prevalent proslavery arguments. Harry becomes an upstanding schoolteacher and Lady Ludlow lifts her literacy ban, all to the good of the small English village. Finally, if we read the story through the lens of transatlantic relations, *My Lady Ludlow* seems to adapt slave narrative conventions in order to pay tribute to British progressivism. From its comfortable midcentury vantage point, Britain may congratulate itself on having abolished slavery and the slave trade, and of educating (however ambivalently) its workers in the early part of the century. America, meanwhile, lags behind, harnessed to a backward slave economy and antiquated beliefs.

Then again, perhaps Gaskell is less interested in indicting America, England, or even France, than in arguing for a universal complicity when it comes to acts of social injustice. Mrs. Dawson repeatedly characterizes her story as having "neither beginning, middle, nor end" (LL, 1), a rejection of Aristotelian plot unity that is reflected in the narratological structure of *My Lady Ludlow*, where multiple temporal moments (1780s, 1810s, and 1850s) coexist with multiple geographic loci (France, England, Scotland, and even America). History is less progressive than recursive, less diachronic than synchronic. By bringing together these disparate narrative threads, Gaskell composes a story that resonates across boundaries of race, class, nation, and time. And while her middle-class sympathies are evident in her gentle treatment of Lady Ludlow and tacit endorsement of gradual change, Gaskell does not allow her own nation and class to escape wholly unscathed.

Nonetheless, the frame narration of *My Lady Ludlow*, like that of "The Grey Woman," does keep the past at a safe remove, even as Gaskell argues for its continued relevance to the present. Her use of the comic and gothic modes likewise distances her narratives from their source in the slave narrative and diffuses some of its political content. With her novel *North and South*, however, Gaskell more forcefully and directly links Britain to its role in the international slave economy. Through the unlikely figure of a sailor, Frederick Hale, she implicates England in global acts of injustice, unmediated by narrative, geographic, and temporal dislocations.

4

The Return of the "Unnative"
North and South

What is the role of Frederick Hale in *North and South?* In the midst of Gaskell's novel of class conflict in the industrial North, the story of Frederick's mutiny, his perilous return to England, his concealment in the Hale House, his near-capture at the train station by the bounty hunter Leonards, and his eventual escape to Cadiz, in southern Spain, seems pure plot contrivance.[1] Rosemarie Bodenheimer and Patsy Stoneman both read Frederick's mutiny as a foil to the union strike, with Bodenheimer arguing that his rebellion "reflects the dangers of Thornton's authoritarian position as well as the corresponding dangers for his striking workers"[2] and Stoneman claiming that his story "provides a powerful argument for working-class solidarity. Frederick is heroic but impotent; a handful of men cannot effectively challenge the armed forces and the law."[3] Deirdre David similarly believes Frederick's story serves as a cautionary tale: "I think that one of Frederick's functions in the novel is to demonstrate Gaskell's belief that to disobey the law is to exile oneself from reason and reconciliation; because Frederick does so, he is permanently exiled from his country and his family."[4] For A. W. Ward, Frederick is a character "of secondary importance only,"[5] and for Stefanie Markovits, his story is "outmoded" and "unrealistic."[6] These readings reduce Frederick to an ancillary character whose purpose is to amplify the primary plot of Margaret Hale's social awakening. In subordinating his tale, however, critics have failed to account for the formal intrusion of Frederick's narrative into the novel's plot. Why would Gaskell devote five central chapters of her novel to Frederick's furtive homecoming, when her narrative is ostensibly about the textile trade?

As a sailor, Frederick belongs to a profession with unparalleled geographic mobility and access to "distant countries and foreign people,"[7] introducing an international context to a novel that has traditionally been read in national terms. Frederick travels to Spain, Mexico, and South America and his peregrinations illuminate the global network in which the novel unfolds. W. A. Craik has observed that in *North and South* Gaskell moves beyond the provincial setting of *Ruth* (1853) to depict "a much wider world than she had done before, of places which exist, and affect life in the most retired or self-absorbed provincial places."[8] This world not only includes a broader swath of England—London, Helstone, Milton, and Oxford—but also the world beyond the nation's borders. Yet from its initial publication, *North and South* has consistently been analyzed along the domestic axis. Partly this can be attributed to Charles Dickens, who recommended that Gaskell change her novel's title from *Margaret Hale* to *North and South*. In a letter to Gaskell, Dickens wrote, "North and South appears to me to be a better name than Margaret Hale. It implies more, and is expressive of the opposite people brought face to face in the story."[9] Bodenheimer points out, "it seems likely that [Dickens] invented a title which would link the new novel with his own [*Hard Times*] and with Disraeli's *Sybil, or Two Nations* [1845], and advertise it as another account of the crisis of social division."[10] Perhaps as a result, critics have generally interpreted the novel's geographic dialectic in strictly national terms. According to Louis Cazamian, Milton becomes "one of the two poles on which England turns," establishing an antagonism between a pastoral, aristocratic, agrarian South and an urban, working-class, industrial North.[11] More recently, critics such as Raymond Williams and Hilary Schor have continued to work within a national framework, the former from a Marxist perspective and the latter from a feminist point of view.[12]

Paul Giles notes, however, that by the mid-nineteenth century the "'condition of England' question that so much troubled Victorian Britain came to be reconceived in transnational terms."[13] In particular, Britain's relationship with America took on added importance during this period, as the two countries found themselves increasingly intertwined economically and politically. Popular travelogues such as Frances Trollope's *Domestic Manners of the Americans* (1832) and Charles Dickens's *American Notes* (1842) helped familiarize British readers with the American landscape while commenting, often disparagingly, on American culture and democracy.[14] As Amanda Claybaugh has shown, the two nations were also connected through various reform movements such as temperance, antislavery, and suffrage, as well as through the literary marketplace.[15]

Transnational relations were further tested during the Anglo-American Enlistment Crisis of 1855–1856. Embroiled in the Crimean War, the British began to recruit volunteers in the United States by offering bounties and establishing enlistment depots in the North American colonies. The United States accused Britain of infringing upon American sovereignty and violating its Neutrality Act of 1818, which outlawed foreign recruitment for service abroad. Adding to Anglo-American political friction was the situation in Central America. J. B. Conacher writes, "the American government charged that the British claim to control the Bay Islands south of Belize (British Honduras) and a protectorate over the Indians of the Mosquito Coast violated the Monroe Doctrine and the

Clayton-Bulwer Treaty of 1850—charges which the British government strongly denied."[16] In 1854, British inhabitants of Greytown clashed with the American minister to Central America, leading to the deployment of the American sloop of war, the *Cayene*, which subsequently bombarded the settlement and destroyed the residence of the British consul.[17] Although the Greytown affair and the enlistment crisis would be resolved without recourse to war, it was clear that British actions in America, as in the Crimea, were not far from the mind of the British public.[18]

Traveling through Europe and the Americas, Frederick comes in close proximity to the major international skirmishes of the mid-nineteenth century. He also highlights the Anglo-American connection most immediately relevant to Lancashire's operatives and manufacturers, that between the British textile industry and its American competitors and suppliers. Émile Montégut, writing at the time of *North and South*'s original publication, shrewdly locates the shadow of America in Gaskell's depiction of northern England, where radical enthusiasm for "American-style democracy" threatens to turn Great Britain into "a new version of the United States."[19] Montégut describes northern manufacturers like Thornton as

a firm, tireless, and courageous bourgeois, always with a spyglass at their eye, like the general of an army, to observe the position or movement of the French, American, or German market, always watching for the direction of the wind, like a sailor, to see why cotton is going up so high or wool is undergoing such a depreciation in value.[20]

In this passage, Montégut compares the global outlook of the textile manufacturer to that of a military officer and a sailor, an analogy that deftly unites the commercial, martial, and maritime fronts and reveals the transnational environment in which trade occurred: against the backdrop of war, and across international waters.

As a mariner, Frederick is the novel's most direct link between the cotton-producing American South and the cotton-manufacturing British North. This alternate "North and South" resituates Gaskell's Condition of England novel in transatlantic terms and offers a new, racialized prism through which to view the narrative's conflict between master and man. Metonymically linked to slavery through the maritime trade, Frederick is also linked through his narrative's formal contiguity to the American slave narrative. Frederick's plight exposes the complexities of cosmopolitan identity in the nineteenth century, as Britain and her citizens struggled to reconcile national and international allegiances in the face of shifting political and economic interests. In depicting Frederick's divided identity, *North and South* also anticipates Gaskell's agonized feelings about the American Civil War, a national conflict that places at its center the global problem of slavery.

Deus Ex Ploio

In *Virtual Americas*, Paul Giles begins the work of reading *North and South* in a transnational context:

In [the] new world of transnational communication, capital, like labor, has become subject to the fluctuations of international markets, but Gaskell extrapolates her organic version of England from the (partial) repression of transatlantic turbulence, thus exemplifying how the attempt to demarcate British culture at this time was uncomfortably shadowed and threatened by the specter of the United States.[21]

Gaskell was living in Manchester (Milton's real-world analogue) during a period of such transatlantic turbulence, when England's textile industry, already suffering under the Corn Laws, found itself squeezed by its American suppliers. Jenny Uglow writes,

The early 1830's had seen a boom in Manchester trade. Cotton goods and yarn made up half of Britain's exports. . . . But the boom was followed by a crash. . . . After a brief recovery a second crash followed in 1839. American banks had been giving credit to planters so that they could hold back cotton and demand high prices. Lancashire manufacturers retaliated by refusing to order and slowing production. Workers were laid off by the thousands and hundreds of mills lay idle.[22]

Uglow traces the events of *North and South* to this period of privation, as foreign pressures, coupled with the growing discontent of Chartists and Anti-Corn Law campaigners, exacerbated an already grim domestic situation. In *North and South*, Thornton complains of competition from "American yarns" (NS, 143), which contributes to the financial woes of Milton manufacturers and laborers, and his own ruin can be traced to imprudent speculation in American markets (NS, 408).[23]

For much of the novel, however, England's entanglement (to use a textile metaphor) in the international textile trade is safely abstracted. In the first chapter, Margaret enjoys the sensual splendor of the Indian shawls and her pleasure is equated to that of a child (NS, 11). Such naïvete underscores Margaret's limited knowledge of the textile industry and her distanced position as the consumer at the end of a long supply-chain. The foreign is safely domesticated or, more accurately, deracinated. When the international context does intrude, it manifests itself with all the subtlety of a deus ex machina: American competition helps trigger the strike at Marlborough Mills, and "making a bad end in America" (NS, 408) through speculation conveniently bankrupts Thornton and throws him upon Margaret's charity.[24] To these two instances we can add the abrupt appearance of Frederick from abroad. But unlike our previous examples, where America and India remain remote even as they affect the lives of our protagonists, the return of Frederick brings the transatlantic world into the Hales' living room.

Frederick Hale is a sailor, but he also becomes the vessel through which Gaskell imports cultural and political debates about industrialization, slavery, and international commerce. It is a weighty load, to be sure, but it is one skillfully borne by members of the maritime community, who were the emissary between disparate classes, races, and nations. To use Paul Gilroy's chronotope, the ship itself became a "living, micro-cultural, micro-political system in motion" and the "living means by which the points within [the] Atlantic world were joined"[25]—a microcosm of national and racial tensions, as well as the vehicle of their circulation. Seen this way, Frederick becomes an updated deus ex machina, interpolating himself into Gaskell's narrative in a nineteenth-century machine, the ship.

Until she learns the details of Frederick's mutiny, Margaret's association of her brother to transatlantic trade is as abstracted as that of the Indian shawls. Margaret retrieves his old letters from her mother's "little japan cabinet" and unties the "silken string" tying them together while noting the "peculiar fragrance which ocean letters have" (NS, 106). Recalling the scene where Margaret "snuff[s] up [the] spicy Eastern smell" (NS, 11) of the Indian shawls, Margaret's knowledge of Frederick is safely bound up in bourgeois knickknacks and benign, if strange, odors. Her reaction is appropriately naïve for until this moment, she had not been deemed "old enough to be told plainly" (NS, 106) about Frederick's plight.

In reading the letters, however, the international background to Frederick's rebellion is brought into sharp relief. Among the responsibilities of the British navy after the abolition of the slave trade in 1807 was to keep slave ships out of British waters. Captain Reid, having spent three years on the *Avenger* "with nothing to do but to keep the slavers off, and work her men, till they ran up and down the rigging like rats or monkeys" (NS, 107) relocates a transatlantic history of physical brutality and subjugation to the *H.M.S. Russell*. His "tyranny" (NS, 107) aboard the ship, his reliance on flogging, his culpability in the death of a crewmember, and his mutinous overthrow by his subordinates eerily recreates, in microcosm, the horrors of slavery.

W. Jeffrey Bolster has drawn parallels between maritime and slave discipline, writing, "Just as slaves could be maimed or killed by their masters with virtual impunity during much of the slave era, sailors aboard British (and later American) merchant ships could be legally—and at times mortally—flogged by their officers well into the nineteenth century."[26] The navy contributed to this culture of brutality through its policy of impressment, a subject Gaskell later addressed in her 1863 novel *Sylvia's Lovers*.[27] Forcibly kidnapped, separated from their families, denied compensation, and ruthlessly flogged, impressed sailors endured abuses typically reserved for slaves.[28] Even those who voluntarily enlisted or who worked aboard merchant carriers likened their situation to that of temporary enslavement, with their vessel a kind of floating plantation.[29]

It seems ironic justice that Captain Reid, set adrift by his men, is eventually picked up "by a West-Indian steamer" (NS, 108) en route, presumably, to its next destination in the infamous triangle trade.

Frederick is neither a slave nor a slaver, but he is implicated in an international system of commerce that could not exist but for slavery. Ships from England transported cotton goods and other supplies to Africa, where they were sold and traded for slaves. Loaded with their human cargo, these ships then sailed to the West Indies and to America, where the slaves were sold to plantation owners in exchange for goods such as raw cotton, sugar, and tobacco. In the third segment of the journey, the ships returned to England, where they unloaded and sold their merchandise. All three English interests prospered in this so-called triangle trade. Textile manufacturers sold their finished cotton goods and received fresh supplies of raw cotton; slave traders kidnapped or bought African slaves, clothed them in English textiles, and sold them to West Indian and American plantation owners; and the mariners were paid for their transportation services and received a cut of the final profit. Mariners, in other words, were the consummate "middlemen," connecting and profiting from various commercial interests.[30] Their role in the textile trade would only increase in the nineteenth century, as Lancashire manufacturers looked to America for greater supplies of "clean" cotton to feed their looms. By the 1840s, Anthony Burton writes, "more than 80 per cent of all cotton spun in Britain came from the American South."[31] By 1856, around the time of *North and South*'s publication, cotton accounted for 54 percent of all American exports.[32]

Frederick may help "keep slavers off" in the British Navy, but he also protects British interests, insuring the safe transport of American slave-produced goods to English ports (an irony that did not go unnoticed by abolitionists). As such, he is integral to the success of the transatlantic textile trade, connecting British textile manufacturers to their supply of American cotton. Moreover, in the daily running of the trade, he occupies a lateral position to that of the slave and the operative: cotton picked by the slave is transported across the Atlantic by the sailor and woven into textile by the operative. In this particularized version of the triangle trade, slave, sailor, and operative are metonymically linked, each occupying a separate node in the transatlantic supply chain.

The contiguity of these three "professions" may account for the active transmission and proliferation of slave metaphors across the global network. Metonymically aligned, slave, sailor, and operative also found themselves metaphorically linked. We have seen how Captain Reid's shipboard tyranny resembles plantation culture, transforming the sailors into oppressed slaves. And on land, too, we see metaphors of slavery color the discourse over industrialization. Catherine Gallagher, in her detailed study of the worker/slave metaphor, writes:

[There were] certain obvious similarities between [workers] and slaves. . . . [Workers] were physically confined and had to work long hours according to the rhythms of the spinning machines; alertness and diligence were too often maintained by corporal punishment, and the sheer size of many textile mills, with their accompanying impersonality, reminded reformers of vast plantations worked by indistinguishable slaves.[33]

Thornton, deploying this rhetoric for his own ends, likens the impending strike to a slave uprising. He cries, "They [the strikers] want to be masters, and make the masters into slaves on their own ground. They are always trying at it; they always have it in their minds; and every five or six years, there comes a struggle between masters and men" (NS, 16). Even his advocacy of "a wise despotism" (NS, 119) mirrors a philosophy of plantation paternalism.[34]

Yet Gaskell moves beyond these popular metaphors in order to emphasize the interdependence of these three "professions"—to demonstrate, in the words of Higgins, that they are "bound in one common interest" (NS, 228) in an informal and unarticulated *global* union. Frederick acts as the "middleman" or lateral mediator between cotton-picking slave and cotton-weaving worker, revealing a transatlantic brotherhood that transcends racial and national boundaries. While Margaret negotiates the vertical, domestic axis, connecting operative to manufacturer to customer, Frederick operates along the horizontal, international axis, connecting supplier to distributor to manufacturer. Later in the novel, Frederick's easy transition from English sailor to Spanish merchant trader can be seen as a geographical and professional move along this international axis. Frederick becomes the novel's Jamesian *ficelle*, peripheral to the narrative yet the device through which Gaskell illumines the complex network in which her story takes place. Given the novel's setting in the textile industry, the term is particularly apt, for Frederick becomes the "string" (*ficelle*) that tugs at the central plot, the horizontal thread of connection that, when pulled, makes visible the cultural and economic matrix in which the narrative occurs.

The intersection of the national and international axes occurs in Milton, at the narrative midpoint of the novel, when Frederick arrives at his mother's deathbed. Concealed behind a door, Frederick glimpses Thornton and imagines him a shopman (much to his sister's chagrin). Later, Thornton glimpses Frederick en route to the train station and imagines him a lover (again to Margaret's chagrin). Both meetings converge on Margaret, the central locus of the novel and the character who must reconcile almost single-handedly the multitudinous tensions in the novel. This, at least, has been the predominant focus of critics, who more often than not see Margaret as the transcendental mediator, an interpretation partially borne out by the novel's original title.

But if we redirect our critical attention to Frederick and his subplot, we may be astonished by just how much narrative real estate he occupies. Alex Woloch has described how narratives function as closed structures or "character-systems" that allocate to characters, both major and minor, a certain portion of "character-space" in which to move.[35] For a minor character, Frederick, it turns out, takes up quite a lot of character-space. Early in the novel, he repeatedly intrudes on Margaret's thoughts while she is at Harley Street, so much so that when Mr. Hale first informs Margaret of his break with the church, her first instinct is to link his decision to Frederick's crime. Mrs. Hale devotes perhaps too much of her own character-space yearning for her son and enumerating his virtues.[36] Thornton is "haunted by the remembrance of the handsome young man" (NS, 246) he glimpses with Margaret at the train station. And in the latter half of the novel, Margaret is consumed by fears for Frederick's safety and hopes for his exoneration. These moments, along with the five central chapters devoted to Frederick's homecoming and flight, comprise a substantial secondary narrative to the primary plot of Margaret's social awakening.

The next section looks more closely at the particular construction of Frederick's narrative as well as the historical moment in which Gaskell wrote in order to further support a transatlantic reading of *North and South*. If Frederick becomes an agent of international cultural transmission, his narrative likewise "circulates" within a transnational context. Set against the nineteenth-century transatlantic antislavery movement, his tale opens up a "contact zone"[37] between Gaskell's novel and the narrative of the American slave.

Doulous Ex Ploio

Markovits describes Frederick's rebellion as "the stuff of romance (as is evidenced by Gaskell's chapter epigraphs from Byron),"[38] while David dismisses Frederick's story as "the conventional saga of the mutiny of a brave young officer against his cruel captain" and points out that "shortly after Margaret learns the details of this story from her mother, the antagonism between Thornton and his workers erupts at the mill."[39] David's argument is supported on the generic level by Margaret Cohen in her analysis of nineteenth-century maritime fiction. Cohen argues that the maritime genre's "fundamental subject matter" is work, namely the degradation of labor, and she links maritime fiction to the industrial novel in their mutual engagement with the problems of an emergent capitalist economy.[40] Seen this way, Frederick's "conventional saga" of a mutinous sailor appears a logical analogue to the Milton strike.

Yet Frederick physically enters the novel *after* the strike, bringing to the foreground the repercussions rather than the provocations of rebellion. His story intersects with Margaret's not at sea but on land, and his immediate concerns are not those of a sailor but those of a fugitive. As such, his tale is less of the "conventional saga" of a seaman, for it moves well beyond the workings and movements of a ship. Earlier I spoke of Frederick Hale as a deus ex machina, but perhaps the most accurate term for his role is *doulous ex ploio*—a slave from a ship. Rather than rehearse the "conventional saga" of a mutinous sailor, he introduces the conventional saga of the run-away slave.[41]

By resituating *North and South* to account for its cosmopolitan dimension, we have seen how slavery impacts the novel. In this alternate "North and South," England is reimagined as part of a global community that links Lancashire to the American South. But it also evokes another geographic division, namely that between the *American* North and South. Paul Giles writes, "Division between the North and South of England, as represented in Gaskell's novel, disconcertingly mirrored those between the northern and southern parts of the United States: on both sides of the Atlantic, the industrial north found itself pitted against the more traditional south."[42] Northern England and New England were the centers of textile production in their respective countries. Southern England and the American South were associated with the landed gentry, large estates, and a "docile servant caste."[43] In this context, Thornton's description of "the aristocratic society down South" with its "slow days of careless ease" (NS, 82) sounds compellingly like an account of American plantation life.

Gaskell's "Condition of England" novel begins to reproduce the condition of America, elevating to the geopolitical level the mutual dependence of the two nations and their inhabitants. In the nineteenth-century global economy, the domestic stability of England depended on the domestic stability of America. An interruption in cotton supplies caused by an American civil war and the abolition of slavery would be devastating to England, creating a ripple effect that would disrupt the manufacturing industry and trigger economic crisis. With the passage of the Fugitive Slave Act of 1850, the conflict over slavery in America became increasingly acrimonious.[44] Exacerbating already existing tensions between the slaveholding South and the free North, the Fugitive Slave Act forced slaves to seek asylum in Canada or England, and in the next ten years, as many as 20,000 slaves made this journey to sovereign British territories.

During this period, the British public was increasingly exposed to the plight of American slaves through the publication of slave narratives. The slave narrative's transatlantic popularity may seem surprising given its cultural specificity, namely its setting in a distinctly American landscape and its focus on the particular horrors of American cotton-slavery. But we have seen how Britain, despite having abolished slavery, continued to find itself politically and economically embroiled in the American slave question—even recreating American internecine tensions.[45] Cohen's argument about the transportability of sea fiction could be applied to the slave narrative, with its culturally resonant scenes of violence, adventure, and degraded labor. Cohen writes, "genres that travel must contain elements that can pass from national literary context to national literary context—flexibility and play, to negotiate cultural difference."[46] The slave narrative becomes the ideal "traveling genre" in two senses. On the one hand, it could straddle (and collapse) cultural difference and thus, be adopted and adapted by writers across the Atlantic. On the other, it literally traveled across the Atlantic, transported by ship and—often—in the guise of the actual fugitive slave.

The most famous fugitive slave was Frederick Douglass, whose narrative was first published in America in 1845 and who fled immediately afterward to England, where he embarked on an extensive lecture tour of the country. Gaskell may have attended one of Douglass's lectures during his tour of England from 1845 to 1847, and we know her close friends, Mary and William Howitt, hosted Douglass and his American abolitionist patron William Lloyd Garrison in their home, the Elms, in Clapton.[47] Frederick Hale's story bears some striking resemblances to Frederick Douglass's narrative, beginning with their shared first name. Margaret's memory of her brother "being in some great disgrace . . . for stealing apples" (NS, 251) evokes a parallel Miltonic allusion in Douglass's narrative of young slaves stealing apples from Colonel Lloyd's garden.[48] In another parallel episode, Frederick Hale finds refuge in Cadiz, a port city in the heart of Moorish Spain, where he changes his surname in order to preserve his anonymity. As Mrs. Hale points out to Margaret, "[Frederick] is not called Hale; you must remember that. . . . Notice the F.D. in every corner of the letters. He has taken the name of Dickenson" (NS, 106, 108). Frederick Douglass likewise changes his name after fleeing to the North, adopting "Douglass" to replace his given surname "Bailey."[49] Indeed, Frederick Douglass and Frederick Hale-cum-Dickenson share not only the same first name but also the same initials.[50]

Yet the novel moves beyond such superficial connections as apples and initials to reveal a shared emphasis on seminal moments of violence and emancipation. Captain Reid recreates the horrors of slavery aboard his ship, and it is his flogging (and murder) of a fellow sailor that incites Frederick to rebel. Set against the historical background of the 1850s, with the heightened transatlantic traffic of runaway slaves and slave narratives following the Fugitive Slave Act, his defiance evokes the slave's struggle against a tyrannical master. Later, bounty hunter and slave catcher converge in the character of Leonards, whose attempted arrest of Frederick at the train station can be read as a literalized enactment of the dangers of the underground railroad, as the fugitive is transported out of the country and into safety.[51] It seems no coincidence that both episodes are linked to vehicles: the ship and the train. Both offer Frederick a means of escape from England but also a means of connection to alternate cultures.

Frederick Hale's cultural mobility manifests itself in his physical appearance, further linking him to a racialized other. Upon seeing her brother for the first time in many years, Margaret describes Frederick as having "delicate features, redeemed from effeminacy by the swarthiness of his complexion, and his quick intensity of expression" (NS, 242). She continues, "His eyes were generally merry-looking, but at times they and his mouth so suddenly changed, and gave her such an idea of latent passion, that it almost made her afraid. . . . [It was] the instantaneous ferocity of expression that comes over the countenances of all natives of wild or southern countries" (NS, 243). Frederick's time at sea and his "travels to Mexico, South America, and elsewhere" (NS, 245) have made him a cosmopolite; his nationality, race, and even gender have become indeterminate. He now exhibits the unpredictability of the "natives," at one moment docile, at another uncontrollable, suggesting an ontological as well as physical metamorphosis.

Frederick's cosmopolitanism, in turn, helps to explain his mutinous actions aboard the ship. Mrs. Hale and Margaret vehemently defend Frederick, the former declaring, "I am prouder of Frederick standing up against injustice, than if he had been simply a good officer" (NS, 109) and the latter agreeing, "Loyalty and obedience to wisdom and justice are fine; but it is still finer to defy arbitrary power, unjustly and cruelly used" (NS, 109). Frederick's allegiances are not to his country but to something loftier—to universal ideals of justice untethered to any particular individual or nation. But as a result, Frederick becomes an enemy of the state and an "outlaw," vilified in newspapers as a "traitor of the blackest dye" and "a base, ungrateful disgrace to his profession" (NS, 35). Mr. Hale explains to Margaret,

> it is necessary, of course, for government to take very stringent measures for the repression of offences against authority, more particularly in the navy, where a commanding officer needs to be surrounded in his men's eye with a vivid consciousness of all the power there is at home to back him, and take up his cause, and avenge any injuries offered to him, if need be. (NS, 203)

The legal system, too, is rigged against him, for Frederick lacks access to witnesses and faces the bias of the maritime court. Frederick finds himself caught between his status as a British subject and his status as a cosmopolite—between his place at "home" and his place in the world. His exile and eventual renunciation of England suggests the impossibility of dual citizenship: once a citizen of all nations, Frederick becomes the citizen of none.

One could argue for other points of connection between Frederick Hale and Frederick Douglass, but a more productive exercise might be to consider *why* Gaskell appropriates the slave narrative in *North and South*. On the stylistic level, the decision seems curious, for Frederick's narrative is often clumsily introduced and integrated. Certain elements of the slave narrative are adopted (episodes of violent resistance and furtive flight) while others are elided (scenes of literacy). Yet the fragmentary and disjunctive quality to the slave narrative's appearance suggests a kind of genre tectonics, a collision between two separate but adjacent genres. Thematically, we have seen how industrial, slave, and maritime discourse participate in a common language of oppression, a universal tongue spoken by each constituent of the international textile trade. The appearance of the slave narrative in Gaskell's industrial novel gestures toward a global *literary*, as well as commercial, community—one in which industrial novel, slave narrative, and maritime fiction are internationally circulated and metonymically aligned. Frederick's liminal status, his ability to traverse national, social, and economic boundaries, also allows him to traverse *generic* boundaries. Earlier, he laments, "No one would read a pamphlet of self-justification so long after the deed, even if I put one out" (NS, 254), but the novel allows him to access a contiguous "pamphlet" in the way he accesses contiguous cultures.

The interpolation of the slave narrative reaffirms the global reach of slavery, which underpins the novel on the economic and generic level. It also erodes Giles's distinction between the work of an American slave narrator like Douglass and that of a British industrial novelist like Gaskell. Giles contends that "Douglass's narratives render with a brutal literalism the corporate and corporeal strife that, in the case of English writers like Gaskell, is kept discreetly under wraps or sublimated metaphorically into harmonious, if unlikely, reconciliations."[52] This is perhaps true in the case of Higgins and Thornton, who learn to break bread together, and Thornton and Margaret, who wed one another. But for Frederick the "corporate and corporeal strife" of his mutiny is never satisfactorily reconciled. At the end of the novel, he remains geographically estranged from his family and, despite Henry Lennox's efforts, no closer to exonerating himself.

Frederick's failure to achieve harmonious closure has led Deidre David to conclude that Frederick "is a social exile by virtue of his immaturity and impetuosity—qualities which render him unfit for life in modern England."[53] And Audrey Fisch reads his expulsion from the text—as well as his initial absence—as further confirmation of slavery's distortive effects on British domestic tranquility.[54] But perhaps there is an alternate reason for Frederick's dissatisfying narrative end, one that has less to do with his bad attitude and propensity for violence than with his conflicted status in the world. At once a British citizen and cosmopolite, Frederick must negotiate two seemingly antagonistic identities. It is not his immaturity or impetuosity that expels him from modern England but rather his inability to sublimate or reconcile this ontological divide. In depicting Frederick's contested status, Gaskell brings to the forefront the problems of global citizenry in the last half of the nineteenth century.

The Return of the "Unnative"

In one of his last letters to Margaret, Frederick passionately disavows his country, wishing he could "unnative himself" and declaring that "he would not take his pardon if it were offered him, nor live in the country if he had permission to do so" (NS, 335). The verb "unnative" (a unique inflection of Gaskell's, according to the *Oxford English Dictionary*) suggests the ability to shed one's birthright, to nullify one's ties to a particular locale or culture. Yet the desire is expressed in the subjunctive—"he wished he could unnative himself"—suggesting the impossibility of such a feat. It is the prerogative of Frederick's native country, Britain, to bestow or revoke citizenship, leaving Frederick in a position of powerlessness. Mr. Hale tells

Margaret, "[The British authorities] spare no expense, they send out ships,—they scour the seas to lay hold of the offenders,—the lapse of years does not wash out the memory of the offence" (NS, 203). Frederick's status as a British subject is as indelible a mark as his crime, resistant to the attenuating effects of distance and time.

By marrying into a Spanish family, Frederick embraces an alternate national identity, one that must contend with his native British status. Neither fully British nor fully Spanish, Frederick occupies the ambiguous position of the cosmopolite, who is caught between all nations and none. His physical situation is correspondingly precarious, for at any moment, Frederick might be discovered in Cadiz and extradited. A presumed traitor in one country, he resides under a false name in another, jeopardizing his status in both nations. Frederick's hybrid status particularly troubles Margaret, who notes "how far the idioms of his bride's country were infecting him" (NS, 335) and harbors suspicions that he has converted to Catholicism, the religion of his adoptive country. Frederick, she fears, is metamorphosing from Englishman to Spaniard. He has become "infected" and hispanicized, as if nationhood is a disease that crosses somatic boundaries.

Margaret's xenophobia is notable for its seeming inconsistency with her own cultural hybridity. Her mother criticizes her use of "horrid Milton words" and "factory slang" (NS, 233), to which Margaret replies, "Edith picked up all sorts of military slang from Captain Lennox, and aunt Shaw never took any notice of it" and "if I live in a factory town, I must speak factory language when I want it" (NS, 233). In both cases, however, the cosmopolitanism that is depicted does not threaten British nationalism. Margaret's use of Northern dialect does not make her less British but more so. Similarly, Edith, though far from England, resides in a British Protectorate and adopts the language of British soldiers, not the foreign Corfiotes. Frederick's cosmopolitanism, on the other hand, imperils national cohesion. In Margaret's mind, his linguistic hybridity is a sign of foreign corruption and "infect[ion]," a threat to a holistic British identity.

Margaret's ambivalence can be traced to the specifically racialized, transnational character of Frederick's cosmopolitanism. Frederick, she had earlier observed, exhibits "the instantaneous ferocity of expression that comes over the countenances of all natives of wild or southern countries" (NS, 243). According to the *Oxford English Dictionary*, "native" here could refer to "a person born in bondage" (derived from the Latin *nativus*), to "a member of an indigenous ethnic group," or to "a black person of African origin or descent" in "Britain and the United States during the period of colonialism and slavery."[55] Frederick's cosmopolitanism exceeds linguistic or national boundaries. It portends, instead, a more transgressive racial and ontological hybridity. Given the racial double meaning of "native," Frederick's subsequent wish to "unnative himself" takes on additional complexity. Frederick rejects the bonds of Great Britain for the bonds of "wild or southern countries." He disavows one native identity (white, British) for another (racialized, cosmopolitan).[56]

"If I had a country, I would be a patriot," Frederick Douglass had pro-
claimed in an 1847 speech, lamenting the plight of the slave, born into a
nation that denies him citizenship yet treats him as a traitor.[57] Douglass,
by virtue of his status as an African-American, is forced into a cosmopolitan existence, and he appeals to the world community—Americans and
Britons, alike—to recognize their shared humanity and to eradicate slavery.[58] It is a cry renewed by W. E. B. Du Bois later in the century in his
struggle to reconcile his Negro and American identities and to access a
"kingdom of culture" that transcends race and nationhood.[59] Frederick
Hale seeks refuge in this "Black Atlantic" space of hybrid culture and
global community, a space of multiple nationalities and ethnicities that is
inveterately linked to slavery and the black diaspora. His expressed desire
to "unnative" himself anticipates the cry of nineteenth-century black
cosmopolitanism, and his designation as a "traitor of the blackest dye"
suggests a solidarity with the racial other.

Frederick's hybrid cosmopolitanism, however, has mixed consequences.
Although he is valorized by his mother and sister, he is physically estranged
from his family, criminalized by his country, and indirectly responsible for
the hangings of his fellow sailors. He is placed in an ethical and ontological bind, caught between ideals of justice and global citizenship on the one
hand and his responsibility to his family, nation, and friends on the other.
Frederick becomes a casualty of this rift, unable to reconcile his cosmopolitan and his national identities and relegated, as a result, to the narrative and geographic margins. In some ways, he is sacrificed for
national stability and a safer, more localized brand of cosmopolitanism.
Once Margaret accepts that Frederick is "lost to [her]" (NS, 373) and
chooses not to follow him to Cadiz, she is able to "return[] to the present
life" (NS, 401) and resolve more immediate domestic tensions. By expel-
ling Frederick from England, the novel can ensure the corporate and
corporeal health of the nation.

Given the novel's privileging of national ties over global, it is interesting
to consider Gaskell's response to the American Civil War, perhaps the most
famous battle between "North and South" of the nineteenth century.
Although Gaskell's novel was published six years before the war, we have
seen how it refracted American internecine tensions through its geographic parallelism and its allusions to the international textile trade. This
cat's cradle of connections would become increasingly snarled with the
outbreak of the war. As feared, the disruption of American cotton supplies
plunged the British textile industry into economic crisis. The Confederacy
had hoped such economic distress would prompt England to support their
cause, but they were sorely disappointed. In Burton's words, "Britain was
not about to go to war on behalf of unemployed cotton workers, even if
there were a quarter of a million of them."[60] Still, Lancashire rallied
around the American South, a fact Gaskell mentions in a letter to her
friend, the American abolitionist Charles Eliot Norton: "You know I live in
S. Lancashire where all personal & commercial intimacies are with the
[American] South."[61] Yet again, transatlantic alliances coalesced around

geographic lines, this time with the British North generally aligning itself with the American South and the British South aligning itself with the Union.[62]

Gaskell found herself caught in an ethical and ontological bind reminiscent of that experienced by Frederick Hale. Torn between her abolitionist sympathies and her concern for her fellow Mancunians, between her cosmopolitan ideals of freedom and her British allegiances, Gaskell appeals to Norton, "Take myself and Meta [Gaskell's daughter] for average specimens of English people,—*most* kindly disposed to you, our dear cousins, hating slavery intensely, but yet thoroughly *puzzled by* what is now going on in America."[63] Gaskell's "puzzle[ment]" becomes a symptom of ontological distress, a psychomachia that pits her commitment to her American "cousins" against her commitment to those at home. Yet even as she reiterates her hatred for slavery, Gaskell clings to the hope of peaceful reconciliation. In a gingerly proffered suggestion, she writes, "I should have thought (I feel as if I were dancing among eggs) that separating yourselves from the South was like getting rid of a diseased member."[64] Gaskell's support of secession here takes on corporeal overtones, as if amputation is the only cure for the diseased American body. It evokes Margaret's comment about Spanish idioms "infect[ing]" Frederick's speech and suggests that for Gaskell, any threat to the national body is suspect and foreign. With this statement, Gaskell signals her own tentative privileging of the national over the global. She proposes an uneasy compromise that effectively condones Southern secession and slavery in order to salvage the corporeal and corporate harmony of Britain and the American North. This compromise would not ultimately come to pass, but it reveals Gaskell's dream of reconciliation, one that sacrificed her commitment to abolition and to the ideal of hybrid cosmopolitanism for a more pragmatic and limited vision of British nationhood.

5

Fugitive Plots in *Great Expectations*

In 1842, Dickens embarked on a tour of the United States, traveling as far south as Virginia, where he witnessed American slavery for the first time. In his travelogue *American Notes*, published soon after his return to England, he recalls taking the train from Fredericksburg to Richmond: "In the negro car [of the train] . . . were a mother and her children who had just been purchased; the husband and father being left behind with their old owner. The children cried the whole way, and the mother was misery's picture."[1] Over the next several days, Dickens visited a tobacco manufactury, "where the workmen were all slaves," a plantation, where he "went down with the owner of the estate, to 'the quarter,' as that part of it in which the slaves live is called, [although] I was not invited to enter into any of their huts,"[2] and the town of Richmond, where slavery seemed to lurk in the "decay and gloom" of the streets. He observes that "there are laws against instructing slaves, of which the pains and penalties greatly exceed in their amount the fines imposed on those who maim and torture them,"[3] and it is with great relief that he finally leaves Virginia and boards a steamboat back to Washington. Even then, slavery shadows him in the form of "two constables on board the steam-boat, in pursuit of runaway slaves."[4]

Slavery sickened Dickens and underscored what he saw as the hypocrisy of America, a democracy in which African Americans were treated undemocratically. In *American Notes* he inserts, toward the end of the narrative, a codalike chapter devoted to slavery. The chapter is seemingly out of place, disrupting the chronological order of Dickens's tour. Jerome Meckier reads this as a manifestation of the warping influence of slavery, and Sidney Moss sees in it a displacement of Dickens's anger over international copyright.[5] In fact, the chapter is not an account of Dickens's eyewitness experience but is, in large part, a reprinting of Theodore D. Weld's antislavery pamphlet, *American Slavery As It Is*.[6] Dickens lists several fugitive slave advertisements and rages against public opinion, which he blames for condoning the pursuit and recapture of runaway slaves. This chapter, as well as Dickens's criticisms of American greed, corruption, and ill manners, led to an outcry among his American readers. Dickens responded by skewering American slavery and hypocrisy further in his novel *Martin Chuzzlewit* (1843–44), published immediately after *American Notes*. Patricia Ingham writes, "In South Carolina there was even an attempt to ban the circulation of [*American Notes*] on the grounds that the treatment of slavery breached a law that forbade any white man to circulate in print or writing any paper intended 'to disturb the peace and security of slaves.'"[7] Frederick Douglass, speaking to a British audience in 1846, urged them to "read the chapter on slavery in Dickens's Notes on America" for proof of the American slave's plight.[8] Two years later, Dickens returned the literary favor, recommending that Macready read a copy of Douglass's narrative before his tour of America.

During the 1850s, Dickens became interested less in exposing the horror of American slavery than in finding peaceable solutions to the problem. In the September 18, 1852 issue of *Household Words*, he contributed to an article entitled "North American Slavery."[9] Arthur Adrian describes the essay as "less belligerent in tone and certainly less inflammatory than the slavery chapter in *American Notes*."[10] It ends with a plea for the peaceful abolition of slavery through gradual emancipation, education, and eventually emigration to Liberia.[11] In a letter to Mrs. Edward Cropper from 1852, Dickens explains that he no longer wished to shock people with images of slavery or to be used as an abolitionist spokesman:

> If I wanted to exhibit myself on this subject [of slavery], I know perfectly well that a few pages of fiery declamation in Household Words would make their way (wafted by the Anti-Slavery Societies) all over the civilised earth. But I want to help the wretched Slave. Now I am morally certain that when public attention has been called to him by pathetic pictures of his sufferings and by the representation in deservedly black colors of his oppressors, the way to save him, is, *then* to step in with persuasion and argument and endeavor to reason with the holders, and shew them that it is best, even for themselves, to consider their duty of abolishing the system.[12]

Dickens recognized the limits of "pathetic pictures" and betrays frustration with the increasing intractability of the American conflict. At the same time, he was redirecting his literary energies to issues of local and national reform, from sanitation to the abolition of capital punishment. It was during these years that Dickens wrote what Amanda Claybaugh describes as "his great novels of reform," works that "tend[ed] to ridicule any attention to the world beyond the nation."[13]

Yet American slavery was both an intensely local and an intensely global conflict. It was geographically specific, grounded in the American landscape and the internecine struggle between North and South. But it also resonated globally, transcending its American context to become an issue of general humanitarian concern. In an 1854 letter to Mrs. Frances Colden, Dickens frets over "the Massachusetts Slavery Question, on which a great deal of importance to the whole world seems to hang."[14] Dickens was referring to the seizure of Anthony Burns, a fugitive slave from Virginia who was returned to his master under the auspices of the Fugitive Slave Law of 1850. Burns's 1854 trial in Boston was accompanied by widespread riots and the declaration of martial law, and it reinvigorated the abolitionist cause while intensifying the animosity between the American North and South. Burns's capture became a test case of state versus federal authority, of Massachusetts' jurisdiction over runaway slaves versus federal legislation that dictated Burns be returned to his Virginian owners. Yet Dickens also saw the episode as one of international urgency, significant to the fate of "the whole world." In the same letter, he writes, "It is sad to consider such a state of things. I know of nothing in the world presenting such a prodigious moral phenomenon, as the whole proceedings of the last audacious seizure at Boston, in a country existing under the great declaration of Independence."[15] Burns's capture exceeds its local circumstances, becoming an indictment of national policy and a "moral" crisis of global proportion.

Written on the eve of the American Civil War, *Great Expectations* appears a steadfastly national text, advocating social reform and chronicling English provincial life. Yet its preoccupation with class divisions and connections is radically informed by the genre of American slave narrative. Resituating the slave narrative in a British context, Dickens applies its generic paradigm to issues of class mobility, freedom, colonialism, literacy, and self-fashioning. The chronotope of the fugitive slave shapes the narrative, from the critical opening scene in which Pip collides with the literal fugitive, Magwitch, to Pip's own journey from indentured apprentice to gentleman. The novel is organized around such scenes of incarceration, clandestine reading, violence, and illicit escape. It is at these moments that, according to Bakhtin, the "knots of narrative are tied and untied."[16] In the case of *Great Expectations*, the more apt image might be of chains: the fugitive slave chronotope shows how events and characters are linked and unlinked.

The image of chains evokes the novel's obsession with metonymic connections. As Alex Woloch writes, the chain comes "to thematically signify contiguity itself" and "is rooted in the dynamics of subordination and distortion."[17] The novel attempts to reconnect alienated labor (Magwitch) with the wealth it has produced (Pip and his inheritance), revealing the link between England and its criminal underclass. The privileging of metonymy in *Great Expectations* simultaneously recalls the metonymic network of slavery and its undergirding of British nation- and empire-building.[18] This network is inferred in the novel through the generic influence of the slave narrative but also through Magwitch's identification of his degraded status with slavery. Magwitch's impoverished background, his economic exploitation, and his subsequent imprisonment and flight nativize the American slave experience to the British context.

Great Expectations employs the slave narrative to help structure what is ultimately a class narrative.

Dickens, who had been a harsh critic of American slavery in the 1840s, was by the 1860s deeply skeptical of the American North's commitment to abolition and of the wisdom of preserving the American union. This ambivalence, which he shared with fellow British authors such as Elizabeth Gaskell, may account for Dickens's compulsive reimaginings of the fugitive plot and his fixation upon the complications of freedom.

In *Great Expectations*, the slave narrative is absorbed, parodically stylized, and revised, paralleling Dickens's own attempts to integrate—and then escape—the fugitive plot.

Literacy, Mastery, Metonymy

The organizing center of *Great Expectations* is Magwitch. Like Frederick Hale in *North and South*, he is peripheral to the narrative yet the device through which Dickens reveals the complex network in which his story takes place. And like Frederick, he introduces into the novel the chronotope of the fugitive slave. From his first appearance, he acts as a centripetal force, drawing Pip into his orbit and subsequently influencing the rest of the events in the novel. As Bakhtin writes, "all the novel's abstract elements—philosophical and social generalizations, ideas, analyses of cause and effect—gravitate towards the chronotope and through it take on flesh and blood, permitting the imaging power of art to do its work."[19] He is, to paraphrase Woloch, a *major* "minor character," socially, economically, and even geographically marginalized, yet central to the narrative plot.

In Magwitch, we see a layering of the "social" contact zone of slavery and empire, and the textual contact zone of slave narrative. The first bridges the novel and the larger world; the second bridges the novel and other genres. Yet Magwitch also represents a *narrative* contact zone—what Bakhtin calls "character zone" and what Woloch calls "character-space." "A character in a novel," Bakhtin writes, "always has, as we have said, a zone of his own, his own sphere of influence on the authorial context surrounding him, a sphere that extends—and often quite far—beyond the boundaries of the direct discourse allotted him."[20] And Woloch describes "character-space" as "that particular and charged encounter between an individual human personality and a determined space and position within the narrative as a whole."[21] In *Great Expectations*, Magwitch's character zone expands to include not just his own discourse and actions, but also those of Pip.

But what, exactly, is the fugitive slave chronotope, and how does it manifest itself in the novel? Derived from the slave narrative, the fugitive slave chronotope is attached to experiences of suffering and violence, of familial and natal alienation, of unfreedom and terror, of the Hegelian struggle between master and slave. It attaches to artifacts such as chains, brands, irons, and whips. It structures life according to "fugitive-time," or pre- and post-emancipatory eras, and its teleology is toward freedom and rebirth. Its escape geography is the road, the swamp, the river, and the sea. Its escape vehicles are the ship and the train. It inhabits scenes of literacy and the struggle for knowledge. Above all, it is affiliated with pursuit, with geographic instability, with homelessness and the fear of capture.

The fugitive slave chronotope is closely allied with the convict chronotope, which enters the novel through the Newgate novel and convict narrative. Where the two differ is in the former's overwhelming emphasis on the fugitive status of the protagonist, with its corresponding need for concealment and secrecy. As Jonathan Grossman points out, the Newgate novel centers on climactic trial scenes and the juridical context, scenes that are notably subordinated in *Great Expectations*.[22] The novel's climactic scenes occur not when Magwitch is tried and found guilty, but rather when he is caught—the first time on the marshes, the last time on the Thames. Nonetheless, there were many sympathetic resonances between the plight of the convict and that of the slave. In his study of the convict labor market, Stephen Nicholas writes that contemporary politicians saw colonial New South Wales as a slave society because of the brutality of the convict labor system and the limitations placed on freedom.[23] Some convicts even exploited such connections in modeling their narratives after slave narratives. In 1846, Linus Miller, an American convict, published *Notes of an Exile to Van Dieman's Land* chronicling his transportation to present-day Tasmania. (Transportation to New South Wales had ended in 1840 but continued to places like Van Dieman's Land.) Cassandra Pybus writes, "By the time [Miller] returned to New York in 1846, an effective mode for his counter-response was readily apparent in the burgeoning genre of slave narratives, which were the Yankee abolitionists' most effective weapon in the fiercely combative debate over slavery."[24] Convict narratives did not enjoy the widespread readership of slave narratives, appearing more often in local newspapers or in the form of short pamphlets.[25] Matthew Mauger estimates that between 1787 and 1868, roughly sixty convict narratives were published. Compare this to the hundreds of slave narratives published in the same period, as catalogued by William H. Andrews.

Great Expectations opens with Pip's collision with Magwitch, a moment that mirrors the generic collision of slave narrative with what initially appears a fictional autobiography or bildungsroman. This literalized contact zone, which has often been read as the novel's primal scene, more accurately sets up the novel's primal *narrative*. Peter Brooks writes, "What the novel chooses to present at its outset is precisely the search for a beginning. . . . With Pip, Dickens begins as it were with a life which is for the moment precedent to plot, and indeed, necessarily in search of a plot."[26] That plot, it becomes clear, is provided by Magwitch. In a scene of *narrative* birth, Pip, forlorn among the tombstones, begins to cry, eliciting the attention of his "father-to-be." Conscripted into the narrative by this "fearful man, all in coarse grey, with a great iron on his leg,"[27] Pip begins to parallel the fugitive's ordeal, from his constant fear of exposure and incarceration to his humorous description of the bread-and-butter "load upon my leg (which made me think afresh of the man with the load upon *his* leg)" (GE, 45). The narrative of the slave becomes the master narrative of the novel; Pip is conscripted into a narrative that itself details the problem of involuntary imprisonment.

To underscore the radical appropriation of Pip's narrative, Dickens has Magwitch flip Pip head over heels, literally enacting how Pip's life is turned upside down: "[Magwitch] gave me a tremendous dip and roll, so that the church jumped over its own weather-cock. Then he held me by the arms, in an upright position on top of the stone, and went on in these fearful terms: 'You bring me, to-morrow morning early, that file and them wittles" (GE, 38). Following this act of physical and epistemological destabilization, Magwitch steadies Pip and indoctrinates him into his new narrative, one that comically mimics the act of religious conversion. When the church finally "came to itself," Pip is called to the ministry—namely, the ministry of Magwitch, who is both fettered and starving. In this ironic revision of the spiritual narrative, Pip is converted not from nonbeliever to Christian, but from orphan to fugitive. From this moment, his mission is emancipation—his own, as well as Magwitch's.

Already, the slave narrative has bumped up against several contiguous genres—the autobiography, the bildungsroman, the spiritual narrative, even the ghost story. It litters the chapter with chronotopic artifacts—the leg iron, the file, chains. Through Magwitch, it triggers the first, fundamental narrative event of the novel, and it situates that event in "marsh country, down by the river, within, as the river wound, twenty miles of sea" (GE, 35). It reappears, in comic incarnation, in a second collision, when Pip "ran head foremost into a party of soldiers with their muskets: one of whom held out a pair of handcuffs to me" (GE, 61). And it appears a third time, in the Hegelian struggle between Compeyson and Magwitch on the marshes, followed by their capture and return to the "black Hulk" (GE, 71).

The slave narrative later emerges in Magwitch's first-person account of his life, which Pip describes as the "book of his remembrance" (GE, 364) and which emphasizes the contingent nature of his freedom. Facing Pip and Herbert, Magwitch begins, "'Dear boy and Pip's comrade. I am not a going fur to tell you my life, like a song or a story-book. But to give it you short and handy, I'll put it at once into a mouthful of English. In jail and out of jail, in jail and out of jail, in jail and out of jail'" (GE, 360). Magwitch rejects the genre of song and storybook, with its fictionalized arc and fairy tale diction. Instead, he reduces his narrative to two eras: "in jail and out of jail," preemancipation and postemancipation. His life is marked by natal alienation, geographic instability, violence, and haphazard literacy. "'I've no more notion where I was born, than you have'" (GE, 360), he says, and "'I've been carted here and carted there, and put out of this town and put out of that town, and stuck in the stocks, and whipped and worried and drove'" (GE, 360). He learns how to read from "a deserting soldier in a Traveller's Rest" and how to write from a "traveling Giant" (GE, 361).

Magwitch's identification with the slave becomes explicit when he describes his relationship to Compeyson, the gentleman thief who takes Magwitch as his partner. "That man got me into such nets as made me his black slave," he recounts. "I was always in debt to him, always under his thumb, always a working, always a getting into danger. He was younger than me, but he'd got craft, and he'd got learning, and he overmatched me five hundred times told and no mercy" (GE, 364). Using the language of captivity, Magwitch describes his situation as one of physical entrapment and subjugation. Though he is not (at that moment) in jail, he is still unfree. Moreover, Compeyson exploits Magwitch's labor through intellectual as well as physical means. "He'd got learning," Magwitch explains, and it is Compeyson's access to formal education that doubly ensures Magwitch's continued subjugation.

Pip's response to Magwitch's story underscores the centrality of the fugitive plot, with its reordering of the world around the threat of pursuit and capture. "A new fear had been engendered in my mind by [Magwitch's] narrative," Pip reveals, "or rather, his narrative had given form and purpose to the fear that was already there. If Compeyson were alive and should discover his return, I could hardly doubt the consequence . . . that, any such man as that man had been described to be, would hesitate to release himself for good from a dreaded enemy by the same means of becoming an informer" (GE, 367). Pip is again conscripted into the teleology of the slave narrative, with its quest for freedom and concomitant fear of capture. He internalizes and literalizes the fugitive plot; he dreams of "pursuers, going swiftly, silently, and surely, to take [Magwitch]" (GE, 394), he is shadowed by Compeyson at Mr. Wopsle's play, he is even captured and bound by Orlick.

Together, they engineer Magwitch's final escape over the river Thames, which echoes Magwitch's opening flight across the marshes and again emphasizes the geography of escape, across both land and sea.[28] Fugitive, captor, and escape vessel collide, as they did in *North and South* with the fugitive Frederick Hale, the bounty hunter Leonards, and the train. In both cases, the captor perishes, though it is unclear whether or not it is by the fugitive's hand. Magwitch tells Pip that "they had gone down, fiercely locked in each other's arms, and that there had been a struggle under water" (GE, 456). The struggle between Compeyson and Magwitch, which had begun on land, continues "under water," traveling from one symbolic locus (the marshes) to another (the sea). Both are Hegelian struggles for mastery and freedom that occur at sites of what Daphne Brooks calls "fugitive liberation."[29]

The fugitive slave chronotope is associated, above all, with an ontology of freedom and unfreedom. Magwitch tells Pip:

"If you knowed . . . what it is to sit here alonger my dear boy and have my smoke, arter having been [concealed] day by day betwixt four walls, you'd envy me. But you don't know what it is."
"I think I know the delights of freedom," I answered.

"Ah," said he, shaking his head gravely, "But you don't know it equal to me. You must have been under lock and key, dear boy, to know it equal to me."(GE, 447)

In Magwitch's articulation of fugitive-time, life is divided into moments spent in hiding "betwixt four walls" or imprisoned "under lock and key," and moments that are not. Yet Magwitch is speaking not simply in physical terms. Fugitive-time is unrelenting and all-encompassing, altering the individual's perceptual field. Pip wonders, "perhaps freedom without danger was too much apart from all the habit of his existence to be to him what it would be to another man" (GE, 447). The fugitive slave chronotope has the ability to reshape everything from literacy to geography to ontology. It conscripts others into its world and subsequently alters the very signification of everyday objects and experiences.

The fugitive slave chronotope, which first enters the text through Magwitch, begins immediately to reorder the narrative of Pip's life. Following the events of Magwitch's arrest, Pip describes his nascent literacy and eventual apprenticeship to Joe, biographical facts that coalesce around the familiar contours of the slave narrative. In a lengthy scene with Joe in front of the hearth, the fugitive slave chronotope manifests itself in Pip's struggle to read and write:

I struggled through the alphabet as if it had been a bramble-bush; getting considerably worried and scratched by every letter. After that, I fell among those thieves, the nine figures, who seemed every evening to do something new to disguise themselves and baffle recognition. But, at last I began, in a purblind groping way, to read, write, and cipher. (GE, 75)

Pip's literacy attempts are depicted as a pursuit through unfriendly terrain. They echo the recent chase through the marshes and also prefigure Magwitch's account of being "carted here and carted there" and being "worried and drove" (GE, 360). Fugitive-time now invades even learning time.

Yet fugitive-time contains within it the very struggle for literacy. Freedom is affiliated with literacy, unfreedom with illiteracy. Likewise, literacy takes on fugitive overtones: it must take place in secret and is haunted by the fear of discovery. In the previous passage, the alphabet is figured as a bramble bush, the "nine figures" as thieves. They become obstacles that must be mastered and subdued before freedom is attained, and they echo Magwitch's account of Compeyson's tyranny: "He'd got craft, and he'd got learning, and he overmatched me five hundred times told and no mercy" (GE, 364). The convergence of the fugitive experience with that of learning is further emphasized in Pip's placing of "an alphabet on the hearth at my feet for reference" (GE, 75), as if writing requires the use of the legs as well as the hands. Composing a letter to Joe on his slate, Pip creates what he calls a "hilly" document that begins, "mI deer JO I hpE U r krWitE wEll"

(GE, 75). Orthography intersects with topography, as Pip's letter visually represents the arduous journey toward literacy.

Joe's illiteracy also orients itself around the fugitive slave chronotope, as he recounts a childhood filled by his father's "hammering" (GE, 76) and his mother's "drudging and slaving" (GE, 79–80): "My mother and me we ran away from my father, several times . . . and [my mother would] put me in school. . . . And then [my father] took us home and hammered us. Which, you see . . . were a drawback on my learning" (GE, 76–77). The association of learning with escape and insubordination prompts Joe to warn Pip, "Mrs. Joe mustn't see too much of what we're up to. [Reading and writing] must be done, as I may say, on the sly. And why on the sly? I'll tell you why, Pip. . . . Your sister is given to government. . . . Which I meantersay the government of you and myself" (GE, 79). Borrowing the slave narrative's trope of literacy as resistance, Joe articulates the fear of slave owners everywhere—that literacy will "spoil" a slave and make him ungovernable. In a passage that echoes Lady Ludlow's fear of working-class literacy, Joe tells Pip, "[Mrs. Joe] an't over partial to having scholars on the premises [. . .] and in partickler would not be over partial to my being a scholar, for fear as I might rise. Like a sort of rebel, don't you see?" (GE, 79). Mrs. Joe is a "master-mind" (GE, 79–80), and Joe, by extension, is a "fugitive-mind," a fact that may partially account for his sympathy for the actual fugitive, Magwitch, whom he deems a "poor miserable fellow-creatur" (GE, 71).

The fugitive-slave chronotope reorders the life of Mrs. Joe, as well. She is comically depicted as a paternalistic tyrant, who brings Joe and Pip up "by hand" and "do drop down upon [them] heavy" (GE, 79) with her polished cane, the Tickler. Brooks distinguishes this plotline, which he calls the "naterally wicious/bringing up by hand" plot, from that of Magwitch, which he calls the "communion with the convict/criminal deviance" plot.[30] But like the literacy plot, the "bringing up by hand" plot intersects with the fugitive plot. Mrs. Joe may terrorize the household, acting as a "Buster" and "Mo-gul" (GE, 79), but she also characterizes herself as "a slave with her apron never off" (GE, 53) and asks "Joe why he hadn't married a Negress Slave at once?" (GE, 126). This collection of images becomes a parodic manifestation of the slave narrative, with the language of mastery and slavery bridging the criminal world of Magwitch to the domestic world of Mrs. Joe. Her disapproval of learning, her disciplinary government, her complaints of forced servitude can be read as an expansion of Magwitch's own character-zone and "sphere of influence."

Their two worlds likewise collide in literal fashion, through the broken leg-iron that Orlick uses to subdue Mrs. Joe. An artifact of Magwitch's escape, the leg-iron is a metonymic extension of the fugitive. Pip immediately identifies it as "the iron I had seen and heard [Magwitch] filing at, on the marshes—but my mind did not accuse him of having put it to its latest use" (GE, 148). The link (literal *and* figurative) between Magwitch and Mrs. Joe is not one of assailant and victim, but of victim and victim; their relationship is based not on hierarchy, but contiguity. Her assault is the result of a power struggle not with Magwitch, but with Orlick, and it is provoked by the question of who is the "master" (GE, 141). Overhearing Joe give Orlick a half-holiday, Mrs. Joe cries, "I wish *I* were [Orlick's] master" (GE, 141), to which Orlick retorts, "You'd be everybody's master, if you durst" (GE, 141). This question of mastery is only settled with another Hegelian struggle, this one between Joe and Orlick.

Orlick's retaliation upon Mrs. Joe is a continuation of this struggle for mastery, and it reverses the trajectory toward literacy and freedom that Pip had begun. Subordinated and severely injured, Mrs. Joe regresses to an almost prelinguistic state. This is poignantly depicted when Pip attempts to interpret Mrs. Joe's scrawl on his slate. What Pip first interprets as the letter "T" is not a letter at all, or the first letter of a word like "tar," "toast," or "tub." Words detach themselves from their corresponding image, creating a signifying rupture. Mrs. Joe, instead, draws a pictogram; the "T" is really a "sign [that] looked like a hammer" (GE, 150). From this discovery, Pip moves along the metaphorical axis, first bringing an actual hammer, then items that look like a hammer, such as a crutch, "the shape being much the same" (GE, 151). Yet, as Biddy soon figures out, Mrs. Joe is signifying not metaphorically, but metonymically: "She had lost [Orlick's] name, and could only signify him by his hammer" (GE, 151). When Orlick appears at her bedside, she has "the bearing of a child towards a hard master" (GE, 151). Stripped of literacy, Mrs. Joe regresses from master to victim.

Even as Mrs. Joe loses certain powers of literacy, however, she retains her grasp of metonymic connection. The leg-iron that metonymically represents Magwitch is linked to the hammer that metonymically represents Orlick. Both are instruments of physical suppression, but both are also instruments of *knowledge* suppression. Mrs. Joe draws a hammer on a slate, summoning up Joe's tale of paternal "hammering" that leads to his own illiteracy. It likewise evokes Pip's passage toward literacy, with letters and numbers, instead of chains, becoming impediments to unencumbered flight. It evokes yet a third image, that of "the old Battery out on the marshes" (GE, 137), a "place of study" for Joe and Pip, where "a broken slate and a short piece of slate pencil were our educational implements" (GE, 137). A former emplacement to guard London from attack, the Battery serves here as shelter for the illicit acts of reading and writing.[31]

The durability of the metonymic axis contrasts with the relative flimsiness of the metaphoric axis. Woloch describes the over-saturation of metaphor that characterizes the Miss Havisham plotline: "In Satis House, physical objects are metaphors, designed to signify not through their physical contiguity but through the similarity of their connotations . . . Satis House catalyzes Pip's own mode of metaphoric apprehension, and the text soon begins to generate typical, romantic metaphors."[32] He points to Estella's criticism of Pip, which "turns on the metaphoric significance of Pip's own hands and boots," and describes Pip's susceptibility to overmetaphorization. The fairy-tale plot competes with the fugitive plot in Pip's narrative and appears to dominate his self-perception for most of the novel.

Yet the fugitive plot does not recede completely, despite Pip's attempts to suppress it. Instead, it enters Pip's narrative in parodic guise, contributing to the tragicomic tone of his story. After the introduction of the Satis House plotline, Dickens reshapes the fugitive slave chronotope to create a space for criticism—criticism of Pip's metaphorical extravagance, but criticism, too, of the genre of slave narrative.

Parodic Revision

"The novel parodies other genres (precisely in their role as genres)," Bakhtin writes. "It exposes the conventionality of their forms and their language."[33] He finds particularly rich examples of this in the English comic novel, from those of Fielding and Smollett to those of Thackeray and Dickens. "In the English comic novel," he writes, "we find a comic-parodic re-processing of almost all the levels of literary language, both conversational and written, that were current at the time."[34] Analyzing several passages from *Little Dorrit*, Bakhtin demonstrates Dickens's parodic stylization of parliamentary discourse, epic language, and legal jargon. Dickens, he argues, creates an authorial distance from the language he parodies: "he steps back and objectifies it, forcing his own intentions to refract and diffuse themselves through the medium of this common view that has become embodied in language (a view that is always superficial and frequently hypocritical)."[35]

In *Great Expectations*, Dickens employs parodic stylization of the slave narrative, especially as it obtains to Pip. While Dickens applies the fugitive slave chronotope to Magwitch, Joe, and Mrs. Joe to arouse pity or sympathy, he applies it to Pip primarily for comic or ironic purposes. Pip becomes what Bakhtin calls a "parodic double"—not a chronotope of the fugitive slave but a parody of the slave narrative genre.[36] When Pip slips his bread-and-butter down his pants and thinks of "the man with the load on *his* leg" (GE, 45), or when he runs into the arms of a soldier brandishing handcuffs, his actions provoke more laughter than sympathy. Such moments are increasingly ironized after Pip is introduced to Estella, revealing the tension between the fairy-tale plot and the fugitive plot.

One such moment occurs when Pip gazes at the sails on the river and begins to interpret them as emblems of his romantic quest:

> It was pleasant and quiet, out there with the sails on the river passing beyond the earthwork. . . . Whenever I watched the vessels standing out to sea with their white sails spread, I somehow thought of Miss Havisham and Estella, and whenever the light struck aslant, afar off, upon a cloud or sail or green hill-side or water-line, it was just the same.—Miss Havisham and Estella and the strange house and the strange life appeared to have something to do with everything that was picturesque. (GE, 137)

Pip imbues the "white sails" with metaphoric qualities: they are unattainable, they are vestal, they are ghostly, and they are linked, in his mind, to Miss Havisham and Estella. Gazing at the ships, Pip is moved to cry out to Biddy, "'I want to be a gentleman . . . I am not at all happy as I am. I am disgusted with my calling and with my life. I have never taken to either, since I was bound'" (GE, 154). In contrast to his own "bound" status, the sails appear unencumbered and free.

The above passage appears a fairly straightforward case of what Woloch calls "the oversignification of landscape,"[37] with its evocation of romantic longing. What has not been noticed is the passage's parodic stylization of a scene from Douglass's *Narrative*. Pip watches the sails from the marshes and the Battery, sites of fugitive flight and of literacy. His vantage point echoes that of Douglass, who describes his own youthful longing for freedom while surveying the ships on the Chesapeake. "Our house stood within a few rods of the Chesapeake Bay, whose broad bosom was ever white with sails from every quarter of the habitable globe," Douglass writes. "Those beautiful vessels, robed in purest white, so delightful to the eye of freemen, were to me so many shrouded ghosts, to terrify and torment me with thoughts of my wretched condition."[38] For Douglass, the white sails are not simply icons of unattainability, purity, and ghostliness; they are potential escape vehicles that may ferry the slave to freedom. He is moved to "pour out [his] soul's complaint, in [his] rude way, with an apostrophe to the moving multitude of ships:—'You are loosed from your moorings, and are free; I am fast in my chains, and am a slave.'"[39] Pip's prospect of the sails and his complaint to Biddy become parodic stylizations of Douglass's ontological despair.

This passage in *Great Expectations* is at once a comparison of white indentured servitude to black slavery and a criticism of that very comparison. Earlier, Pip describes the signing of his indentures at the Town Hall, an experience that evokes the carceral background of the fugitive plot and the historical tendency to find commonality between the plight of the apprentice and the plight of the slave. Hilary Beckles describes the situation of the white indentured servant in the West Indies as a form of "proto-slavery,"[40] and Aaron S. Fogleman categorizes slaves, convicts, and indentured servants as the unfree.[41] As a child, Frederick Douglass mingles with the poor white children of his neighborhood who, like Pip, are indentured apprentices. Douglass identifies one major difference, however: "You will be free as soon as you are twenty-one," he tells them, "*but I am a slave for life.*"[42] Despite this, Pip's life continues its "comic-parodic reprocessing" of Douglass's narrative. Pip is roughly the same age as Douglass when he first becomes disenchanted with his plight and tormented over his degraded condition; he too begins to "hunger for information" and horde "intellectual crumbs" (GE, 137) and to contemplate running away by "[going] for a soldier or sailor" (GE, 135).[43]

Dickens parodies the slave narrative genre in order to expose Pip's own hypocrisy. In the way he integrates high epic style to mock public perception of Merdle in *Little Dorrit*, he integrates the language of the slave narrative to mock Pip's perception of himself.[44] Pip fancies himself a slave, and he clumsily reprocesses the most superficial conventions of the slave narrative; yet these very moments are suffused with irony. Pip's apprenticeship to Joe is far from enslavement, and prior to his seduction by Estella and the fairy-tale plot, he believes the forge to be "the glowing road to manhood and independence" (GE, 134). Pip's extravagant self-pity and overblown images of his plight create an ironic-parodic distance between his narrative persona (who recognizes his youthful absurdity) and his character persona (who does not).

This ironic-parodic distance arises a second time soon after the signing of Pip's indentures, and it is again triggered by his misguided fascination with Estella. Pip begins in his narrative persona: "What I wanted, who can say? How can *I* say, when I never knew?" (GE, 136). Pip then transitions into his childhood persona:

> What I dreaded was that in some unlucky hour I, being at my grimiest and commonest, should lift up my eyes and see Estella looking in at one of the wooden windows of the forge. I was haunted by the fear that she would, sooner or later, find me out, with a black face and hands, doing the coarsest part of my work, and would exult over me and despise me. (GE, 136)

This passage employs "hybrid construction," defined by Bakhtin as "an utterance that belongs, by its grammatical (syntactic) and compositional markers, to a single speaker, but that actually contains mixed within it two utterances, two speech manners, two styles, two 'languages,' two semantic and axiological belief systems."[45] It begins in the autobiographical or confessional register, displaying the adult Pip's self-recrimination. It slides into a second register, that of the child Pip, whose hypocrisy and ingratitude are revealed through the comic-parodic reprocessing of the slave narrative.

The forge is transformed into a prison and Pip into an inmate, the subject of Estella's carceral gaze. Pip's shame is further augmented by his "black face and hands," an image that turns Pip into a clownlike figure, a blackface blacksmith. By revealing Pip's sensitivity to phenotype—he is not black, but he looks black—Pip is turned into a racial parody. The young Pip may imagine himself mocked by Estella, but it is the adult Pip who, from his retrospective vantage point, mocks his former self. Pip has never truly been enslaved, but his preoccupation with the superficial markers of degradation—the coarse clothing, the darkened skin—demonstrate his willingness to "play" a certain role, one that indulges his childish and overblown perceptions of his plight. The scene recalls his susceptibility to overmetaphorization, from his conviction that the coarseness of his hands and thickness of his boots is linked to the coarseness and thickness of his mind, to his belief that the white sails on the Thames are avatars of Miss Havisham and Estella. The blackness of his face and hands, Pip imagines, are signs that he *is* black.[46]

With his "emancipation" (GE, 173) from his indentures, Pip moves from one parodic guise to another, mimicking the manners and lifestyle of a gentleman. To borrow—and pervert—Frederick Douglass's famous phrase, we have seen how a man was made a "slave"; now we shall see how a slave was made a (gentle)man. Pip narrates,

> I had got on so fast of late, that I had even started a boy in boots—top boots—in bondage and slavery to whom I might have been said to pass my days. For, after I had made the monster (out of the refuse of my washerwoman's family) and had clothed him with a blue coat, canary waistcoat, white cravat, creamy breeches, and the boots already mentioned, I had to find him a little to do and a great deal to eat; and with both of those horrible requirements he haunted my existence. (GE, 240)

In a scene reminiscent of Thackeray's send-up of the servant Morgan in *Pendennis*, Pip escapes enslavement only to enslave (or be enslaved by) another. The passage's allusion to Mary Shelley's *Frankenstein* supports the novel's preoccupation with failed parent-child relations.[47] But it also heralds back to the image of Pip, with black face and hands, in the forge, who becomes a monster of his own creation. In another form of racial parody, Pip creates a kind of blackface dandy, a boy "in bondage and slavery" who mimics, in vulgar fashion, the dress (and eventually the leisurely life) of a gentleman. This Anglicized Zip Coon, with his flashy clothes and impertinent manner, becomes a further indictment of Pip and his pretensions.

The return of Magwitch reorients the novel to the fugitive plot, but along with the novel's other plotlines, it ultimately surrenders to what Brooks has called "the generalized breakdown of plots."[48] Magwitch dies in jail, and Pip nearly dies as well after being arrested for debt. The fairy-tale plot disintegrates with Magwitch's reappearance, Estella's betrothal to Bentley Drummle, and Miss Havisham's death. The marriage plot too evades Pip, as Biddy marries Joe and Pip is left unwed and childless. In the feverish dreams that haunt Pip after Magwitch's death, Pip struggles to extract himself from the narrative edifice. He is a "brick in the house wall" who "entreat[s] to be released from the giddy place where the builders had sent me" (GE, 471); he is a "steel beam of a vast machine" that he wishes to have stopped, and his part "hammered off" (GE, 472). Pip, as Brooks describes it, wishes to "escape from plot"[49]—even the fugitive plot, the plot that has radically reordered his life. On the metanarratival level, Pip is a fugitive *from* plot.

The incorporation, parodic revision, and eventual failure of the fugitive plot raises the question of whether Dickens shares his narrator's critical distance from the slave narrative. The fugitive plot is so unyielding and so systemic that it threatens to destroy its protagonists in its "vast machine." The violence that haunts the novel—from Magwitch's battle with Compeyson, to Orlick's assault of Mrs. Joe, to Orlick's attempted murder of Pip—challenges the ethical paradigm set up by the slave narrative. Can slavery and injustice best be resolved by blind resistance or by running away? And are "the delights of freedom" worth their human cost?

The novel offers an alternative through the figure of Joe, who while comically suffering under Mrs. Joe's "government," manages to break the cycle of violence that had begun in his childhood. Nursing Pip at the end of the novel, he muses, "'I done what I could to keep you and Tickler in sunders, but . . . if I put myself in opposition to [Mrs. Joe] but that she dropped into you always heavier for it'" (GE, 478). Resistance only exacerbates Mrs. Joe's wrath and multiplies the punitive consequences for Pip. As a result, Joe chooses accommodation over blatant "opposition," pacifism and nonviolent resistance over overt rebellion. He tolerates "minor" injustices—the abuse of Pip and his own self at the hands of Mrs. Joe—to preserve something much more important: domestic stability. Joe's own childhood is marked by itinerancy and insecurity, and it is partially to erase this legacy that Joe refuses to run away or to rebel. Given Joe's convictions, his wife's domestic "government" is worth enduring, for the alternative—domestic unrest and a fractured household—is too great a price to pay.

Yet quietly, on the very margins of the plot, Joe manages to achieve his own narrative success, marrying Biddy and learning to read and write. Partly this testifies to Pip's self-absorption and preoccupation with his own narrative "plots," but it also testifies to Joe's quiet revision of the fugitive plot. Joe does not rise against Mrs. Joe; nor does he attempt escape. Instead, he subscribes to gradual, peaceable change. His acquisition of literacy occurs "off the page," away from Pip's gaze, invoking a trope of the slave narrative in order to adapt it. Watching Joe compose a letter to Biddy, Pip describes how he "choos[es] a pen from the pen-tray as if it were chest of large tools, and tuck[s] up his sleeves as if he were going to wield a crowbar or sledgehammer" (GE, 474). The scene recalls Mrs. Joe's pictogram of a hammer on Pip's slate and Joe's own "hammering" by his father. The two images converge in this scene, as the act of writing and the act of hammering become one and the same. Joe peacefully resolves the tension between literacy and suppression. Pip observes, "Occasionally, he was tripped up by some orthographical stumbling-block"—an image that evokes Pip's childhood struggle through the alphabet—"but on the whole he got on very well indeed" (GE, 474).

Joe has written, or "hammered," his way to narrative freedom. In the wake of "the generalized breakdown of plots," as Pip desperately dreams of being "hammered off" the vast narrative machine, Joe has already successfully done so, detaching himself from an overly prescriptive plot and emerging in Pip's dreams as the sole model of stability: "there was an extraordinary tendency in all these people [in my dreams], sooner or later, to settle down into the likeness of Joe" (GE, 472). In *Great Expectations*, Dickens incorporates the fugitive slave chronotope, parodically stylizes it, and finally critiques its conventionality, paralleling the slave narrative's historical trajectory from new and engaging literary genre to one whose popularity and conventionality made it ripe for satire. Despite Magwitch's sympathetic embodiment of the fugitive slave chronotope and Pip's comic-parodic one, it is ultimately Joe who revises the fugitive plot in favor of nonviolence and domestic harmony and who enjoys the greatest narrative success.

Dickens's reworkings of the fugitive plot in *Great Expectations* take on additional significance when situated against the American Civil War, a domestic conflict that threatened to consume the nation with violence. Serial installments of *Great Expectations* frequently appeared beside articles on the America slave situation in *All the Year Round*. For example, the December 29, 1860 number, which recounts Pip's first visit to Satis House (chapter 8 in volume form), appears immediately before an article on "Black Weather in the South," an account of American slavery that describes the cruel public whipping of a slave girl. And the February 16, 1861 number, which chronicles the "end of the first stage of Pip's expectations" (chapter 19 in volume form), appears immediately before an article on slave labor in South Carolina. This is in addition to many other articles about America, from "American snake stories" to "A Scene in the Cotton Country" to "American Cotton," all of which included depictions of American slaves. Also appearing concurrently with *Great Expectations* in *All the Year Round* was Gaskell's "The Grey Woman," published in January 1861 and revealing its own reworking of the fugitive plots of Harriet Jacobs and of William and Ellen Craft. The plight of the American slave, like the fugitive plot in *Great Expectations*, was becoming culturally inescapable, even on the pages of Dickens's magazine.

Yet Dickens stubbornly resisted ascribing the American Civil War to the conflict over slavery, instead questioning Northern motives and accusing the Union of hypocrisy. In a letter to W. F. De Cerjat dated 16 March 1862, he writes:

> I take the facts of the American slave quarrel to stand thus. Slavery has in reality nothing on earth to do with it. . . . Every reasonable person may know, if willing, that the North hates the Negro, and that until it was convenient to make a pretence that sympathy with him was the cause of the War, it hated the abolitionists and derided them up hill and down dale.[50]

Dickens accuses the North of adopting the role of "generous or chivalrous" rescuer who is preoccupied with the emancipation of the American slave. Even the government, it turns out, rehearses the fugitive plot. Dickens, however, attributes the war not to the struggle over slavery but to a dispute over money. The unscrupulous North, he writes, has "taxed the South most abominably for its own advantage."[51] Two articles appearing in *Household Words* in December of 1861, one entitled "American Disunion" and the other, "The Morrill Tariff," come to the same conclusion. Neither is signed by Dickens, but Arthur Adrian looks to them as confirmation of Dickens's deeply ambivalent feelings toward the war.[52] The former article vilifies slavery but favors the secession of Southern states over the preservation of the Union. The latter article deems the Civil War "solely a fiscal quarrel" rather than a struggle for slave emancipation.

Dickens was not alone in his distrust of the North. Douglas Lorimer describes how some British observers became so disillusioned with the

Union's refusal to come out against slavery that they threw their support behind the South, believing that abolition stood a better chance in a seceded, independent Confederacy than in the Union. Furthermore, British loyalties to the Confederacy or Union did not fall neatly along lines of politics, class, or region. Lorimer writes, "Englishmen of a broad range of social backgrounds and political viewpoints found it difficult to support a war fought for union and not freedom."[53] Even the British and Foreign Anti-Slavery Society maintained a neutral stance in the American Civil War, endorsing the North only after Lincoln signed the Emancipation Proclamation in January 1863, explicitly naming slavery one of the causes of the war.

The passage of the Emancipation Proclamation, however, did little to assuage Dickens's suspicion of the North. On 6 January 1863, he wrote to Captain Elisha Morgan,

> And you think the [American] south will come back [to the Union], within the winter and spring?—May I whisper (at this distance from Fort Lafayette), that *I* don't? I wish to God, for the interests of the whole human race, that the War were ended. But I don't see that end to it, no, not anything like that end, with my best spectacles.[54]

A few months later, with the passage of the First Conscription Act, Dickens persisted in his belief that the North would fail in its bid to preserve the Union. Writing to Frederick Lehmann, who had just returned from America and who was certain the North would prevail, Dickens vowed, "I can *not* believe that the Conscription will do otherwise than fail, and wreck the War. I feel convinced, indeed, that the War will be shattered by want of Northern soldiers."[55] His prediction, of course, proved false, yet stubborn as always, Dickens continued to question the integrity of Northern motives, even as the War turned increasingly in the North's favor.

While Dickens's irritation with the North, as well as his refusal to see slavery as central to the Civil War, could be signs of his growing conservatism, it may also reflect his exhaustion with fugitive plots in general.[56] From tearing out Douglass's frontispiece and sending his *Narrative* to Macready, to incorporating scenes from the *Narrative* in *Great Expectations*, Dickens had cycled through every possible role in relation to the slave narrative: reader, editor, publisher, writer, parodist, and critic. The shift in Dickens's role can be seen as a barometer of the slave narrative's increasing influence in the literary marketplace. As a reader, Dickens saw the genre as abolitionist propaganda that effectively exposed the plight of the American slave. As an editor and publisher, he marketed the genre to friends with abolitionist sympathies. As a writer, he began to mine the genre for its narrative structure and chronotopes. As a parodist, he ironized and exaggerated those narrative conventions. And as a critic, he revised and subsequently rejected the fugitive plot. The slave narrative's rise from ephemera to cultural artifact leads Dickens to treat the genre with correspondingly greater care: what had been clumsily defaced and easily loaned is now institutionalized and memorialized in his fiction. *Great Expectations* becomes a fitting conclusion to the trajectory of the slave narrative's influence on the Victorian novel, for in it, the slave narrative achieves cultural saturation. The fugitive plot is transformed into the master plot of the novel.

Epilogue

The Plot Against England
The Dynamiter

In 1863, President Lincoln issued the Emancipation Proclamation, an executive order that conferred freedom to slaves in the Confederate States of America. Nearly three years later, the Thirteenth Amendment, prohibiting slavery throughout the nation, was officially ratified.[1] It was a moment of triumph for British and American abolitionists, who saw the culmination of several decades of fierce protest. For the emancipated American slaves, however, the struggle for equality was just beginning. After the initial optimism that attended the end of the American Civil War, the country now faced the difficult task of Reconstruction. The Freedmen's Bureau (officially the Bureau of Refugees, Freedmen, and Abandoned Lands) was founded in 1865 to supervise the resettlement of emancipated slaves. It provided food, housing, medical care, and legal aid, and also established more than 4,000 schools, thereby beginning to undo centuries of opposition to African American education. In 1868, the Fourteenth Amendment was passed, overturning the Dred Scott case of 1856 and granting citizenship to African Americans. Two years later, the Fifteenth Amendment extended to African Americans the right to vote. Despite the passage of these laws, freedmen continued to battle widespread racism and economic exploitation. Southern states instituted Jim Crow laws that effectively disenfranchised black voters and mandated racial segregation, and the sharecropping system that replaced slavery ensured that former slaves remained impoverished and oppressed.

For American abolitionists, the failure of Reconstruction to integrate freedmen fully into the postbellum social order led to a renewed call for support. In 1875, Frederick Douglass attended a reunion meeting of Philadelphia abolitionists and exhorted them to mobilize once again. Yet, as James McPherson notes, "Most of the original abolitionists were too old to start up the machinery of organized agitation again";[2] many, too, were disheartened by the "sordid materialism of the Gilded Age"[3] and feared that the age of moral conviction and heroism had passed. In England, only the British and Foreign Anti-Slavery Society continued to operate into the 1870s, but its energies were now focused on the suppression of the slave trade in Africa (where England had extended its imperialist reach), as well as the "the struggles for abolition in Brazil and Cuba, slave-trading in Polynesia, and the traffic in indentured labour all round the world."[4] The Royal Navy continued to police the seas for slavers, but domestic concerns over labor reform and Irish home rule began to take over the national consciousness. As the nation entered the 1860s and beyond, Lorimer describes a shift in British racial attitudes, away from the humanitarian views of the early antislavery movement to a more hardened racist ideology linked to the new field of ethnic anthropology.[5] The Morant Bay Rebellion of 1865, which began with an uprising of black Jamaican settlers and ended with the declaration of martial law and execution of the rebel George William Gordon by Governor Edward John Eyre, was further proof of the hazards of the postemancipatory era.[6]

With the dissipation or redirection of abolitionist sentiment, the slave narrative declined in popularity on both sides of the Atlantic. The slave narrative, however, did not disappear entirely. William L. Andrews and Frances Smith Foster estimate that between the Civil War and the Great Depression, at least fifty more slave narratives were published, the most famous of which was Booker T. Washington's *Up From Slavery*, published in 1901.[7] In contrast to the antebellum narratives, postbellum slave narratives dwelt less on the horrors of slavery, instead emphasizing racial uplift and success. Stripped of one of its defining characteristics—the call for abolition—the slave narrative reshaped itself into a more anodyne form.[8]

The "classic phase" of the slave narrative may have passed, but the genre would appear in its antebellum guise at least one more time in a work of Victorian fiction. In 1885, Robert Louis Stevenson and his American wife Fanny Van De Grift Stevenson published a collection of stories called *The Dynamiter*. Set against the Fenian dynamite bombings in London of the early 1880s, *The Dynamiter* is comprised of several "as-told-to" narratives, among them the "Story of the Fair Cuban." A fanciful, exoticized version of a slave narrative, the "Story of the Fair Cuban" has generally been dismissed as the mediocre work of Fanny Stevenson and subsequently ignored in any holistic analysis of the work. Yet the story repeatedly emphasizes England's vaunted role in the global eradication of slavery, recalling a national mythology that by the mid-1880s was under increasing attack by Irish nationalists. Formerly the world's antislavery "policemen," England was now forced to police her own cities to fend off internal threats to cohesive nationhood. Read against the history of abolition and transatlantic reform, *The Story of the Fair Cuban* exposes England's dwindling moral authority in the late-Victorian period.

In her introduction to the Tusitala edition, Fanny Stevenson describes *The Dynamiter*'s inception during a stay in Hyères, France in 1883. The chronically ill Louis, having developed sciatica, hemorrhage, and "contagious Egyptian ophthalmia," lay convalescing for months in his bedroom.

Forbidden to read, speak, or even move, he enlisted his wife's help to pass the time. Fanny Stevenson writes, "I was to go out for an hour's walk every afternoon . . . and to invent a story to repeat when I came in—a sort of Arabian Nights Entertainment where I was to take the part of Schehe-razade and he the sultan."[9] In addition to claiming sole authorship for "The Destroying Angel" (a Mormon tale) and "The Fair Cuban," Fanny claims to have devised the "impotent dynamite intrigue as the thread to string my stories on."[10] Once Louis had fully recovered, Fanny's stories were forgotten until a few years later when, desperate for money, the couple "set to work to write out what we could remember of [the stories]. We could recall only enough to make a rather thin book, so my husband added one more to the list, *The Explosive Bomb*."[11] Marketed as a sequel to Louis's earlier collection of stories, *New Arabian Nights* (1882), *The Dynamiter* also went under the title, *More New Arabian Nights*. In Fanny's words, the collection sold well enough to "replenish[ ] our depleted bank account" and "was as well received as we could have hoped."[12]

The Dynamiter's dual authorship has led to a blinkered analysis of the work, with critics choosing to focus only on those parts that can be attrib-uted to Louis—namely, everything but the *Story of the Destroying Angel* and the *Story of the Fair Cuban*. Alan Sandison, for example, pointedly ignores the two stories in his reading of *The Dynamiter* as a burlesqued detective tale and proto-Modernist attack of Realism. Yet Fanny Stevenson's contri-butions, when read against *Zero's Tale of the Explosive Bomb*, as well as the frame narrative as a whole, testify to England's increasingly tenuous authority in the world community. Unlike the other narratives in the collec-tion, which take place in various London drawing rooms and a cigar divan, Fanny's stories take place on foreign soil—in America and in Cuba. Adding a dose of transatlantic exoticism to the bourgeois frame narrative, Fanny's stories simultaneously critique English earnestness and quixoticism.

The Dynamiter opens with the *Prologue of the Cigar Divan*, in which three feckless young Englishmen named Challoner, Somerset, and Des-borough meet at a cigar shop in Soho owned by a Thomas Godall (a dis-guised Prince Florizel from the *New Arabian Nights*). Bored, broke, and described by Somerset as "three futiles,"[13] the men vow to become ama-teur detectives and to seek adventure in the London streets, after which they plan to reconvene at the cigar shop to share their stories. The first man to encounter adventure is Challoner, who glimpses a woman fleeing from a smoking building and eagerly offers his aid. The woman gives her background in *The Story of the Destroying Angel*, an absurd tale that depicts her as the only daughter of Mormon missionaries in Utah who are mur-dered by Brigham Young. The woman, who claims her name is Asenath Fonblanque, is sent to England, where she is watched by Mormon spies and set to marry the Mormon mad scientist Dr. Grierson, when his botched experiments cause a house explosion from which Miss Fonblanque flees. Challoner "thrill[s] to every incident" (69) of her narrative and is enlisted to help in her escape, only to discover later that Miss Fonblanque is a Fenian dynamite bomber. This same Miss Fonblanque, now going under the name Teresa Valdevia, subsequently dupes Desborough, who believes her to be a Cuban runaway slave, the mulatta daughter of a Scottish-born father and slave mother. In *The Story of the Fair Cuban*, Teresa describes her father as a prominent plantation owner who, after her mother's death, becomes bankrupt and faces selling his daughter to repay his creditors. Before he dies, he buries a hoard of jewels in the swamp, which Teresa retrieves and brings with her as she flees to England. Wary of Cuban spies, Teresa asks Desborough's help in smuggling the jewels, now packed in a brown box, out of the country. The box actually contains a bomb, which detonates prematurely and exposes Teresa as no runaway slave but covert terrorist.

While *The Destroying Angel* probably derives from Fanny Stevenson's experiences in Mormon country, liberally embellished to exploit popular fears of religious cultism, *The Fair Cuban* relies most heavily on the familiar framework of the American slave narrative. To be sure, the story is set in Cuba, not America, but this appears a strategic decision based on the fact that Cuba and Brazil were the only two nations who had yet to abolish slavery in 1885, when *The Dynamiter* was published. Of course the island also provides an exotic locale against which to set a story of jewel theft and "Hoodoo" sorcery, elements Fanny Stevenson added to the basic slave narrative structure to create a kind of literary pastiche. The result is what Robert Kiely calls a tale of "adolescent sensationalism"[14] that combines the most provocative details of its constitutive genres: stolen gems, violence, erotic display, murder. Particularly vulnerable to such narrative lures is Desborough, a youth who is "neither rich, nor witty, nor successful" and who, as a result, is immediately seduced by Teresa Valdevia's foreign appearance, her Spanish-inflected speech, and her mysterious past life.

Teresa's supposed identity as a runaway slave becomes the seminal "hook" to her story, the secret Desborough "accidentally" exposes in his initial flirtation with Teresa on the terrace of his house. After sharing her Cuban tobacco with the kind "Señor," Teresa sorrowfully recalls her "dear home, dear Cuba!" to which she will "never . . . ah, never, in Heaven's name" return (186). "Are you then resident for life in England?" Desborough innocently asks, but Teresa gives the cryptic answer, "'You ask too much, for you ask more than I know'" (186). Captivated, Desborough purchases for her "a little book" written in Spanish, but Teresa, with a series of well-timed blushes, reveals that she had deceived Desborough: "'Spanish is, of course, my native tongue,' she says, '[but] how shall I confess to you the truth—the humiliating truth—that I cannot read?'" (189). Desborough's response is incredulous: "'Read?' repeated Harry. 'You!'" (189). Teresa's sophisticated manner, as well as the whiteness of her skin, which "gleam[s]" (184) through her lace mantilla, belie the fact of her illiteracy. But betrayed by this marker of slave status, Teresa finds herself compelled to "tell [Desborough] without disguise the story of my life" (189), a statement that recalls the testimonials of "unvarnished" truth-telling accompanying the slave narratives of William Wells Brown, Solomon Northup, James Williams, and others.

Claiming a mixed racial heritage typical of many slave narrators, Teresa invokes the trope of the tragic mulatta who is forced, by her black blood, to confront the insidious legacy of slavery. With the opening caveat, "I am not what I seem," Teresa describes a lineage "from grandees of Spain" and "the Patriot Bruce" on her father's side, and from a "line of [African] kings" on her mother's (191). Despite this illustrious pedigree, Teresa learns that her "mother was a slave" (198) and that it was her father's design "to sail to the free land of Britain, where the law would suffer me to marry her: a design too long procrastinated; for death, at the last moment, intervened" (196). Facing financial ruin, Señor Valdevia finds he cannot even emancipate his own daughter. He tells her, " 'You are a chattel; a marketable thing; and worth—heavens, that I should say such words!—worth money. Do you begin to see? If I were to give you freedom, I should defraud my creditors; the manumission would be certainly annulled; you would be still a slave, and I a criminal' "(197). From enjoying the life of a plantation mistress, Teresa now endures the degradation of slavery. Madame Mendizabal—herself a former slave freed by marriage to an English nobleman—assesses Teresa with malevolent glee, informing her, " 'I should take a pleasure . . . in bringing you acquainted with a whip' " (194). And Caulder, one of Señor Valdevia's creditors, coarsely evaluates Teresa's physical attributes, asking, " 'Is your hair all your own?' " and then testing it as if she were "a horse" (204).

With her father's death and the subsequent sale of his estate, Teresa must seek the protection of Sir George Greville, owner of an English yacht docked on the north side of the island. Her passage to freedom crosses through swamp country, that traditional "site of protection and subterfuge" for the runaway slave. Daphne A. Brooks has noted that "swamp lands posed both a threat to and an opportunity for the resourceful fugitive,"[15] thrusting the slave into an inhospitable environment while simultaneously providing necessary refuge from white pursuers. Here, the Cuban swamp is overrun with tropical vegetation, wild animals, and insects, and it proves literally toxic to those with white blood. Señor Valdevia succumbs to tropical fever soon after concealing his jewels deep within the jungle. Similarly, Caulder, guided by Teresa to the hiding spot, is overcome with nausea and hallucinations and quickly dies. Teresa, on the other hand, is protected by "the black blood that [she] now knew to circulate in [her] veins" (200). Although the swamp is "inimical to [white] life" (214), it provides a space for black sedition and emancipation. It is to the swamp that Teresa lures the ignorant Caulder, exploiting his greed for the jewels and deceiving him with her counterfeit loyalty. And it is in the swamp where Caulder "breathe[d] his last" and where Teresa finally "knew that [she] was free" (214). Taking the jewels, as well as Caulder's pocketbook and revolver, Teresa "resolve[s] rather to die than to be captured" and "set[s] forward towards the north," running, in her case, not to Canada but to the north coast of the island (214).

The swamp, however, is also the locus of Hoodoo ritual for Negro slaves under the spell of the sorceress, Madame Mendizabal. Teresa's sinister double, Madame Mendizabal represents the emancipated slave gone awry. Señor Valdevia recalls,

> Twenty years ago, [Madame Mendizabal] was the loveliest of slaves; to-day she is what you see her—prematurely old, disgraced by the practice of every vice and every nefarious industry, but free, rich, married, they say, to some reputable man, whom may Heaven assist! and exercising among her ancient mates, the slaves of Cuba, an influence as unbounded as its reason is mysterious. (195)

A mulatta like Teresa, but one who exploits her liminal position to incite her African followers to mutiny and human sacrifice, Madame Mendizabal becomes the high priestess of a de facto maroon community. Unlike Teresa, the runaway slaves under Madame Mendizabel's power do not seek to emerge from the swamp. Instead they cling to the rites of a primitive, precarceral past, establishing a renegade presence in the heart of the wilderness. Rejecting this alternate slave community, Teresa describes the Hoodoo spectacle as "barbarous" and "bloody" and calls the worshipers "a mob of cannibals" (219). Her epistemological and racial alienation reaches a peak when she witnesses Madame Mendizabal about to sacrifice a slave girl. Teresa's involuntary scream occurs almost simultaneously with a freak tornado that conveniently kills Madame Mendizabal, destroys the Hoodoo chapel, and safely expels Teresa from the swamp. With this meteorological deus ex machina, Teresa avoids the fate of other runaway slaves, who escape white domination only to submit to black witchcraft.

But perhaps the most cunning manipulation of the slave narrative occurs in Teresa's invocation of English national superiority. Teresa repeatedly insists that "a slave . . . is safe in England" (231) and that England is "the natural home of the escaped slave" (228). In so doing, she perpetuates a myth of British moral preeminence that was a common feature in American slave narratives from the late eighteenth to mid-nineteenth century. Although implicated in West Indian slavery and a major player in the transatlantic slave trade, Britain enjoyed a reputation, according to Frances Smith Foster, as a "more enlightened and hospitable country than the United States."[16] Foster writes that "when Parliament abolished slavery in Britain and all British colonies in 1833, the pro-British flavor of the narratives became even more pronounced."[17] In paying homage to Britain's antislavery attitudes, slave narrators understood that "many Americans still deferred to Great Britain as a model for cultural and social living."[18] Moreover, after the passage of the Fugitive Slave Law of 1850, Britain was one of the few safe havens from recapture and repatriation. Even though her story takes place in the 1880s, well after the glory days of British antislavery, Teresa taps into this powerful history in charting her own escape. She chooses to make the longer trip to "Old England," even though Sir Greville's yacht briefly docks in New Orleans, where slavery had been abolished for some twenty years. It is England, as much as freedom, that composes Teresa's narrative *telos*.

Of course, Teresa, we learn, is no runaway slave but a criminal named Clare Luxmore, who "was never nearer Cuba than Penzance" (346). Yet she successfully appropriates the conventions of the slave narrative, from the scenes of physical degradation, to the flight northward through swampland, to the repeated glorification of England. Her opportunistic use of these generic features is a testament to the slave narrative's cultural durability in the years after the American Civil War, but it simultaneously confirms the political demise of the genre. From an abolitionist vehicle that promised rare access to "the *heart* of the poor slave,"[19] the slave narrative had now achieved such cultural saturation that it had become, in effect, a cliché. Clare Luxmore may not know the Cuban landscape and may not possess a drop of African blood, but this does not prevent her from parlaying the familiar tropes of the slave narrative to "pass" as a runaway slave.[20] Never mind that her guise frequently slips or that her narrative inclines toward the absurd; that she claims to be illiterate but then describes how she "drew out Mr. Caulder's pocket-book and turned to the page on which the dying man had scrawled his testament" and cries, "How shall I describe the agony of happiness and remorse with which I read it!" (229).[21] *The Story of the Fair Cuban* becomes a parody of the slave narrative, as ridiculous and exaggerated as the frame narrative as a whole.

Desborough's willful blindness to the inconsistencies in Clare Luxmore's story becomes an indictment of British national vanity. If we look at the scenes that precede and follow *The Story of the Fair Cuban*, we see that Clare seduces Desborough by flattering his English character. "English gentlemen," Clare claims, "could be fast friends, respectful, honest friends; could be companions, comforters, if the need arose, or champions, and yet never encroach" (187). They are mythological heroes she has "heard of since my childhood" (187) and "longed to meet" (187), guardians of morality and arbiters of justice. Clare lauds everything from English "aplomb" (188) (which she contrasts to her Cuban manner, which is "too constrained, too cold" [184]) to the English language (which she describes as an "expressive tongue" [185]) to the English chivalric tradition. In a rhapsodic ode to the country, she cries,

> But here, in free England—oh, glorious liberty! . . . here there are no fetters; here the woman may dare to be herself entirely, and the men, the chivalrous men—is it not written on the very shield of your nation, *honi soit?*[22] Ah, it is hard for me to learn, hard for me to dare to be myself. You must not judge me yet awhile; I shall end by conquering this stiffness, I shall end by growing English. (185)

She praises Desborough's "national seriousness of bearing" (187) and appeals to his protection from Cuban spies, whom she claims seek her extradition for jewel theft.[23] Desborough, for his part, swells with patriotism and gallantry. "'Count upon me,'" he tells her "with bewildered fervour" (234). He seeks out and reads every book on Cuba he can find. He asks himself, "What should he do, to be more worthy? by what devotion, call down the notice of these eyes to so terrene a being as himself?" (235). So ardent is he in his desire to "protect Teresa with his life" that he begins to shadow her every move, prompting her to tease him, "'Do I understand that you follow me, Señor? . . . Are these the manners of the English gentleman?'" (236).

Desborough becomes a model not of English cultural preeminence, but of English futility, a "knight-errant" who inspires amusement rather than respect. In another example of his bumbling, if well-meaning, efforts, Desborough spies a strange man visiting Clare and, imagining him to be a "Cuban emissary" (235) in disguise, attempts to scare him off. When he reports the exchange to Clare, she responds, "'Don Quixote, Don Quixote, have you again been tilting against windmills? . . . how you must have terrified [my solicitor's clerk]'" (239). As a vigilante policeman and detective, Desborough proves more hindrance than help to Clare. Moreover, this self-appointed guardian to a runaway slave is in fact the unwitting accomplice to a traitor and terrorist. Instructed by Clare to deliver the brown box to an Irish packet steamer, Desborough dutifully complies, ignoring the "delicate ticking" (243) that emanates from the container. When the plans suddenly change and Clare orders Desborough to retrieve the ticking box, he takes advantage of the situation to "display his strength" (245) and carry the box on his shoulders. Only when the bomb explodes with more of a whimper than a bang does Desborough realize he is no hero but a patsy. Instead of defending England's jurisdiction from Cuban spies, Desborough has in fact undermined national security by abetting Fenian conspirators.

The movement for Irish independence had taken a particularly violent turn in the second half of the nineteenth century, as members of the Irish Republican Brotherhood and sister groups like the Irish-American Clan a Gael fomented rebellion against the British state. In 1867, in an attempt to liberate Irish Republican Brotherhood member Richard Burke, Fenian sympathizers detonated two hundred pounds of gunpowder at Clerkenwell Prison in London, decimating an entire neighborhood, killing twelve people, and injuring at least one hundred and twenty others. The vast physical destruction reflected a shattered sense of national security. The British felt themselves under siege, but instead of battling a foreign adversary, they were battling insurgents from within. As K. R. M. Short writes, "The Englishman in his castle 'knew' he had much to fear from the Irishman at his gate but much more so from the Irishman *within* the gate."[24] In 1882, the public was again shocked when the Irish National Invincibles, an extremist group that had broken off from the Irish Republican Brotherhood, murdered Lord Frederick Cavendish and Thomas Henry Burke, the Chief Secretary and Permanent Under Secretary for Ireland. The gruesome and audacious nature of the murders—Cavendish and Burke were stabbed as they crossed Phoenix Park in Dublin—earned the public condemnation of Irish nationalist leader Charles Stewart Parnell and even the disapproval of some Fenian sympathizers.

With technological advances in dynamite in the 1870s, radical Irish nationalists discovered a new, potent weapon for their anticolonial campaign. As Sarah McLemore writes, "it was [now] possible to build a bomb which would cause a massive explosion and could be manufactured, transported, and placed with relative ease and security."[25]

While the Irish Republican Brotherhood eventually disavowed the use of dynamite bombs, questioning their benefits given public outrage, collateral damage, and potential reprisals against Irish citizens, Irish-American Fenian groups saw in dynamite terror an effective means of forcing British withdrawal from Ireland. In Short's words, "London was to be held to ransom."[26] Beginning in 1881, Irish-American Fenians bombed the Tower of London, Westminster Palace, London Bridge, and Scotland Yard, as well as sites in major British cities such as Liverpool and Glasgow. Unlike anarchist and Russian revolutionary groups, which used dynamite to target specific individuals, Irish-American Fenians generally directed their attacks against cultural and political symbols of English power. As Zero tells Somerset in *The Dynamiter*, "You might, perhaps, expect us to attack the Queen, the sinister Gladstone, the rigid Derby, or the dexterous Granville; but there you would be in error" (158). The Fenians instead aimed for a more generalized, even democratic, brand of terror, one that touched both the loftiest government official and the humblest British citizen. In the case of *Zero's Tale of the Explosive Bomb*, the (parodied) target is an effigy of Shakespeare in Leicester Square, chosen because the playwright is "claimed as a glory by the English race" (160). To destroy a statue of Shakespeare would be to assault Englishness itself, to take on the nation's sacred cow. Zero gloats, "Guilty England would thus be stabbed in the most delicate quarters" (160) and the nation's corporate health crippled.

According to Fanny Stevenson, *The Dynamiter* is based on "several dynamite outrages in London about this time, the most of them turning out fiascos."[27] She was almost certainly referring to the dynamite attacks perpetrated by Clan a Gael members James Gilbert Cunningham and Henry Burton. In December of 1884, Cunningham smuggled into the country a brown Saratoga trunk—the probable inspiration for Desborough's brown box—filled with sixty pounds of dynamite. Burton, who had bombed London railway stations earlier that year, arrived in Liverpool a short time after and subsequently took rooms in a London boarding house, from which he planned the attacks. On January 2, 1885, Cunningham launched his first dynamite attack, targeting a train on the Metropolitan Line. Next was a coordinated attack on the Tower of London and House of Commons on January 24. Cunningham, concealing a bomb under a large overcoat, slipped into the Tower with some tourists and deposited the device in the Banqueting Room. Meanwhile, two other bombers, one possibly dressed as a woman to conceal the explosives under a skirt, entered Westminster Hall and separated, one heading for the Crypt and the other for the Bar of the House. At 2:00 P.M., the Tower bomb exploded, but Short writes that Cunningham had "either misjudged the amount of time required to make his exit or the fuse prematurely detonated" and was detained at the gates. Short continues,

At about 2:10 pm, a woman in the Crypt cried out, "I think one of your mats is on fire." Constable Cole, seeing that it was in fact a smoking parcel, grabbed it and made a dash up the stairs for Westminster Hall but it exploded before he reached the top. At the sound of the blast the constable in the Chamber of the House [Constable Cox] left his post, and the second bomb was dropped into the chamber with a short fuse; minutes later it exploded causing extensive damage.[28]

The two bombers escaped safely, but Burton was arrested soon after, having been identified as a colleague of Cunningham's by a London detective. In May of 1885, Cunningham and Burton went to trial, were found guilty, and were sentenced to life imprisonment. Constable Cole was promoted to sergeant and given the Albert Medal for Lifesaving, named in memory of the Prince Consort.[29]

Cunningham and Burton are likely the inspiration for Zero, or "the man in a sealskin coat," the self-professed "dynamiter" who assembles bombs and seeks "the fall of England, the massacre of thousands, the yell of fear and execration" (156). Clare Luxmore and Patrick M'Guire are his confederates, who execute Zero's plans, sometimes to humorous effect. In the course of *The Dynamiter*, they are revealed to be "three futiles" to rival Somerset, Challoner, and Desborough, as inept in their dynamiting as the three Englishmen are in their detecting. But beneath the Stevensons' wry treatment of the dynamite bombers and the English gentlemen is a serious indictment of what I will call "vigilante nationalism." Whether it is an Irish nationalist planting bombs to liberate "green Erin" or an English citizen playing "knight-errant" to Mormon maiden or Cuban fugitive slave, such acts do not promote Irish or English nationalism so much as parody it. The only true heroes—and patriots—are the unnamed policemen who periodically appear in the narrative, their suspicions awakened by "unguarded trunks" (104), as in the *Narrative of the Spirited Old Lady*, or by the nervous behavior of dynamite bombers, as in *Zero's Tale of the Explosive Bomb*. In a tribute to these unsung guardians of national security, the Stevensons specifically dedicated *The Dynamiter* to "Messrs. Cole and Cox, Police Officers," the constables on duty at the Tower of London and Westminster Palace bombings, both of whom were injured in their efforts to protect the public. "Courage and devotion, so common in the ranks of the police, so little recognised, so meagrely rewarded, have at length found their commemoration in an historical act" (6), they write.

In praising Cole and Cox, however, the Stevensons simultaneously criticize the ineffectuality of the nation's official representatives, politicians such as Gladstone and Parnell, who, they believe, lack the moral courage and integrity to lead the country both abroad and at home. They conclude *The Dynamiter*'s dedication with the damning statement, "History, which will represent Mr. Parnell sitting silent under the appeal of Mr. Forster, and Gordon setting forth upon his tragic enterprise, will not forget Mr. Cole carrying the dynamite in his defenceless hands, nor Mr. Cox coming coolly to his aid" (6). Louis was an outspoken critic of Gladstone, the

British Prime Minister whose reluctance to send aid to General Charles Gordon in the Battle of Khartoum (1884–85) led to the British expulsion from Sudan and General Gordon's death by beheading. Louis was likewise critical of Charles Stewart Parnell, the Irish M.P. with reputed ties to the Irish Republican Brotherhood who clashed with William Edward Forster over the Coercion Bill of 1881, which gave the Irish government the right to arrest and imprison suspected conspirators without trial. Together, these men jeopardized Britain's international and domestic authority, leading the loyal imperialist and Unionist Louis to lament that "England stands before the world dripping with blood and daubed with dishonour."[30] In this postheroic age, Louis writes in a letter, "Police-Officer Cole is the only man I see to admire. I dedicate my New Arabs [*The Dynamiter*] to him and Cox in default of other great public characters."[31]

Within *The Dynamiter*, the Stevensons lambasts the British government most directly in *Zero's Tale of the Explosive Bomb*, making clear that while leaders like Gladstone may occasionally thwart dynamite plots, their success is more a factor of Fenian ineptitude than government competence. According to Zero, some "chicken-souled [Fenian] conspirators" (160) inform government authorities of a possible attack on Leicester Square, with the result that the "Government had craftily filled the place with minions" (161). M'Guire, who has been dispatched to set the bomb (concealed, pointedly, in a Gladstone bag), panics, embarking on a ludicrous tour of London in which he attempts to save himself by foisting the ticking bomb on a small child, a woman, and a cabdriver before flinging the bag into a river, where it harmlessly explodes underwater. Louis pokes fun at M'Guire's dubious morality, as his lofty nationalist ideals give way to base self interest. Yet M'Guire's actions only mirror that of the "Machiavellian Gladstone" (160), who may superficially defend the public against terrorist attack, but who, in Louis's mind, enables such activity by accommodating Irish nationalists like Parnell. Such wavering moral authority places Gladstone on the same level as the cowardly M'Guire. The two are complicit in threatening national stability, and in fact, work in concert with each other. A Fenian turncoat tips off the government; the government provides cover for Fenian activity; both parties are morally stained by the "collaboration."[32]

Louis's preoccupation with England's public humiliation and "dishonour" and what he saw as the government's lack of moral integrity takes on added poignancy when read through *The Story of the Fair Cuban*. Desborough's eagerness to help Teresa Valdevia and his embrace of the English chivalric ideal hearken back to a period in which "great public characters" were possible, when England's position as global antislavery policeman reflected its sense of moral and political integrity. In this idealized past, as opposed to the confused present, the country resided squarely on the side of justice—the side now occupied by the local constable. Heroism now seems possible only on the smallest scale, on the level of the humble policeman who steps in where the nation's leaders fail. Cole and Cox, not Gladstone and Parnell, are the nation's defenders from the threat of domestic terrorism. And Challoner, Somerset, and Desborough, *The Dynamiter*'s three amiable "futiles," metonymically represent the bumbling nation, easily flattered by past glory but hopelessly ineffective in the present. They may fancy themselves "men of the world" who, Somerset boasts, are "possessed of an extraordinary mass and variety of knowledge" and who are "planted at the strategic centre of the universe" and "in the midst of the chief mass of people, and within ear-shot of the most continuous chink of money on the surface of the globe" (14). Yet this privileged situation renders the three men complacent, easy prey to hoaxes and humiliation, saved only by sheer luck or the valiant efforts of the Metropolitan Police.

The dedication to *The Dynamiter* therefore celebrates more than the mere bravery of Cole and Cox; it celebrates the moral clarity of their actions. "Whoever be in the right in this great and confused war of politics;" the Stevensons write, "whatever elements of greed, whatever traits of the bully, dishonour both parties in this inhuman contest;—your side, your part, is at least pure of doubt" (5). *The Story of the Fair Cuban*, set against this prefatory note, becomes a narrative of nostalgia, pointing to an idealized past in which England's moral responsibility to eradicate slavery is unfettered by political contingencies. In a particularly devastating piece of irony, it is an Irish terrorist who takes on the guise of the runaway slave, thus exploiting popular, pseudoscientific racial theories equating the Irish to the "Negro" race only to turn the comparison on its head: Irish colonial rebel affects grateful black slave in order to attack the metropole.[33]

That the story is fabricated by Clare Luxmore to further her own interests further confirms the moral bankruptcy of this age, where even the slave narrative, that nineteenth-century morality play, may be appropriated for corrupt ends. As for Desborough, Clare's malevolent motives do not prevent him tossing aside his idealistic pretences and marrying his deceiver. *The Dynamiter* ends on a mordant note as Fenian bomber and bumbling Englishman end up not enemies but bedmates, signifying a world in which the absence of any clear moral leadership leads to such questionable alliances and affiliations.

Of course the story of *The Dynamiter* is also the story of Fanny Stevenson and the literary partnership she embarked upon with her husband, an alliance that was regarded with skepticism and even hostility. Critics have not been kind to Fanny. To H. Bellyse Baildon, she was "not herself possessed of great artistic genius."[34] T. C. Livingstone deems *The Dynamiter* "inferior to [*New Arabian Nights*], largely because it has to carry Mrs. Stevenson's competent but uninspired contributions."[35] And Frank McLynn is even less magnanimous, describing Fanny as "developing delusions of grandeur about her status as a writer" and dismissing *The Dynamiter* as "mediocre stuff indeed, so much so that some scholars think it almost entirely Fanny's work."[36] Fanny herself was "bitterly resentful that her contribution was downgraded, that critics did not give her her due."[37] In a letter to her mother-in-law, she complains of "being Louis's scapegoat" and of being "treated as a comma, and a superfluous one at that."[38] Her preface to the Tusitala edition of *The Dynamiter* represents her belated attempt to "set the record straight" and to claim ownership of a contested work. But even then critics such as McLynn derogate the "feminine hand"[39] that sullies the work, while lauding the "occasional sign of the authentic RLS presence."[40]

McLynn's comments, focused as they are on questions of authenticity and legitimacy, recall the narrative's own obsession with truth and deception. Nearly every character is something he or she is not, from Clare Luxmore (aka Asenath Fonblanque, aka Teresa Valdevia) to Prince Florizel (aka Thomas Godall) to the three knights-errant, Challoner, Somerset, and Desborough. Based on this observation, Kiely offers a psychoanalytic reading of *The Dynamiter*, claiming that "Stevenson is almost compulsive about forcing his various narrators in these tales to plead guilty to telling lies. In a way he seems to feel the guilt is his as well as theirs . . . he implicitly casts aspersions on the validity of certain kinds of narrative art, especially adventure fiction, and on the integrity of artists like himself who write it."[41] Yet if we take Fanny Stevenson at her word and read *The Dynamiter* as mostly her own work, then it is Fanny who is the true fabulist, she who creates the most extravagant tales and plays Scheherazade to Louis's sultan. *The Dynamiter* boasts Robert Louis Stevenson's literary sponsorship, but it is ultimately Fanny's story.

Ironically, many of the charges levied against Fanny Stevenson—outlandishness, mediocrity, inauthenticity—recall the critical misgivings that dogged the slave narrative for years. To be sure, the trials of validation that greeted the slave narrative were racially driven, centering on issues of white abolitionist authentication and collaboration, historical accuracy, and propagandistic bias.[42] In Fanny's case, critical enmity has focused on issues of gender (her "feminine hand"), nepotism, and dilettantism. Still, for all her supposed faults, Fanny succeeds in updating an antebellum American genre for a late Victorian text, enacting on the literary level the transatlantic collaboration between herself and her husband. The result is not just a critique of Gladstonian ethics, but an unlikely testament to the formidable afterlife of the slave narrative.

Notes

Introduction

1. Charles Dickens, "To W. C. Macready," 17 March 1848, *The Letters of Charles Dickens*, ed. Madeline House, Graham Storey, and Kathleen Tillotson, vol. 5 (New York: Oxford University Press, 1965–2002), 262.

2. Charles T. Davis and Henry Louis Gates, Jr., introduction, *The Slave's Narrative* (New York: Oxford University Press, 1985), xvi. This was Macready's second American tour. It was marred by the Astor Place Riot, which broke out on May 10, 1849, in New York City and resulted in twenty-two deaths. The riot pitted fans of Edwin Forrest, an American actor, against fans of the British Macready. At Macready's first performance of *Macbeth* at the Astor Place Theatre, he was pelted with rotten eggs and potatoes. The paths of Macready and Douglass may have crossed around this time. Dennis Berthold describes Forrest's supporters as "racist, xenophobic, anti-Catholic bigots" who taunted Macready with the cry, "Three cheers for Macready, Nigger Douglass, and Pete Williams" during a May 7 performance. He writes, "Williams, an African American saloon keeper in the Five Points area, ran a tavern notorious for interracial dancing. Frederick Douglass, in town to address the American Anti-Slavery Society Convention, had scandalized New Yorkers on 5 May by walking down Broadway arm-in-arm with two white women. The nativist Democrats who hated Macready, also hated blacks, abolitionists, and foreigners, making Macready into a complex political symbol of Whig elitism and comparative racial tolerance" (Dennis Berthold, "Class Acts: the Astor Place Riots and Melville's 'The Two Temples,'" *American Literature* 71 [1999], 434).

3. Charles Dickens, "To W. C. Macready," 17 March 1848, *Letters*, 262.

4. It is unclear which edition of Douglass's *Narrative* Dickens owned and passed on to Macready. The frontispiece to the first British edition (Dublin 1845) departs from the frontispiece in the earlier American editions. Subsequent British editions reverted to the American frontispiece. Douglass's *Narrative* is not listed in the *Catalogue of the Library of W. C. Macready*. Given Dickens's cultural preeminence and known antislavery sympathies, he would have likely received a first British edition of Douglass's

Narrative as a gift from the publisher or author. I read Dickens's strong reaction to this British frontispiece as a condemnation of its racial distortion. Yet the American frontispiece could also, in its own way, be considered "hideous and abominable," albeit for reasons of technical incompetence.

5. My thanks to Susan Dackerman, curator of prints at the Harvard University Art Museums, who informed me that "delt" is an abbreviation for "delineavit" ("drawn by") and "sc" is an abbreviation for "scuplsit" ("incised by"). Therefore, it seems that Bell made the drawing for the frontispiece and Adlard engraved the copperplate. Kraig Binkowski at the Yale Center for British Art pointed out the resemblance between the 1845 Dublin edition frontispiece and the Douglass painting, currently housed at the National Portrait Gallery in Washington, D. C.

6. Ezra Greenspan, *The Cambridge Companion to Walt Whitman* (Cambridge: Cambridge University Press, 1995), 144.

7. Marcus Wood, *Blind Memory: Visual Representations of Slavery in England and America* (Manchester: Manchester University Press, 2000), 103, 137.

8. Frederick Douglass, *The North Star*, April 7, 1849.

9. Ibid.

10. See John Stauffer, *The Black Hearts of Men: Radical Abolitionists and the Transformation of Race* (Cambridge: Harvard University Press, 2002).

11. Frederick Douglass, "My Experience and My Mission to Great Britain: An Address Delivered in Cork, Ireland, on October 14, 1845," Cork *Examiner* 15 October 1845, *The Frederick Douglass Papers: Series One—Speeches, Debates, and Interviews*, ed. John Blassingame, et al., vol. 1 (New Haven: Yale University Press, 1979), 36. One wonders if B. Bell read this description of Douglass and correspondingly adjusted his portrait.

12. John Estlin, "To Samuel May," 12 January 1847," quoted in Clare Taylor, *British and American Abolitionists: An Episode in Transatlantic Understanding* (Edinburgh: Edinburgh University Press, 1974), 305. For more on the racial and gender anxiety that accompanied Douglass's popularity, see Claire Midgely, *Women Against Slavery: The British Campaigns, 1780–1870* (New York: Routledge, 1992), 140–41.

13. Douglas Lorimer, *Colour, Class, and the Victorians* (Bristol [England]: Leicester University Press, 1978), 13.

14. Augusta Rohrbach, *Truth Stranger Than Fiction: Race, Realism, and the U.S. Literary Marketplace* (New York: Palgrave, 2002), 31.

15. Davis and Gates, Jr., *Slave's Narrative*, xvi.

16. Marion Wilson Starling, *The Slave Narrative: Its Place in American History* (Washington: Howard University Press, 1988), 108.

17. Davis and Gates, Jr., *Slave's Narrative*, xvi.

18. Starling, *Slave Narrative*, 36.

19. Charles H. Nichols, *Many Thousand Gone: The Ex-Slaves Account of Their Bondage and Freedom* (Bloomington: Indiana University Press, 1969), 150–51.

20. Starling, *Slave Narrative*, 107.

21. R. J. M. Blackett, *Building an Antislavery Wall: Black Americans in the Atlantic Abolitionist Movement, 1830–1860* (Baton Rouge: Louisiana State University Press, 1983), 17.

22. Starling, *Slave Narrative*, 145. In his travelogue, *Three Years in Europe, or, Places I have Seen and People I have Met*, William Wells Brown

describes staying "under the hospitable roof of Harriet Martineau" (William Wells Brown, *Three Years in Europe or, Places I have Seen and People I have Met* [London: Charles Gilpin, 1852]), 197. In the *Memoir of William Wells Brown* that prefaces his travelogue, Brown is described as being elected an honorary member of the Whittington Club, "an institution numbering nearly 2000 members, among whom are Lords Brougham, Dudley Coutts Stuart, and Beaumont; Charles Dickens, Douglass Jerrold, Martin Thackeray, Charles Lushington, M.P., Monckton Milnes, M.P., and several other of the most distinguished legislators and literary men and women in this country" (Ibid., xxiv).

23. Blackett, *Building an Antislavery Wall*, 3.

24. Ibid, 14.

25. Howard Temperley, *British Antislavery 1833–1870* (London: Longman, 1972), 32–33.

26. Ibid., 223. For more on Henry Box Brown's public reenactments of his escape from slavery, see Daphne A. Brooks, *Bodies in Dissent: Spectacular Performance of Race and Freedom: 1850–1910* (Durham, NC: Duke University Press, 2006). See also Samuel Rowse's 1850 lithograph of "The Resurrection of Henry Box Brown at Philadelphia."

27. See Audrey Fisch, *American Slaves in Victorian England: Abolitionist Politics in Popular Literature and Culture* (New York: Cambridge University Press, 2000).

28. Henry Mayhew, *London Labour and the London Poor*, 4 vols. (London: Dover, 1968), 193. Douglas Lorimer speculates that Mayhew's descriptions of "negro beggars" in his survey could be those of American fugitive slaves fallen on hard times. He points to the Report of the Ladies' Society to Aid Fugitives from Slavery for 1854, which describes eight fugitive slaves employed as apprentices, waiters, carpenters, and cooks. See Lorimer, *Colour, Class and the Victorians* (Bristol [England]: Leicester University Press, 1978), 42.

29. The American counterpart to the BFASS was the American Anti-Slavery Society, which was founded in 1833 by William Lloyd Garrison and Arthur Tappan. In 1840, the anti-Garrisonian American and Foreign Anti-Slavery Society, led by Lewis Tappan, broke off from the American Anti-Slavery Society over disputes such as the admission of women into the society. For more, please see Midgley, *Women Against Slavery*, 123–24.

30. Ibid.

31. Temperley, *British Antislavery*, 196.

32. Ibid., 196, 222.

33. Fisch, *American Slaves in Victorian England*, 55. Kelly J. Mays supports Fisch's point when she notes that Thomas Burt, a former miner and M.P., "greatly admired *The Narrative of Frederick Douglass*" and in his 1924 working-class autobiography hopes that "by recounting his own efforts 'to acquire discipline under extreme difficulties,' he 'may encourage youths of the working class, with better opportunities than [his], to put forth their utmost efforts in the same direction'" (Kelly J. Mays, "When a 'Speck' Begins to Read," *Reading Sites: Social Difference and Reader Response*, ed. Patrocinio P. Schweickart and Elizabeth A. Flynn [New York: MLA, 2004], 129).

34. John Bugg, "The Other Interesting Narrative: Olaudah Equiano's Public Book Tour," *PMLA* 121 (2006), 1427.

35. Robin W. Winks, introduction, *Four Fugitive Slave Narratives* (Reading: Addison-Wesley Publishing Co., 1969), vi.

36. Fisch, *American Slaves in Victorian England*, 54.

37. Blackett, *Building an Antislavery Wall*, 25.

38. Frances Smith Foster, *Witnessing Slavery: The Development of Ante-Bellum Slave Narratives* (Madison: University of Wisconsin Press, 1994), 85.

39. Jacques Derrida writes, "Every text participates in one or several genres, there is no genreless text" (Jacques Derrida, "The Law of Genre," trans. Avital Ronell, *Critical Inquiry* 6 [1980], 65). The slave narrative both participates in other genres and constitutes its own genre.

40. James Olney, "'I was born': Slave Narratives, Their Status as Autobiography and as Literature," *Calalloo* 20 (1984), 50.

41. Ibid., 50.

42. Ibid.

43. William Andrews believes the slave narrative achieved its "classic form and tone" in the period between 1840 and 1860 (William Andrews, "The Representation of Slavery and Afro-American Literary Realism," *African American Autobiography: A Collection of Critical Essays*, ed. William L. Andrews [Englewood Cliffs, NJ: Prentice Hall, 1993], 78). Charles Heglar has a slightly more expansive time frame, designating classic slave narratives those published between 1830 and 1861 (Charles Heglar, *Rethinking the Slave Narrative* [Westport: Greenwood Press, 2001], 8). In both cases, the time frame roughly corresponds with that of the interabolition period (1833–1863).

44. Recently, Vincent Carretta has cast doubt on the truthfulness of Equiano's narrative, citing evidence that Equiano was born not in Africa, as he claimed, but in South Carolina. See Vincent Carretta, *Equiano, the African: Biography of a Self-Made Man* (New York: Penguin, 2007). See also Bugg, "The Other Interesting Narrative," 142.

45. Other early examples of slave narratives include Briton Hammon, *A Narrative of the Uncommon Sufferings, and Surpizing Deliverance of Briton Hammon, A Negro Man* (Boston: Green and Russell, 1760); John Marrant and William Aldredge, *A Narrative of the Lord's Wonderful Dealings with John Marrant, a Black* (London: Gilbert and Plummer, 1785); and Ottobah Cugoano, *The Narrative of the Enslavement of Ottobah Cugoano, a Native of Africa, Published by Himself, In the Year 1787* (London: Hatchard and Company, 1825).

46. Starling, *Slave Narrative*, 66.

47. Ibid.

48. William Lloyd Garrison, founder of the American Anti-Slavery Society and the antislavery newspaper, *The Liberator*, was an ardent supporter of immediate and complete emancipation.

49. Starling, *Slave Narrative*, 222.

50. See Ibid., 228–29.

51. *Liberator* 16:35, reprinted in Starling, *Slave Narrative*, 253. For further discussion of the literary negotiations between white abolitionist patrons and black slave narrators, see John Sekora, "Black Message/White Envelope: Genre, Authenticity, and Authority in the Antebellum Slave Narrative," *Callalloo* 10 (1989): 482–515.

52. See John W. Blassingame, *The Slave Community: Plantation Life in the Antebellum South* (New York: Oxford University Press, 1979). Blassingame was one of the first historians to use slave narratives as historical artifacts, a methodology that was criticized by those who questioned the reliability of slave recollections.

53. Quoted in Davis and Gates, Jr., *Slave's Narrative*, xxi.

54. Ibid., 19.

55. "Black Letters," *Graham's Magazine* 42 (January 1853): 215, quoted in Starling, *Slave Narrative*, 2.

56. Ibid., 215.

57. Paul Gilroy, *The Black Atlantic: Modernity and Double Consciousness* (Cambridge: Harvard University Press, 1993), 4, 15.

58. Ibid., 4.

59. Helen Thomas, *Romanticism and Slave Narratives: Transatlantic Testimonies* (Cambridge: Cambridge University Press, 2000), 11, 12.

60. Fisch, *American Slaves in Victorian England*, 10.

61. Amanda Claybaugh, "Toward a New Transatlanticism: Dickens in the United States," *Victorian Studies* 48 (2006) 439–60. Claybaugh offers a cogent overview of the state of transatlantic studies. She writes, "The difference in focus on the Anglo-American world has tended to entail a difference in method. Those scholars who focus on the Anglo-American world have tended to excavate the material networks that constituted it, such as the slave trade (Paul Gilroy and Joseph Roach) and black newspapers in the United States, Europe, and Africa (Brent Edwards). Those scholars who focus on the relations between Great Britain and the United States have tended, by contrast, to focus on relations that are imagined, not material. For Robert Weisbuch, the relevant paradigm in Freudian. . .for Buell, the relevant paradigms come from post-colonial theory. . .more recently, Paul Giles has taken a different approach, proposing that what he calls 'the trans-Atlantic imaginary' is not structured in any stable way, but is rather a space of projection and free play into which any author, British or American, can enter at will" (ibid., 443). See also Amanda Claybaugh, *The Novel of Purpose: Literature and Social Reform in the Anglo-American World* (Ithaca: Cornell University Press, 2006) and Susan Manning and Andrew Taylor, eds. *Transatlantic Literary Studies: A Reader* (Baltimore: Johns Hopkins University Press, 2007).

62. Alex Woloch has described how the nineteenth-century novel "creates a formal structure that can imaginatively comprehend the dynamics of alienated labor, and the class structure that underlies this labor" (Alex Woloch, *The One v. the Many* [Princeton: Princeton University Press, 2003], 27). He argues that the novel's asymmetric distribution of "character-spaces" (ibid., 14) reflects and enacts contemporaneous concerns about class and social inequality. Working within this same "imprecise juncture between form and history" (ibid., 30), I propose broadening Woloch's outlook from character-space to chronotope (literally, "time-space"), from the history of the English working class to the history of Atlantic slavery. The Victorian novel is a multivoiced, heteroglot system that is implicated by and reflective of the originary form of alienated labor, slavery.

63. Gilroy, *Black Atlantic*, 4.

64. Meredith McGill, *American Literature and the Culture of Reprinting, 1834–1853* (Philadelphia: University of Pennsylvania Press, 2003), 31.

65. Mary Louise Pratt, *Imperial Eyes: Travel Writing and Transculturation* (New York: Routledge, 2007), 4.

66. Ibid., 7.

67. Blackett, *Building an Antislavery Wall*, 13.

68. Frederick Douglass, "Farewell Speech to the British People, at London Tavern, London, England, March 30, 1847," *Frederick Douglass:*

Selected Speeches and Writings, ed. Philip S. Foner (Chicago: Lawrence Hill Books, 2000), 70.

69. For more on Atlantic slavery's shaping influence on the modern world, see David Brion Davis, *The Problem of Slavery in the Age of Revolution, 1770–1823* (New York: Oxford University Press, 1999) and *The Problem of Slavery in Western Culture* (New York: Oxford University Press, 1988).

70. Frederick Douglass, "An Appeal to the British People, reception speech at Finsbury Chapel, Moorfield, England, May 12, 1846," *Frederick Douglass: Selected Speeches and Writings,* ed. Philip S. Foner (Chicago: Lawrence Hill Books, 2000), 39.

71. My use of this chemical metaphor is indebted to Homi Bhabha and his discussion of free radicalism in Joseph Conrad's *Lord Jim.* ENG 165b lecture, Harvard University, Spring 2003.

72. Douglass, "An Appeal to the British People," 38.

73. M. M. Bakhtin, "Forms of Time and Chronotope in the Novel," *The Dialogic Imagination: Four Essays,* trans. Caryl Emerson and Michael Holquist (Austin: University of Texas Press, 1981), 250.

74. Ibid., 250–51.

75. Ibid., 243–47.

76. Ibid.," 85.

77. See Orlando Patterson, *Slavery and Social Death: A Comparative Study* (Cambridge: Harvard University Press, 1982).

78. Bakhtin, "Epic and Novel," in *Dialogic Imagination,* 11.

79. Bakhtin, "Discourse in the Novel," in *Dialogic Imagination.,* 321.

80. Douglass, "An Appeal to the British People," 31.

81. For further discussion of *tenor* and *vehicle,* see I. A. Richards, *The Philosophy of Rhetoric* (New York: Oxford University Press, 1965).

82. Douglass, "An Appeal to the British People," 39.

83. Edward W. Said, *Culture and Imperialism* (New York: Knopf, 1993), 71.

84. Ibid., 96.

85. Ibid., 71. I refer to Said's argument about Jane Austen's *Mansfield Park* in my first chapter and his argument about Dickens's *Great Expectations* in my fifth chapter.

86. Catherine Gallagher, *The Industrial Reformation of English Fiction: Social Discourse and Narrative Form 1832–1867* (Chicago: University of Chicago Press, 1985).

87. Roman Jakobson distinguishes between the metaphoric and metonymic poles of language, with the former attaining primacy in Romantic poetry and the latter in Realist prose. "Following the path of contiguous relationships," he writes, "the Realist author metonymically digresses from the plot to the atmosphere and from the characters to the setting in space and time" (Roman Jakobson, *Two Aspects of Language.* Reprinted in *The Norton Anthology of Theory and Criticism,* ed. Vincent B. Leitch [New York: Norton, 2001], 1267). While Jakobson's formulation is perhaps overly schematic, his depiction of language's dualism is useful here. Slavery manages to negotiate both the metaphoric and metonymic axes.

88. Douglass, "To William Lloyd Garrison," January 1, 1846, *Frederick Douglass: Selected Speeches and Writings,* 18.

89. Ibid.

90. Douglass, "Farewell Speech to the British People," in ibid., 74–75.

Chapter 1

1. Susan Meyer, *Imperialism at Home: Race and Victorian Women's Fiction* (Ithaca, NY: Cornell University Press, 1996), 71.

2. David Turley, *The Culture of English Antislavery, 1780–1860* (New York: Routledge, 1991), 197.

3. To prevent the wholesale abandonment of the plantations by newly freed slaves, the British installed a transitional apprenticeship system, in which ex-slaves were required to remain on their plantations for a period of six years. The plan was a failure and was terminated in 1838.

4. In a prefatory letter to Frederick Douglass's *Narrative*, Wendell Phillips uses the term "West Indian experiment" to describe the recent abolition of slavery in the British West Indies:

> I remember that, in 1838, many were waiting for the results of the West India experiment, before they could come into our [American abolitionists'] ranks. Those 'results' have come long ago; but alas! Few of that number have come with them, as converts. A man must be disposed to judge of emancipation by other tests than whether it has increased the produce of sugar,—and to hate slavery for other reasons than because it starves men and whips women,—before he is ready to lay the first stone of his anti-slavery life.

5. Jenny Sharpe writes, "Britain's moral stand against slavery underwrote its self-designated mission to free enslaved peoples across the globe. As the first European nation to abolish slavery, it saw itself as a more humanitarian master. . . .In the years between the end of the African slave trade in 1807 and the Emancipation Act of 1834, abolitionists were the self-appointed consciences of Europe" (Jenny Sharpe, *Allegories of Empire: The Figure of Woman in the Colonial Text* [Minneapolis: University of Minnesota Press, 1993], 27).

6. Meyer, *Imperialism at Home*, 37. For other postcolonial readings of *Jane Eyre*, see Sharpe, *Allegories of Empire* and Gayatri Chakravorty Spivak, "Three Women's Texts and a Critique of Imperialism." *Critical Inquiry* 12 (1985): 243–61.

7. Humphrey Gawthrop, "Slavery: *Idée Fixe* of Emily and Charlotte Brontë." *Brontë Studies* 28 (2003): 113–21.

8. Rebecca Fraser, *Charlotte Brontë: A Writer's Life* (London: Methuen, 1998), 54.

9. As children, the Brontës created their own miniature versions of *Blackwood's Edinburgh Magazine*, examples of which can be seen at Harvard University's Houghton Library.

10. Charlotte Brontë, "An American Tale," 9 September 1929, *Juvenilia: 1829–1835* (New York: Penguin, 1997). The sketch begins, "'The Mill wheel of America is going downwards' said Scipio Africanus CLARKSON a zealous partizan [sic] of JOHN Quincy Adams as he read the account of General Andrew Jacksons [sic] succes [sic] in the Boston Manufacturer [.]"

11. In 1774, John Wesley published the antislavery pamphlet, "Thoughts Upon Slavery." His last letter was addressed to William Wilberforce; in it, he writes, "Go on, in the name of God and in the power of his might, till even American slavery (the vilest that ever saw the sun) shall vanish before it."

The Brontës were also avid readers of William Cowper, an Evangelical Anglican and abolitionist poet whose poem *The Castaway* "they all at times appreciated, or almost appropriated," (Quoted in Mary Taylor, *Mary Taylor, Friend of Charlotte Brontë*, ed. Joan Stevens [Wellington: Oxford University Press, 1972], 164).

12. Quoted in Elizabeth Gaskell, *The Life of Charlotte Brontë* (New York: Penguin, 1997), 153–54.

13. Fraser, *Charlotte Brontë*, 69–71. According to Gayle Graham Yates, Martineau was "the first Englishwoman to make the analogy between the American woman's lot and the slave's" in her popular travel narrative *Society in America*, published in 1837. In a letter to W. S. Williams, written just before she was to meet Martineau for the first time, Brontë admits, "For her [Martineau's] character—as revealed in her works—I have a lively admiration—a deep esteem."

14. In letters to Ellen Nussey from? 28 May 1836, October/November 1836, 15 April 1839, and 2 June 1840, Brontë mentions planned visits to Gomersal.

15. Charlotte Brontë, "'*All this day I have been in a dream,*'" *Jane Eyre*, ed. Richard J. Dunn (New York: Norton, 2001), 404.

16. Charlotte Brontë, "To Ellen Nussey," 30 June 1839, *The Letters of Charlotte Bronte*, ed. Margaret Smith, vol. 1 (Oxford: Clarendon, 1995–c.2004), 194.

17. Brontë, "To Ellen Nussey," 2 October 1838, *Letters*, vol. 1, 182.

18. Brontë, "To Ellen Nussey," 1 July 1841, *Letters*, vol. 1, 258. Brontë quotes from Exodus 13:14.

19. See Jane Austen, *Emma* (New York: Norton, 2000), 196.

20. Howard Temperley, *British Antislavery* 1833–1870 (London: Longman, 1972), 222.

21. Claire Midgley writes, "[The first World Anti-Slavery Convention] was largely a transatlantic convention of British and American abolitionists, and it became the arena in which British campaigners' decision to focus primarily on slavery in the United States was clarified" (Claire Midgley, *Women Against Slavery: the British Campaigns 1780–1870* [New York: Routledge, 1992], 123).

22. R. J. M. Blackett writes, "In early 1841, Remond spoke twenty-three nights out of thirty on slavery, prejudice, and colonization and lost his voice for his pains" (R. J. M. Blackett, *Building an Antislavery Wall: Black Americans in the Atlantic Abolitionist Movement, 1830–1860* [Baton Rouge: Louisiana State University Press, 17]).

23. Moses Grandy, *Narrative of the Life of Moses Grandy; Late a Slave in the United States of America* (London: C. Gilpin, 1843), 72.

24. In "History of the Year 1829," quoted in Gaskell's *Life of Charlotte Brontë*, Brontë writes, "We take the *Leeds Intelligencer, Tory*, and the *Leeds Mercury*" (19).

25. Fraser, *Charlotte Brontë*, 105.

26. Ibid., 126.

27. A. C. Benson, *The Life of Edward White Benson* (quoted in Fraser, *Charlotte Brontë*, 126).

28. Marion Wilson Starling, *The Slave Narrative: Its Place in American History* (Washington: Howard University Press, 1988), 107.

29. Moses Roper, "Letter from Moses Roper to the Committee of the British and Foreign Anti-Slavery Society, May 9, 1844," *The Black Abolitionist Papers: The British Isles, 1830–1865*, ed. C. Peter Ripley, et al., vol. 1 (Chapel Hill: University of North Carolina Press, 1985), 134–36.

30. Moses Roper, *Narrative of the Adventures and Escape of Moses Roper, from American Slavery* (London: Warder Office, 1839), 21.

31. Charlotte Brontë, *Jane Eyre*, ed. Richard J. Dunn (New York: Norton, 2000), 109–10. Hereafter cited within the text. Critics such as Kari J. Winter have also noted similarities between *Jane Eyre*'s Bertha Mason, the "madwoman in the attic," and *Incidents in the Life of a Slave Girl*'s Harriet Jacobs, who is concealed for years in a garret "only nine feet long and seven wide." While it is tempting to speculate that Brontë may have known of Jacobs's plight before writing *Jane Eyre*, *Incidents in the Life* was only published in 1861 (though parts of it were serialized in the New York *Daily Tribune* as early as 1853). Therefore, Brontë could not have known of Jacobs's story when composing *Jane Eyre*, which was published in 1847. Jacobs, however, probably knew of *Jane Eyre* when composing *Incidents in the Life*. After fleeing north, Jacobs went to work as a nursemaid for Nathaniel Parker Willis, the poet and editor, and his wife. (Willis's second wife, Cornelia Grinnell Willis, would later help Jacobs purchase her freedom.) According to Jean Fagan Yellin, *Jane Eyre* was one of the books in the Willises' library. See Jean Fagan Yellin, *Harriet Jacobs: A Life* (New York: Basic Civitas Books, 2004), 145.

32. Sandra Gilbert and Susan Gubar, *The Madwoman in the Attic: The Woman Writer and the Nineteenth-Century Literary Imagination* (New Haven: Yale University Press, 2000), 339.

33. Jane's experience in the Reed household resonates with Frederick Douglass's experience in the Auld household. Having discovered that "education and slavery were incompatible with each other," Douglass vows to read as much as possible.

34. Jane's language echoes the abolitionist William Lloyd Garrison's in the first issue of *The Liberator* (1831): "I do not wish to think, speak, or write with moderation. . .I am in earnest—I will not equivocate—I will not excuse—I will not retreat a single inch—AND I WILL BE HEARD."

35. Marcus Wood, *Slavery, Empathy, and Pornography* (New York: Oxford University Press, 2002), 335–36.

36. Ibid., 335. Wood also figures Mrs. Reed and her children as representatives of the "slave power" (334).

37. Marcus Wood echoes this point in *Slavery, Empathy, and Pornography*: "Wondering how to 'achieve escape from inescapable oppression,' Jane thinks of the two classic forms of slave resistance beside insurrection, flight and suicide, running away or voluntary starvation" (226).

38. Frederick Douglass, "An Appeal to the British People, reception speech at Finsbury Chapel, Moorfield, England, May 12, 1846," *Frederick Douglass: Selected Speeches and Writings*, ed. Philip S. Foner (Chicago: Lawrence Hill Books, 2000), 31.

39. This is not to say that the slave narrative is wholly uninflected by elements of the gothic; indeed, as I described in the introduction, the slave narrative borrowed from a host of preexisting genres, including the sentimental novel, the spiritual autobiography, and the adventure tale. Kari J. Winter devotes an entire book-length study to the shared attributes of slave narrative and gothic novel, focusing on analogous depictions of female imprisonment and exploitation. But Winter herself admits that the two genres are substantially different, most evidently in their stated literary purpose; she writes, "the [gothic novel] is encoded as 'fantasy and pleasure' and the [slave narrative] as 'politics and propaganda'" (Kari J. Winter, *Subjects of Slavery, Agents of Change: Women and Power in Gothic Novels and Slave Narratives, 1790–1865*[Athens: University of Georgia

Press, 1995], 13). The gothic novel may reveal much about the political plight of eighteenth- and nineteenth-century women, but it is still a work of fiction. The slave narrative, on the other hand, resolutely markets itself as a work of non-fiction, written to educate readers and to eradicate slavery. Jane's loss of interest in *Gulliver's Travels* and *The Arabian Tales* suggests a more profound shift in literary taste from the fantastic to the real.

40. Lisa Sternlieb, *Hazarding Confidences: The Female Narrator in the British Novel* (New York: Palgrave, 2002), 21.

41. Many of Jane's biblical selections overlap with those quoted by American slaves in their narratives. It was common to equate the slaves' plight to that of the enslaved and exiled Israelites. Harriet Tubman was figured as a modern "Moses" who led fugitive slaves from their imprisonment in the South to the "promised land" of the north. Douglass invokes the story of Daniel in the lion's den in his narrative. He was also a millennialist, believing in an upcoming Day of Judgment in which God's kingdom would be realized on earth (and the higher law of God would trump the corrupt law of man). His viewpoint resonates with that of St. John Rivers, whose invocation of Revelation closes *Jane Eyre*: "'My Master,' he says, 'has forewarned me. Daily he announces more distinctly,—'Surely I come quickly' and hourly I more eagerly respond,—'Amen; even so come, Lord Jesus!'" (385).

42. Elizabeth Rigby, "*Vanity Fair*—and *Jane Eyre*." *Quarterly Review* 84:167 (December 1848). Reprinted in Charlotte Brontë, *Jane Eyre*, ed. Richard J. Dunn (New York: Norton, 2000), 452. Douglass, anticipating these same accusations to his narrative, includes an appendix in which he clarifies his stance toward Christianity: "I love the pure, peaceable, and impartial Christianity of Christ: I therefore hate the corrupt, slaveholding, women-whipping, cradle-plundering, partial and hypocritical Christianity of this land" (118).

43. Ibid.

44. Ibid.

45. She demonstrates her scrappy nature when she turns on Master John a second time, striking him with her knuckles: "John thrust his tongue in his cheek whenever he saw me, and once attempted chastisement; but as I instantly turned against him, roused by the same sentiment of deep ire and desperate revolt which has stirred my corruption before, he thought it better to desist and ran from me, uttering execrations, and vowing I had burst his nose. I had indeed leveled at that prominent feature as hard a blow as my knuckles could inflict; and when I saw that either that or my look daunted him, I had the greatest inclination to follow up my advantage to purpose" (Brontë, *Jane Eyre*, 22).

46. Sharon Marcus describes how at this moment, Jane becomes the object of "sadistic visual attention" and becomes "more conscious of her body" (Sharon Marcus, "The Profession of the Author: Abstraction, Advertising, and *Jane Eyre*," *PMLA* (1995), 209).

47. William Lloyd Garrison, Douglass's abolitionist patron, likewise vouched for Douglass' veracity in his prefatory testimonial to Douglass's narrative. He writes, "I am confident that [the narrative] is essentially true in all its statements; that nothing has been set down in malice, nothing exaggerated, nothing drawn from the imagination. . . .The testimony of Mr. Douglass. . .is sustained by a cloud of witnesses, whose veracity is unimpeachable" (William Lloyd Garrison, introduction, *Narrative of the Life*

of Frederick Douglass [New York: Signet 1968], x, xiii). The similarity of name is provocative.

48. Gilbert and Gubar, *Madwoman in the Attic*, 86.

49. Meyer, *Imperialism at Home*, 7.

50. See also Ruth Bernard Yeazell, "More true than real: Jane Eyre's 'Mysterious Summons,'" *Nineteenth Century Fiction* 29 (1974): 127–43.

51. Spivak, "Three Women's Texts," 247.

52. Gilbert and Gubar, *Madwoman in the Attic*, 489.

53. See Brontë's Roe Head journal for more autobiographical detail of her rage and anger at governessing slavery (Brontë, *Jane Eyre*, 403–4).

54. Often appended as an introduction to Frederick Douglass's *Narrative*, Wendell Phillips's letter alludes to the West Indian "experiment" of 1838, when England abolished slavery throughout its empire.

55. *Jane Eyre* should not, by this token, be read as a political allegory of West Indian and American slavery, but rather as a testament to the multiple ways in which Atlantic slavery infiltrates the narrative.

56. Having led the Israelites out of slavery in Egypt, Moses ascended Mount Sinai to receive the Ten Commandments. In his absence, the Israelites created an idol in the form of a golden calf. Upon returning, Moses burned the calf and destroyed the tablets, chastising the Israelites for straying from God.

57. John Ruskin, *Modern Painters* (New York: John Wiley and Son, 1866), 377.

58. According to Simon Schama, "The Slave-Ship" was "mocked by the reviewers as 'the contents of a spittoon,' a 'gross outrage to nature,' and so on. The critic of the *Times* thought the seven pictures—including "Slavers"—that Turner sent to the Royal Academy that year were such 'detestable absurdities' that 'it is surprising the [selection] committee have suffered their walls to be disgraced with the dotage of his experiments'" (Simon Schama, "The Patriot: Turner and the Drama of History" *The New Yorker*, September 24, 2007). Mark Twain, writing in 1878, described the painting as "Slave Ship—Cat having a fit in a platter of tomatoes."

59. Orlando Patterson, *Slavery and Social Death: A Comparative Study* (Cambridge: Harvard University Press, 1982), 41.

60. Marcus Wood, *Blind Memory: Visual Representations of Slavery in England and America* (Manchester: Manchester University Press, 2000), 87–88.

61. Douglass in fact changed his name several times. He was born "Frederick Augustus Washington Bailey" and took the name "Stanley" when fleeing Baltimore. Upon reaching New York, he changed his name to "Frederick Johnson," but after moving to New Bedford, changed his name a last time to Frederick Douglass.

62. Jane's escape from the margins could also signal the successful escape from the legacy of Pamela, the first and most famous scribbling woman whose tale she enjoys as a child at Gateshead.

63. It's difficult not to think of Frederick Douglass's parallel experience in his *Narrative* when, learning how to write, he scrawls "in the spaces of Master Thomas's copy-book, copying what he had written" (58). As Daneen Wardrop writes, "[Douglass's] enforced marginalization by a paternalistic, logocentric power structure shows in that he has to write, literally, in the margins of the copy-book. It is a palimpsest of a particular kind; the black slave pens over the white spaces" (Daneen

Wardrop, "'While I am Writing': Webster's 1825 Spelling Book, the Ell, and Frederick Douglass's Positioning of Language," *African American Review* 32 [1998]: 653.)

64. In what Sternlieb describes as "a series of parallel confidence games" (18), Jane now controls the dissemination of knowledge. When Rochester begins to regain his sight, the first item he sees is the "gold watch-chain" (384) around Jane's neck. Some readers see this as proof that Jane is still "enslaved" to Rochester through the patriarchal convention of marriage. Earlier, however, Rochester had told Jane, "'I'll just—figuratively speaking—attach you to a chain like this' (touching his watch-guard)" (231). Jane now wears the watch-chain; she is the one who now leads Rochester around "by the hand" (384).

Chapter 2

1. Henry Kingsley, "Thackeray," *Macmillan's* (Feb 1864), *Thackeray: The Critical Heritage*, ed. Geoffrey Tillotson and Donald Hawes (London: Routledge, 1966), 340.

2. See Craig Howes, "Pendennis and the Controversy on the 'Dignity of Literature,'" *Nineteenth-Century Literature* 41 (1986), 269–98.

3. David Masson, in the *North British Review* of May 1851, compared Dickens to Thackeray in the following way: "Mr. Thackeray, though more competent, according to our view of him, to appear in the character of a general critic or essayist, seems far more of a *procurante* than Mr. Dickens...he has taken up *procurantism* as a theory, we have no means of saying; but certain it is, that in the writings he has given forth since he became known as one of our most distinguished literary men, he has meddled far less with the external arrangements of society than Mr. Dickens, and made far fewer appearances as a controversialist or reformer (David Masson, "Thackeray," *North British Review* May 1851, *Thackeray: The Critical Heritage*, ed. Geoffrey Tillotson and Donald Hawes [London: Routledge, 1966], 113).

4. Theodore Martin, "Thackeray," *Westminster Review* (April 1853), in Tillotson and Hawes, 171.

5. W. M. Thackeray, *The Book of Snobs*, ed. John Sutherland (New York: St. Martin's, 1978), 72.

6. W. M. Thackeray, *Vanity Fair*, ed. Peter Shillingsburg (New York: Norton, 1994), 84.

7. In the following chapter (IX), Thackeray segues from the abolitionist slogan to a tongue-in-cheek assessment of the younger Pitt Crawley, whose earnestness and ambition lead him to write "a pamphlet on Malt" and take "a strong part in the negro emancipation question [and become] a friend of Mr. Wilberforce's whose politics he admired" (*Vanity Fair*, 87–88). Pitt is presumably named after William Pitt, an antislavery advocate and friend of Wilberforce.

8. W. M. Thackeray, *The History of Pendennis*, ed. Peter Shillingsburg (New York: Garland, 1991), 372. Hereafter cited within the text as "P."

9. [Unsigned Review] *Athenaeum* (7 Dec 1850), in Tillotson and Hawes, 90–91.

10. J. R. Findlay, "Thackeray," *Scotsman* (18 Dec 1850), in Tillotson and Hawes, 94.

11. Masson, "Thackeray," in Tillotson and Hawes, 117.

12. Peter Shillingsburg, *Pegasus in Harness: Victorian Publishing and W. M. Thackeray* (Charlottesville: University of Virginia Press, 1992), 55.

13. W. M. Thackeray, *Letters and Private Papers of William Makepeace Thackeray*, ed. Gordon N. Ray. Vol. 1 (London: Oxford University Press, 1945–46), 667.

14. Charles Dickens, "In Memoriam," *Cornhill Magazine* (Feb 1864), *Thackeray: The Critical Heritage*, ed. Geoffrey Tillotson and Donald Hawes (London: Routledge, 1966), 129–32.

15. Shillingsburg, *Pegasus in Harness*, 9.

16. Marcus Wood, *Slavery, Empathy and Pornography* (New York: Oxford University Press, 2002), 368.

17. Thomas Carlyle, "The Occasional Discourse on the Negro Question," *Fraser's Magazine for Town and Country* (London: February 1849). In 1853, Carlyle expanded and reprinted his essay in pamphlet form as "The Occasional Discourse on the Nigger Question."

18. Thomas Carlyle, "No. 1: The Present Time," *Latter Day Pamphlets*. Volume xx of *Centenary Edition of the Works of Thomas Carlyle in Thirty Volumes* (London: Chapman and Hall, 1896), 25–26.

19. "English Authors—American Booksellers," *Punch, or the London Charivari*, Jan–Jun 1847, quoted in Richard Altick, *Punch: The Lively Youth of a British Institution 1841–1851* (Columbus: Ohio State University Press, 1997), 178.

20. Ibid. Italics in text.

21. In fundraising speeches for the Royal Literary Fund, Thackeray admitted, "I feel deeply interested in the ends of a Society which has for its object to help my brother in similar need" (quoted in Shillingsburg, *Pegasus in Harness*, 8), but his investment in such a literary brotherhood was erratic, at best. Writers, Thackeray felt, should be prepared for the inevitable ups and downs of the literary profession.

22. Quoted in John Sutherland, *Thackeray at Work* (London: Athlone Press, 1974), 94.

23. Dickens, *American Notes For General Circulation* (New York: Penguin, 2000), 265.

24. Sidney P. Moss argues that Dickens's excoriation of American slavery is a displacement of his anger over American disregard of international copyright. See Sidney P. Moss, *Charles Dickens' Quarrel with America* (Troy: Whitson, 1984).

25. Frederick Douglass, "An Appeal to the British People, reception speech at Finsbury Chapel, Moorfield, England, May 12, 1846," *Frederick Douglass: Selected Speeches and Writings*, ed. Philip S. Foner (Chicago: Lawrence Hill Books, 2000), 33.

26. Ibid.

27. Carlyle, "No. 1: The Present Time," 26.

28. Ibid.

29. Thomas L. Jeffers, "Thackeray's Pendennis: Son and Gentleman." *Nineteenth-Century Fiction* 33 (1978), 178.

30. Ibid., 177.

31. Meredith McGill, *American Literature and the Culture of Reprinting, 1834–1853* (Philadelphia: University of Pennsylvania Press, 2003), 31.

32. Ibid., 114.

33. John Sutherland, *Thackeray at Work* (London: Athlone Press, 1974), 78.

34. Deborah A. Thomas, *Thackeray and Slavery* (Athens: Ohio University Press, 1993), 86.

35. See Franco Moretti, *The Way of the World: The Bildungsroman in European Culture* (New York: Verso, 2000).

36. The serial of *Pendennis* was suspended during Thackeray's illness.

37. Sarah Rose Cole points out that Thackeray modeled the robbers after Irish highwaymen.

38. Catherine Peters, *Thackeray's Universe* (Boston: Faber and Faber, 1987).

39. Thomas, *Thackeray and Slavery*, 77.

40. Mary Leatheley, *Large Pictures with Little Stories* (London: Darton, *c*. 1855) 27–28. For more on this image, see Wood, *Blind Memory*, 275–76.

41. John Sutherland, "Thackeray as Victorian Racialist," *Essays in Criticism* 20 (1970), 443.

42. For more on Mrs. Carmichael-Smyth's evangelical influence, see Thomas, *Thackeray and Slavery*, 13–15.

43. Turner was hanged on November 11, 1831. He was beheaded, skinned, and quartered and his body parts were distributed as souvenirs.

44. Thomas, *Thackeray and Slavery*, xvi. I would argue that Thackeray's fiction in general waned in creative power after *Henry Esmond*.

45. In *The Virginians* (1857–59) Thackeray actually portrays American slavery through Gumbo, George's servant. This was facilitated by the novel's setting in eighteenth-century America.

46. W. M. Thackeray, *The Adventures of Philip*, vol. 1 (London: Smith, Elder, & Company, 1887), 196.

47. W. M. Thackeray, "To Mrs. Carmichael-Smyth," 26 January 1853, *Letters and Private Papers of William Makepeace Thackeray*, ed. Gordon N. Ray and Edgar Harden, Vol. 1 (London: Oxford University Press, 1945–46).

48. Thackeray, "To Mrs. Carmichael-Smyth," 13 February 1853, in ibid.

49. Thackeray, "To Anne Thackeray," 3 March 1853, in ibid.

50. Thackeray, "To Harriet Thackeray," 11 March 1853, in ibid.

51. Thackeray, "To Mrs. Brian Waller Procter," 4 April 1853, in ibid.

52. W. M. Thackeray, "To Mrs. Baxter," 3 June 1853, in ibid. Thackeray writes, "In place of the woman I had imagined to myself after the hideous daguerreotype I found a gentle almost pretty person with a very great sweetness in her eyes and smile." His comment recalls Dickens's horror at the "hideous and abominable portrait" that prefaced Douglass's *Narrative*.

53. Thomas partially attributes Thackeray's interest in slavery to his mother's affiliation with evangelical Anglicanism, which was associated closely with the antislavery movement in the eighteenth and nineteenth centuries.

54. Thackeray certainly approached *Uncle Tom's Cabin* with typical irreverence. In a letter to a Mrs. Dunlop from 12 December 1856 he depicts Legree whipping Uncle Tom, using what looks like heart-shaped stamps for the faces of Legree and little Eva and for the lips of Uncle Tom.

55. Thackeray, "To Mrs. Carmichael-Smyth," 13 February 1853, *Letters and Private Papers*.

56. Thackeray, "To Mrs. Carmichael-Smyth," 26 January 1853, in ibid.

Chapter 3

1. Elizabeth Gaskell, "To Charles Eliot Norton," 10 June 1861, *The Letters of Mrs. Gaskell*, ed. J. A. V. Chapple and Arthur Pollard (Cambridge: Harvard University Press, 1966), 654.

2. Gaskell, "To Charles Eliot Norton," April 5th [1860], *Letters*, 606.

3. Ibid.

4. Gaskell, "Lois the Witch," *Gothic Tales* (New York: Penguin Books, 2004), 161. Gaskell's story, with its setting in eighteenth-century Salem, was probably inspired by her reading of Nathaniel Hawthorne's *The Scarlet Letter*. In her biography of Gaskell, Uglow writes that the two authors never met, but that they shared the same group of friends, including the Martineaus, Henry Bright, and Charles Eliot Norton (Hawthorne had served as American consul in Liverpool in 1853). Gaskell's earlier novel *Ruth* (1853) betrays the most evident literary debt to *The Scarlet Letter*. Uglow writes, "Both novels deal with a sexual fall, social hypocrisy and humiliation, a woman's struggle for autonomy—Gaskell's seducer even bears the name of Hawthorne's governor, Bellingham" (Uglow 310). In "Lois the Witch," Gaskell includes a description of one of Hawthorne's ancestors, John Hahorne, a Salem merchant and magistrate.

5. Gaskell, "To Charles Sumner," December 1857, *Letters*, 490.

6. Gaskell, "To Grace Schwabe," [19 June? 1853], *Letters*, 237.

7. See Jenny Uglow, *Elizabeth Gaskell: A Habit of Stories* (Boston: Faber and Faber, 1993), 423. In 1857, Gaskell, Norton, William Storey, and Stowe congregated in Italy, where Stowe regaled them with stories of Sojourner Truth. Stowe would later write an essay for the *Atlantic Monthly* called "Sojourner Truth, the Libyan Sibyl," published in April 1863. Storey would also create a statue of Truth that he would exhibit at the 1862 World Exposition in London.

8. Sarah Parker Remond was a noted abolitionist and the sister of Charles Lenox Remond, the first African American lecturer for the American Anti-Slavery Society.

9. Gaskell, "To Anne Robson," [February 1859], *Letters*, 530.

10. Gaskell, "To Mary Green," ?15 October 1855, *Further Letters of Mrs. Gaskell*, eds. John Chapple and Alan Shelston (Manchester: Manchester University Press, 2000), 142.

11. Elizabeth Gaskell, "The Grey Woman," *Gothic Tales* (New York: Penguin, 2004), 289. Hereafter cited within the text as "GW."

12. Diana Wallace, "Uncanny Stories: The Ghost Story as Female Gothic," *Gothic Studies* 6 (2004): 60.

13. Harriet Jacobs, *Incidents in the Life of a Slave Girl, Written By Herself* (Cambridge: Harvard University Press, 2000), 183. Hereafter cited within the text as "HJ."

14. As far as we know, Jacobs and Douglass did not meet each other in England in 1845. Jacobs was not, as of yet, an antislavery figure, and she was moreover preoccupied with her nursing duties. In 1852, following the publication of *Uncle Tom's Cabin*, Jacobs approached Harriet Beecher Stowe for help in composing and publishing her own narrative. Stowe demurred, much to Jacobs's disappointment and anger. For more, see Jean Fagan Yellin, *Harriet Jacobs: A Life* (New York: Basic Civitas Books, 2004), 120–21 and Jean Fagan Yellin, "Incidents Abroad: Harriet Jacobs and the Transatlantic Movement" in *Women's Rights and Transatlantic Slavery in the Era of Emancipation*, eds. Kathryn Kish Sklar and James Brewer Stewart (New Haven: Yale University Press, 2007), 158–72.

15. See also Claire Midgley, *Women Against Slavery: the British Campaigns, 1780–1870* (New York: Routledge, 1992), 145–46. The Stafford House Address was signed by Dickens's wife and presented to Harriet Beecher Stowe.

16. Yellin, *Harriet Jacobs*, 138.

17. Jenny Uglow writes that Gaskell spent three weeks in London in June 1859 (Uglow, 455). She was in residence at Kildare Terrace, London from 14 June to 27 June 1859. See Gaskell, *Letters*, 198.

18. Elizabeth Gaskell, "To the Duchess of Sutherland," 18 June [?1859], *Letters*, 900. Jacobs had departed for England on May 26, 1859 and presumably arrived in England about two weeks later. This places her date of arrival around June 9, 1859. She would have been at Stafford House for most of June, during the period in which Gaskell had planned to visit the Duchess of Sutherland. Gaskell had hosted Mary Weston Chapman during her trip to Manchester in 1856. Her unease regarding Chapman's vocal antislavery sentiment is reminiscent of her reaction to the fiery abolitionist, Charles Sumner.

19. Yellin, *Harriet Jacobs*, 138.

20. Ibid., 147.

21. Quoted in ibid., 146.

22. Since Anna is pregnant, she cannot pass as a man.

23. Werner Sollors describes how racial passing and cross-dressing appeared earlier in Richard Hildreth's novel, *The Slave; or, Memoirs of Archy Moore* (1836): "Archy decides to let Cassy [Archy's half-sister and wife] dress up as a man and act as his younger brother—a common occurrence of combining racial passing, especially of the sporadic kind, with sexual cross-dressing, and one that was often written up after the legendary escape of William and Ellen Craft in 1848" (Werner Sollors, *Neither Black Nor White Yet Both: Thematic Explorations of Interracial Literature* [New York: Oxford University Press, 1997], 260). The Crafts' escape inspired the cross-dressing plot of William Wells Brown's *Clotel; or, the President's Daughter* (1853), in which Clotel disguises herself as a white man. Cross-dressing also occurs in *Uncle Tom's Cabin* (1852), when Eliza Harris disguises herself as a boy and her son as a girl in order to escape to Canada, an episode that may have found its inspiration in the Crafts' escape.

24. R. J. M. Blackett, "The Odyssey of William and Ellen Craft," in William and Ellen Craft, *Running a Thousand Miles to Freedom* (Baton Rouge: Louisiana State University Press, 1999), 55.

25. Craft, *Running a Thousand Miles*, 17, 19. Hereafter cited within the text as "Craft."

26. Marion Wilson Starling, *The Slave Narrative: Its Place in American History* (Washington: Howard University Press, 1988), 235.

27. Blackett, "Odyssey," 65.

28. Ibid., 66.

29. Reprinted in *The Liberator*, Issue 21, May 23, 1851 (82).

30. Blackett, foreword, in Craft, *Running a Thousand Miles*, ix.

31. Ibid.

32. Salomé Muller's full story appears in George Washington Cable's *Strange True Stories of Louisiana* and also in William Wells Brown's *Clotel*.

33. Marjorie Garber, *Vested Interests: Cross-Dressing and Cultural Anxiety* (London: Routledge, 1997), 283.

34. There is a Babette Muller in "The Grey Woman," who is described as Anna Scherer's great rival.

35. J. R. Watson, "'Round the Sofa': Elizabeth Gaskell Tells Stories," *The Yearbook of English Studies* 26 (1996), 93.

36. Lawrence Stone, "Literature and Education in England, 1640–1900," *Past and Present* 42 (1969), 84.

37. Ibid., 85.

38. Fisch writes, "By mid-century, however, there was an explosion of working-class education. The attempts of working men and women to acquire proof of humanity, however, were met with a concomitant anxiety, on the part of the middle class, about the consequences of education for these new groups of people" (Audrey Fisch, *American Slaves in Victorian England: Abolitionist Politics in Popular Literature and Culture* [New York: Cambridge University Press, 2000], 37).

39. See Richard Altick, *The English Common Reader: A Social History of the Mass Reading Public, 1800–1900* (Columbus: Ohio State University Press, 1998). For more on the fear of mass literacy, see Thomas Laqueur, *Religion and Respectability: Sunday Schools and Working Class Culture, 1780–1850* (New Haven: Yale University Press, 1976); Alan Richardson, *Literature, Education, and Romanticism: Reading as Social Practice, 1780–1832* (Cambridge: Cambridge University Press, 2004); and Patrick Brantlinger, *The Spirit of Reform: British Literature and Politics, 1832–1867* (Cambridge: Harvard University Press, 1977).

40. Fisch, *American Slaves in Victorian England*, 42. Among the assorted personages gathered "round the sofa" is a casualty of the 1848 revolutions, a "Mr. Sperano, the Italian exile, banished even from France, where he had long resided, and now teaching Italian with meek diligence in the northern city."

41. Stone, "Literature and Education in England," 84.

42. Elizabeth Gaskell, *My Lady Ludlow* (Charleston, S.C.: BookSurge Classics, 2004), 14. Hereafter cited within the text as "LL."

43. Harriet Beecher Stowe, *Uncle Tom's Cabin* (New York: Norton, 1994), 206. Hereafter cited within the text as "Stowe."

44. In her reception study of *Uncle Tom's Cabin*, Fisch has shown how some British reviewers feared the novel's influence on the working-class reader, who was incapable of reading the novel "correctly." Fisch writes that *The Times* review of *Uncle Tom's Cabin* worries that the novel "will inevitably succeed in 'enforcing' and 'impressing' its incorrect message on the many 'weak intellects' and 'strong hearts' of *its poorly educated readers*" (Fisch, 22).

45. Stowe based part of *Uncle Tom's Cabin* on Josiah Henson, *The Life of Josiah Henson, Formerly a Slave, Now an Inhabitant of Canada, As Narrated by Himself* (Boston: Arthur D. Phelps, 1849). See Stowe, *The Key to 'Uncle Tom's Cabin'* (Boston: John P. Jewett, 1853), 42–43.

46. Frederick Douglass, *Narrative of the Life of Frederick Douglass, An American Slave* (New York: Signet, 1968), 52. James Williams, writing in 1857, describes a slave "who was instructed in reading and writing, and on that account proved very troublesome. He could imitate the hand-writing of all the neighboring planters, and used to write passes and certificates of freedom for the slaves, and finally wrote one for himself, and went off to Philadelphia, from whence her father received from him a saucy letter, thanking him for his education" (James Williams, *Narrative of James Williams, An American Slave who was, For Several Years a Driver on a Cotton Plantation in Alabama* [New York: The American Antislavery Society, 1838], 28).

47. Frederick Douglass, *My Bondage and My Freedom* (New York: Miller, Orton, and Mulligan, 1855), 146.

48. The pivotal exchange with Harry Gregson prompts Lady Ludlow to recall a similar occurrence during the Revolution, when the ability of a French urchin to read a concealed message leads to the revelation of an escape plot and the death, by guillotine, of two young nobles.

49. Her disapproval is partially overcome by the death of Harry's benefactor, Mr. Horner, and Harry's subsequent crippling from a fall from a tree. Unable to support himself through physical work, Harry now pins his hope on becoming a schoolteacher. He eventually becomes the vicar of Hanbury.

Chapter 4

1. See also Edgar Wright, *Mrs. Gaskell: The Basis for Reassessment* (New York: Oxford University Press, 1965), 144–46. Wright sees Frederick's introduction as "pure plot spinning."

2. Rosemarie Bodenheimer, *The Politics of Story in Victorian Social Fiction* (Ithaca, NY: Cornell University Press, 1988), 59.

3. Patsy Stoneman, *Elizabeth Gaskell* (Bloomington and Indianapolis: Indiana University Press, 1987), 124–25.

4. Deirdre David, *Fictions of Resolution in Three Victorian Novels* (New York: Columbia University Press, 1981), 15.

5. A. W. Ward, "Introduction to *North and South*," in *The Works of Mrs. Gaskell, Volume IV* (London: Smith, Elder & Co., 1906), xi–xxvii.

6. Stefanie Markovits, "*North and South*, East and West: Elizabeth Gaskell, the Crimean War, and the Condition of England," *Nineteenth-Century Literature* 59 (2005), 480.

7. Elizabeth Gaskell, *North and South*, ed. Alan Shelston (New York: Norton, 2005), 243. Hereafter cited within the text as "NS."

8. W. A. Craik, *Elizabeth Gaskell and the English Provincial Novel* (London: Methuen, 1975), 111–20, reprinted in Gaskell, *North and South*, 523–30. Craik argues that Gaskell's references to Corfu, Spain, Scotland, and Europe "all render the work and the reader aware of the whole contemporary world" (ibid., 524).

9. Charles Dickens, letter to Elizabeth Gaskell, January 1855, *The Letters of Charles Dickens: 1844–1846*, ed. Kathleen Tillotson and Nina Burgis (New York: Oxford University Press, 1978).

10. Rosemarie Bodenheimer, "*North and South*: A Permanent State of Change," *Nineteenth-Century Fiction* 34 (1979), 281. Bodenheimer argues against a reductive dialectical model of *North and South*, writing that the novel "is not really organized as a system of contrasts" but is "rather a novel about irrevocable change, and about the confused process of response and accommodation to it" (ibid.).

11. Louis Cazamian, *The Social Novel in England* (1903), trans. Martin Fido (London and Boston: Routledge and Kegan Paul, 1973), 226–31. Reprinted in Gaskell, *North and South*, 499–504. Cazamian sees *North and South* as a more sophisticated version of Disraeli's *Sybil*, and his description of the novel's regional antagonisms is quoted extensively in A. W. Ward's introduction to *North and South*. Émile Montégut also characterizes the North as Anglo-Saxon and Dissenting and the South as Anglo-Norman and Anglican. See Montégut, "Le Roman de Moeurs Industrielles," *Revue des Deux Mondes* (1 October 1855), XII (new period, second series), 115–46; trans. Anne-Marie Hutchings and reprinted in Gaskell, *North and South*, 423.

12. See Raymond Williams, *Culture and Society 1780–1950* (New York: Columbia University Press, 1958) and Hilary Schor, *Scheherezade in the Market-Place: Elizabeth Gaskell and the Victorian Novel* (New York and Oxford: Oxford University Press, 1992). For more feminist readings of *North and South*, see Stoneman, *Elizabeth Gaskell*.

13. Paul Giles, "Narrative Reversals and Power Exchanges: Frederick Douglass and British Culture," in *American Literature* 73.4 (2001), 796.

14. Trollope famously excoriated the American people in *Domestic Manners of the Americans*, writing, "I do not like them. I do not like their principles, I do not like their manners, I do not like their opinions" (Frances Trollope, *Domestic Manners of the Americans* [New York: Penguin Books, 1997], 314). So popular was her travelogue that according to Pamela Neville-Sington, "to 'trollopize,'" that is 'to abuse the American nation,' became a recognized verb in the English language" (Neville-Sington, introduction, *Domestic Manners of the Americans*, vii). Dickens's *American Notes* was no less unflattering, condemning American vulgarity, hypocrisy, and materialism. Both Trollope and Dickens were particularly disgusted by slavery, which they felt contradicted the country's purported allegiance to democratic ideals.

15. See Amanda Claybaugh, "Toward a New Transatlanticism: Dickens in the United States," *Victorian Studies* 48 (2006), 439–60. Claybaugh gives a cogent history of transatlantic literary studies from the nineteenth century to the present.

16. J. B. Conacher, "British Policy in the Anglo-American Enlistment Crisis of 1855–1856," *Proceedings of the American Philosophical Society*, 136 (1992), 533. The Monroe Doctrine (1823) forbade European colonization of American sovereign territories and espoused a position of American neutrality in European wars. Under the terms of the Clayton-Bulwer Treaty, Britain and America agreed not to colonize Central America.

17. See Ibid., 533–34.

18. Stefanie Markovits has attempted to connect *North and South* with the Crimean War, though she traces any influence primarily through the character of Margaret Hale, whom she reads as an analogue to Florence Nightingale. See Markovits, "*North and South*, East and West," 463–93.

19. Montégut, "Le Roman de Moeurs Industrielles," 115–46, trans. Anne-Marie Hutchings and reprinted in Gaskell, *North and South*, 424.

20. Ibid.

21. Paul Giles, *Virtual Americas: Transnational Fictions and the Transatlantic Imaginary* (Durham, NC: Duke University Press, 2002), 38.

22. Jenny Uglow, *Elizabeth Gaskell: A Habit of Stories* (Boston: Faber and Faber, 1993), 138. The Corn Laws were a protectionist measure that encouraged the export and limited the import of corn when prices fell below a certain level. As such, it operated as a subsidy for English landowners but hurt the new class of manufacturers, who were saddled with higher industrial costs. It was the mill workers and not the owners, however, who suffered most. Faced with mass layoffs and rising food costs, many workers "clemmed"—hence, the designation of this period as "The Hungry Forties."

23. Thornton is presumably referring to the textile mills in the American North, such as those in Lowell, Massachusetts. In the nineteenth century, Americans began to develop their own textile industry in New England. The most famous of these entrepreneurs was Francis Cabot Lowell, who visited numerous Manchester mills and imported British

technology to America. In 1821, Lowell opened his own mill in present-day Lowell, Massachusetts. By 1860, cotton manufacturing had overtaken cotton production as the United States' leading industry. See Ronald Bailey, "The Slave(ry) Trade and the Development of Capitalism in the United States: The Textile Industry in New England," *The Atlantic Slave Trade*, ed. Joseph E. Inikori and Stanley L. Engerman (Durham, NC: Duke University Press, 1992), 221–27.

24. For further discussion of the role of deus ex machina in working-class fiction, see Rob Breton, "Ghosts in the Machina: Plotting in Chartist and Working-Class Fiction," *Victorian Studies* 47 (2005), 557–75.

25. Paul Gilroy, *The Black Atlantic: Modernity and Double Consciousness* (Cambridge: Harvard University Press, 1993), 4, 16.

26. W. Jeffrey Bolster, *Black Jacks: African American Seamen in the Age of Sail* (Cambridge, Harvard University Press, 1997), 72.

27. See Elizabeth Gaskell, *Sylvia's Lovers* (New York: Penguin, 1997). Gaskell writes, "The men thus pressed were taken from the near grasp of parents and wives, and were often deprived of the hard earnings of years, which remained in the hands of the masters of the merchantman in which they had served, subject to all the chances of honesty or dishonesty, life or death" (12).

28. Bolster, *Black Jacks*, 71.

29. Ibid., 11.

30. Moreover, seafaring was one of the few trades open to blacks in nineteenth-century England, offering independence and a uniquely integrated work environment. Olaudah Equiano was a seaman, and Douglass successfully passed himself off as one in his escape north.

31. Anthony Burton, *The Rise and Fall of King Cotton* (London: BBC, 1984), 97. As the textile industry boomed in the early nineteenth century, Lancashire had hoped India would become its main cotton supplier, but this scheme fell apart as the colony only managed to supply "dirty" cotton, or cotton mixed with dirt, seeds, and rotten fibers. The United States eagerly stepped into the void left by India. For some time, the South had been looking for another crop to support its plantation system and saw cotton as a tremendous opportunity. Still, it was slow and tedious work for American slaves to handpick seeds and dirt from raw cotton. With the invention of Eli Whitney's cotton gin, however, the last obstacle to American cotton production was eliminated and the United States began to export large quantities of cotton to England. See ibid., 61.

32. Bailey, "The Slave(ry) Trade," 220.

33. Catherine Gallagher, *The Industrial Reformation of English Fiction: Social Discourse and Narrative Form 1832–1867* (Chicago: University of Chicago Press, 1985), 11. While Gallagher does not identify a metonymic connection between slave and worker in *North and South*, she characterizes Gaskell's narrative strategy as fundamentally metonymic in nature. In particular, she contrasts the representation of the public and private spheres in *North and South* to that in Dickens's *Hard Times*: "In *North and South* the spheres of the family and of trade and production are not connected through the kind of metaphoric structural symmetry that Dickens attempts in *Hard Times*, where fathers and children serve as analogues for employers and workers. In Gaskell's novel the private and public spheres are associated through their integration in Margaret Hale's life and through her influence over the manufacturer John Thornton" (Gallagher, *The Industrial Reformation of English Fiction*, 168).

34. See also Peter Fryer, *Staying Power: The History of Black People in Britain* (London: Pluto, 1984) and V. G. Kiernan, *The Lords of Human Kind: European Attitudes Towards the Outside World in the Imperial Age* (London: Weidenfeld & Nicolson, 1969). Fryer writes, "There was an organic connection in nineteenth-century Britain between the attitude the ruling class took to the 'natives' in the colonies and the attitude it took to the poor at home" (169–70). Both were "lesser breeds" and "lower orders," capable of violence and brutality. V. G. Kiernan concurs: "Discontented native in the colonies, labor agitator in the mills, were the same serpent in alternate disguises. Much of the talk about the barbarism or darkness of the outer world, which it was Europe's mission to rout, was a transmuted fear of the masses at home" (316).

35. Alex Woloch, *The One vs. the Many* (Princeton: Princeton University Press, 2003), 14. Woloch identifies two types of minor characters in nineteenth-century realist novels: the "worker" and the "eccentric." The former is "reduced to a single functional use within the narrative" and the latter plays "a disruptive, oppositional role within the plot" (25). Frederick becomes an example of the "eccentric," who "grates against his or her position and is usually, as a consequence, wounded, exiled, expelled, ejected, imprisoned, or killed (within the *discourse*, if not the *story*)" (25).

36. In a telling moment of maternal bias, Mrs. Hale tells Margaret, "you must not be hurt, but [Frederick] was much prettier than you were. I remember, when I first saw you in Dixon's arms, I said, 'Dear, what an ugly little thing!' And she said, 'It's not every child that's like Master Fred, bless him!'" (184).

37. See Mary Louise Pratt, *Imperial Eyes: Travel Writing and Transculturation* (New York: Routledge, 1992). See also Debbie Lee, *Slavery and the Romantic Imagination* (Philadelphia: University of Pennsylvania Press, 2002).

38. Markovits, *North and South*, East and West, 480.

39. David, *Fictions of Resolution*, 14.

40. See Margaret Cohen, "Traveling Genres," *New Literary History* 34 (2003) 481–99. Cohen writes, "My suggestion that the nature and status of work and the worker are at issue in sea fiction would be confirmed if we look at the forms edging it. This contextualization follows the materialist precept that genres take shape in a generic system where different poetic patterns engage the same intractable social questions but respond to them in different ways. The degradation of labor certainly takes center stage in the industrial novel that flourished in the mid-nineteenth century" (492).

41. My reading contests Markovits's claim that Frederick's "transgression against military honor seems. . . (like so much of his story) to be outmoded" (483). If anything, Frederick's resistance is entirely modern, evoking the contemporaneous plight of American fugitive slaves.

42. Giles, *Virtual Americas*, 38

43. Bertha Dodge, *The Plant That Would be King* (Austin: University of Texas, 1984), 124.

44. With the passage of the Fugitive Slave Act of 1850, any person suspected of assisting a runaway slave was subject to imprisonment and a $1,000 fine, while those who aided in the capture of fugitive slaves were offered a monetary reward. The captured slave was denied a jury trial and could not testify on his or her own behalf.

45. See also Audrey Fisch, *American Slaves in Victorian England* (New York: Cambridge University Press, 2000) and Howard Temperley, *British*

Antislavery, 1833–1870 (London: Longman, 1972). Fisch writes that slave narratives offered Victorian readers "the excitement for which they were eager: graphic scenes of torture, murder, sexual violence, and the thrill of escape" (54). While *North and South* cannot claim to be quite so titillating, its account of Frederick's near-capture and escape gives the reader a tantalizing taste of intrigue and danger. Gaskell's readership—educated, middle-class individuals, like Gaskell herself—would have overlapped with the readership of slave narratives. By the 1850s, Temperley writes, "the antislavery struggle [came] to mean simply the sectional controversy in the United States" (222).

46. Cohen, *Traveling Genres*, 496.

47. Douglass writes, "While in England, I saw few literary celebrities, except William and Mary Howitt, and Sir John Bowering. . . .William and Mary Howitt were among the kindliest people I ever met. Their interest in America, and their well-known testimonies against slavery, made me feel much at home with them at their house in that part of London known as Clapton." See Frederick Douglass, *Life and Times of Frederick Douglass* (New York: Collier, 1967), 240. While in London, Douglass also met up with the Chartists William Lovett and Henry Vincent, and he publicly supported Chartist demands for suffrage and reform, seeing commonality in the plight of the British worker and American slave.

48. Frederick Douglass, *Narrative of the Life of Frederick Douglass: An American Slave* (New York: Signet, 1968), 33.

49. In his *Narrative*, Frederick Douglass writes, "The name given me by my mother was, 'Frederick Augustus Washington Bailey'. . .I started from Baltimore bearing the name of 'Stanley.' When I got to New York, I again changed my name to 'Frederick Johnson,' and thought that would be the last change. But when I got to New Bedford, I found it necessary again to change my name. The reason of this necessity was, that there were so many Johnsons in New Bedford, it was already quite difficult to distinguish between them. I gave Mr. Johnson the privilege of choosing me a name, but told him he must not take from me the name of 'Frederick.' I must hold on to that, to preserve a sense of my identity. Mr. Johnson had just been reading the 'Lady of the Lake,' and at once suggested that my name be 'Douglass.' From that time until now I have been called 'Frederick Douglass;' and as I am more widely known by that name than by either of the others, I shall continue to use it as my own." See Douglass, *Narrative*, 114–15.

50. Frederick Douglass typically signed his articles in *The North Star*, "F. D." In 1851, he changed the name of his paper to *Frederick Douglass' Paper* and began to sign his editorials with his full name.

51. In his *Narrative*, Douglass rails against those who would talk in a "very public manner" about the underground railroad, thus turning it into a "upperground railroad" and endangering the lives of fugitive slaves (90).

52. Giles, *Virtual Americas*, 46.

53. David, *Fictions of Resolution*, 14. David's reading is consistent with Markovits' description of Frederick as Byronic throwback.

54. I would like to thank Audrey Fisch for this alternate reading of Frederick Hale's role in the novel. Fisch points out that Frederick's mutiny is linked to Mr. Hale's unexplained defection from the church and to both the Hales' eventual deaths, further illuminating slavery's indirect but devastating effect on British spiritual and domestic life.

55. Oxford English Dictionary Online, http://dictionary.oed.com. ezp2.harvard.edu.

56. This semantic shift is evocative of Henry Louis Gates, Jr.'s mathematical model of signification, where one axis represents the white discursive universe, the other the black. Frederick's liminal residence between these two poles of signification—between one definition of "native" and another—indicates the racially hybrid nature of his cosmopolitanism. See Henry Louis Gates, Jr., *The Signifying Monkey: A Theory of African-American Literary Criticism* (New York: Oxford University Press, 1989).

57. Frederick Douglass, "Speech on American Slavery, September 24, 1847," *The Frederick Douglass Papers: Volume 2, Series One: Speeches, Debates, and Interviews, 1847–1854* (New Haven: Yale University Press, 1982). In a speech before the American Anti-Slavery Society on May 11, 1847, Douglass vows, "I have no love for America, as such; I have no patriotism. I have no country. What country have I? The institutions of this country do not know me, do not recognize me as a man." See Frederick Douglass, "The Right to Criticize American Institutions," *Frederick Douglass: Selected Speeches and Writings*, ed. Philip S. Foner and Yuval Taylor (Chicago: Lawrence Hill Books, 1999), 76–83. In his 1855 autobiography, Douglass describes himself as an "outlaw in the land of [my] birth" (Frederick Douglass, *My Bondage and My Freedom*, ed. Philip S. Foner [New York: Dover, 1969], 368).

58. Gaskell's abolitionist friend Edward Everett Hale, a Boston Unitarian minister and author, would write his own fictional indictment of slavery, a short novel called "The Man Without a Country," published in 1863 at the height of the Civil War. Centered on an American sailor who disavows his country and is exiled to sea, the story is considered a tribute to the sanctity of the American Union. The plot of Hale's story—as well as the coincidence of his surname—has many intriguing connections to the plight of Frederick Hale, a character who also wishes to "unnative" himself and who becomes an Anglo-born "man without a country."

59. See W. E. B. Du Bois, *The Souls of Black Folk*, ed. Henry Louis Gates, Jr., and Terri Hume Oliver (New York: Norton, 1999). More recently, Kwame Anthony Appiah has explored the tension between cosmopolitan and national identities in "Cosmopolitan Patriots," *Critical Inquiry* 23 (1997), 617–39.

60. Burton, *Rise and Fall of King Cotton*, 179. In fact, although the Civil War devastated the British cotton textile trade, it proved a boon to the British maritime trade, which thrived in the absence of American competition. Britain was nearly drawn into war with the United States with the Trent Affair of 1861. The Confederacy, in an attempt to garner support from Britain and France, dispatched two diplomats aboard the *RMS Trent*, a British mail steamer. The ship was stopped by the *USS San Jacinto*, which seized the Confederate diplomats before allowing the *Trent* to continue on its voyage. In an ironic reversal of the Anglo-American Enlistment Crisis, the British accused the Union of violating maritime law and infringing upon British sovereignty, and demanded the release of the diplomats. Loath to enter an international conflict at the same time he was fighting a war at home, Lincoln acquiesced to British demands. In 1862, the Confederate diplomats were released, but they ultimately failed to secure support for the Confederacy from any European nation.

61. Elizabeth Gaskell, letter to Charles Eliot Norton, 10 June 1861, *The Letters of Mrs. Gaskell*, 654. Hereafter referred to as *Letters*.

62. See Burton, *Rise and Fall of King Cotton*, 179. Although Gaskell confirms Lancashire's sympathies with the American South, British working-class reaction to the American Civil War was often difficult to pinpoint. Philip S. Foner, for example, has argued that while many working-class papers supported the South, the workers themselves often did not (Philip Foner, *British Labor and the American Civil War* [New York: Holmes and Meier, 1981], 25–26). Dodge cites a letter from December of 1862 in which John Bright, the Anti-Corn-Leaguer and abolitionist, describes a pro-Union meeting "composed mainly of the industrial classes of Manchester" that took place on the eve of the Emancipation Declaration (quoted in Dodge, *The Plant That Would Be King*, 123). She also notes that in March of 1863, trade unions sent a large number of representatives to a pro-North rally held in London, indicating growing pro-Union sentiment among members of the working class (123).

63. Gaskell, *Letters*, 654.

64. Ibid. Gaskell's skepticism of the American Union is reminiscent of her ambivalence regarding trade union tactics in *North and South*: both groups disregard individual suffering in pursuit of a collective goal, and both resort to violence as a result.

Chapter 5

1. Charles Dickens, *American Notes For General Circulation* (New York: Penguin, 2000), 151.

2. Ibid., 152.

3. Ibid., 154.

4. Ibid.

5. See Jerome Meckier, *Innocent Abroad: Charles Dickens's American Engagements* (Lexington: University of Kentucky Press, 1990) and Sidney P. Moss, *Charles Dickens' Quarrel with America* (Troy: Whitson, 1984). For more on the copyright controversy, see Alexander Welsh, *From Copyright to Copperfield* (Cambridge: Harvard University Press, 1987).

6. For more on Dickens's use of Weld's pamphlet, see Amanda Claybaugh, "Toward a New Transatlanticism: Dickens in the United States," *Victorian Studies* 48 (2006) and Meredith McGill, *American Literature and the Culture of Reprinting, 1834–1853* (Philadelphia: University of Pennsylvania Press, 2003).

7. Patricia Ingham, introduction, *American Notes For General Circulation* (New York: Penguin, 2000), xxvii. Ingham quotes Sidney P. Moss, "South Carolina Contemplates Banning Dickens's *American Notes*," *Dickensian* 80 (1984), 157.

8. Frederick Douglass, "An Appeal to the British People, reception speech at Finsbury Chapel, Moorfield, England, May 12, 1846," *Frederick Douglass: Selected Speeches and Writings*, ed. Philip S. Foner and Yuval Taylor (Chicago: Lawrence Hill Books, 2000), 33.

9. Charles Dickens and Henry Morley, "North American Slavery," *Household Words*, Sep 1852.

10. Arthur Adrian, "Dickens on American Slavery: A Carlylean Slant," *PMLA* 67 (1952), 321.

11. "North American Slavery" was at least partially inspired by the recent publication of Harriet Beecher Stowe's *Uncle Tom's Cabin*, a novel Dickens found problematic for its "very overstrained conclusion and [its] very violent extreme. . .to set up the Colored race as capable of subduing

the White" (Charles Dickens, "To the Hon. Mrs. Edward Cropper, 20 December 1852, *The Letters of Charles Dickens*, ed. Madeline House, Graham Storey, and Kathleen Tillotson, vol. 6 [New York: Oxford University Press, 1965–2002], 826). Dickens contrasted Stowe's radicalism with what he saw as his own, more measured antislavery position. See also Harry Stone, "Dickens and Harriet Beecher Stowe," *Nineteenth-Century Fiction* 12 (1957): 188–202.

12. Dickens, "To the Hon. Mrs. Edward Cropper," 20 December 1852, *Letters*, vol. 6, 826. Dickens's wife, meanwhile, continued to be involved in the transatlantic abolition movement, helping to draw up an antislavery petition entitled "An Affectionate and Christian Address of Many Thousands of Women of Great Britain and Ireland to Their Sisters, the Women of the United States of America" (also known as the Stafford House Address), which was presented to Harriet Beecher Stowe in 1853.

13. See Claybaugh, "Toward a New Transatlanticism," 457.

14. Dickens, *Letters*, vol. 7, 387–88.

15. Ibid. Adrian believes the "audacious seizure" refers to "the vain attempt by Thomas Wentworth Higginson in 1854 to liberate from the federal courthouse in Boston a fugitive slave, Anthony Burns. . . .Though Higginson helped to batter a passage through the courthouse door and struggled with the police, he was never punished for his offense. Studying the publicity given this incident, Dickens must have been deeply disappointed to see the slavery issue taking this drastic turn" (322). I believe Dickens is referring not to Higginson's rescue attempt but to Burns's original arrest.

16. M. M. Bakhtin, "Forms of Time and Chronotope in the Novel," *The Dialogic Imagination: Four Essays*, trans. Caryl Emerson and Michael Holquist (Austin: University of Texas Press, 1981), 250.

17. Alex Woloch, *The One vs. the Many* (Princeton: Princeton University Press, 2003), 199.

18. Herbert describes to Pip his desire to be an "Insurer of Ships" with dreams of trading to the East Indies "for silks, shawls, spices, dyes, drugs, and precious woods" and to the West Indies "for sugar, tobacco and rum" (GE, 207). Elaine Freedgood examines "the global movement of commodities and racial symbolic from the New World to the Old World" in *Great Expectations*, focusing on the fetishistic symbolism of Magwitch's "Negro head" tobacco, which she ties to the Aboriginal genocide. "Negro head" tobacco, she notes, "hails from Virginia" and describes "a strong plug tobacco of a black colour"; in other words, it takes on the appearance of the slaves who pick it. It thus connects Magwitch to American slave labor. See Elaine Freedgood, "Realism, Fetishism, and Genocide: 'Negro Head' Tobacco in and around *Great Expectations*," *Novel: A Forum on Fiction* 36 (2002).

19. Bakhtin, "Forms of Time," 250.

20. Bakhtin, "Discourse in the Novel," in *The Dialogic Imagination*, 321.

21. Woloch, *The One vs. the Many*, 14.

22. See Jonathan Grossman, *The Art of Alibi: English Law Courts and the Novel* (Baltimore: Johns Hopkins Press, 2002).

23. Stephen Nicholas, "The Convict Labour Market," *Convict Workers: Reinterpreting Australia's Past* (New York: Cambridge University Press, 1988), 111.

24. Cassandra Pybus, "The d—Yankee quill-driver," *Chain Letters: Narrating Convict Lives* (Melbourne: Melbourne University Press, 2001), 27.

25. Lucy Frost and Hamish Maxwell-Stewart, Introduction, in *Chain Letters*, 3.

26. Peter Brooks, "Repetition, Repression, and Return: *Great Expectations* and the Study of Plot," *New Literary History* 11 (1980), 505.

27. Charles Dickens, *Great Expectations*, ed. Angus Calder (New York: Penguin, 1985), 36. Hereafter cited within the text as "GE."

28. Recall that during Dickens's first trip to America, he witnessed slave catchers board his steamship in pursuit of runaway slaves.

29. Daphne A. Brooks, *Bodies in Dissent: Spectacular Performance of Race and Freedom: 1850–1910* (Durham, NC: Duke University Press, 2006), 106. Brooks is referring specifically to the swamp, which emerges in the narratives of Henry Box Brown, Solomon Northup, and Henry Bibb as a site of "black agency."

30. Peter Brooks, "Repetition, Repression, and Return," 506.

31. It also ironically serves as a contact zone, connecting London to the larger world, albeit in relations of hostility. For more analysis of metonymic chains in *Great Expectations*, see Woloch 199–201.

32. Woloch, *The One vs. the Many*, 204.

33. Bakhtin, "Epic and Novel," in *Dialogic Imagination*, 5.

34. Bakhtin, "Discourse in the Novel," in *Dialogic Imagination*, 301.

35. Ibid., 302.

36. Bakhtin describes how the parodic sonnets that open *Don Quixote* are not part of the sonnet genre. Rather, the sonnet is the "object of representation" and "the hero of parody" (M. M. Bakhtin, "From the Pre-history of Novelistic Discourse," *The Dialogic Imagination: Four Essays*, trans. Caryl Emerson and Michael Holquist [Austin: University of Texas Press, 1981], 51). In the same way, we can see how Pip does not embody the fugitive slave chronotope, or belong to the genre of the slave narrative. Instead, he parodies the genre and becomes a symbol of something else entirely—of tragicomedy, perhaps, or minstrelsy.

37. Woloch, *The One vs. the Many*, 206.

38. Frederick Douglass, *Narrative of the Life of Frederick Douglass, An American Slave* (New York: Signet, 1968), 76.

39. Ibid.

40. Hilary Beckles, "Plantation Production and White 'Proto-Slavery': White Indentured Servants and the Colonisation of the English West Indies, 1624–1645," *The Americas* 41 (1985): 21.

41. See Aaron S. Fogleman, "From Slaves, Convicts, and Servants to Free Passengers: the Transformation of Immigration in the Era of the American Revolution," *The Journal of American History* 85 (1998): 43–76.

42. Douglass, *Narrative*, 54. Italics within text.

43. Douglass escaped to slavery by disguising himself as a sailor.

44. For Bakhtin's analysis of *Little Dorrit*, see Bakhtin, "Discourse in the Novel," in *Dialogic Imagination*, 303–8.

45. Ibid., 304.

46. This scene also resonates provocatively with blackface minstrelsy, which Eric Lott has argued allows members of the white working-class to negotiate, through race, their class anxieties. See Eric Lott, *Blackface Minstrelsy and the American Working Class* (New York: Oxford University Press, 1993). Many thanks to John Reilly for pointing out this connection.

47. Iain Crawford explores this *Frankenstein* allusion in "Pip and the Monster: The Joys of Bondage," *Studies in English Literature* 28 (1988), 625–48.

48. Peter Brooks, "Repetition, Repression, and Return," 520.

49. Ibid., 522.

50. Dickens, "To W. F. De Cerjat," 16 March 1862, *Letters*, vol. 10, 54–55.

51. Ibid.

52. Adrian, "Dickens on American Slavery," 315–29.

53. Douglas Lorimer, *Colour, Class and the Victorians* (Bristol [England]: Leicester University Press, 1978), 163–64.

54. Dickens, "To Captain Elisha Morgan," 6 January 1863, *Letters*, vol. 10, 190.

55. Dickens, "To Frederick Lehmann," 28 [May] 1863, *Letters*, vol. 10, 255.

56. Michael Goldberg and Arthur Adrian see in Dickens's contrarian attitude the influence of Thomas Carlyle, whose 1849 article, "Occasional Discourse on the Negro Question," mounts an inflammatory defense of slavery. In it, Carlyle points to the poverty and indolence of "Quashee" as proof of the failure of West Indian emancipation, an argument much cited by antebellum slave owners in their defense of American slavery. See Michael Goldberg, "From Bentham to Carlyle: Dickens' Political Development," *Journal of the History of Ideas* 33 (1972): 61–76.

Epilogue

1. The Thirteenth Amendment was ratified by the necessary three-quarters of the states by December of 1865. Kentucky did not ratify the amendment until 1976, and Mississippi until 1995.

2. James McPherson, *The Abolitionist Legacy: From Reconstruction to the NAACP* (Princeton: Princeton University Press, 1975), 36.

3. Ibid.,36.

4. Howard Temperley, *British Antislavery 1833–1870* (London: Longman, 1972), 266. Temperley notes that the BFASS's principal rivals, such as the Glasgow Emancipation Society, had "so identified themselves with the American Unionist cause that when the war ended they soon faded away" (265).

5. Douglas Lorimer, *Colour, Class and the Victorians* (Bristol [England]: Leicester University Press, 1978), 13–14.

6. The Sepoy Rebellion of 1857 (also known as the Indian Mutiny) similarly inflamed racial tensions and magnified British anxiety over its colonial possessions.

7. William L. Andrews and Frances Smith Foster, *Witnessing Slavery* (London: Greenwood Press, 1979), 78.

8. For more on postbellum narratives, see ibid., 60–61, 150–53.

9. Fanny Van De Grift Stevenson, "Prefatory Note," *The Dynamiter* (London: Heinemann, 1923–24), xi.

10. Fanny Van De Grift Stevenson, "Prefatory Note," xii.

11. Ibid.

12. Ibid.

13. Robert Louis Stevenson and Fanny Stevenson, *The Dynamiter* (Fairfield, Iowa: 1st World Publishing, 2004), 13. Hereafter cited within the text.

14. Robert Kiely, *Robert Louis Stevenson and the Fiction of Adventure* (Cambridge: Harvard University Press, 1965), 128.

15. Daphne Brooks points to the narratives of Henry Box Brown, Solomon Northup, and Henry Bibb as texts in which the swamp becomes a site of "fugitive liberation" and "black agency" (106).

16. Frances Smith Foster, *Witnessing Slavery: The Development of Ante-Bellum Slave Narratives* (Madison: University of Wisconsin Press, 1994), 15.

17. Ibid., 16.

18. Ibid., 17.

19. Solomon Northup, *Twelve Years a Slave: Narrative of Solomon Northup, a Citizen of New-York, Kidnapped in Washington City in 1841, and Rescued in 1853* (Auburn: Derby and Miller, 1853).

20. Clare Luxmore is clearly unhindered by the fact that she does not look black. By pretending she is a mulatta, Clare takes advantage of the racial ambiguity that surrounded such light-skinned slaves as Moses Roper and Ellen Craft, both of whom spent time in England and astonished their British patrons by their "white" appearance. Robert Kiely apparently misreads the passage where Teresa-cum-Clare is described as "raising [her] veil" and "show[ing] [Desborough] a countenance from which every trace of colour had fled" to mean that Clare had been "paint[ing] herself brown" (Kiely, *Robert Louis Stevenson*, 128). In fact, blackface makeup would have been unnecessary, for Clare, as a supposed mulatta, could "pass" for white.

21. Clare also leaves a note for Desborough, entrusting him to the care of the brown box. Presumably, a runaway slave who could write, could also read.

22. *Honi Soit Qui Mal Y Pense* ("Shame upon he who thinks evil upon it") is the motto of the chivalric Order of the Garter.

23. Since a slave is ostensibly safe in England, Teresa Valdevia must fabricate another reason why she fears Cuban repatriation. She tells Desborough that Caulder's son wishes to arrest her because she is a jewel thief, not because she is a runaway slave.

24. K. R. M. Short, *The Dynamite War: Irish American Bombers in Victorian Britain* (Dublin: Gill and MacMillan, 1979), 12.

25. See Sarah McLemore's unpublished dissertation chapter, "Homeland Insecurity: Dynamite Terror and the Textual Landscape of London," diss. University of California, Santa Barbara, 2007.

26. Short, *The Dynamite War*, 1.

27. Fanny Van De Grift Stevenson, "Prefatory Note," xi.

28. Short, *The Dynamite War*, 207–8.

29. The Albert Medal was replaced by the George Cross in 1971.

30. Robert Louis Stevenson, [letter], *The Works of Robert Louis Stevenson*, Tusitala Edition, vol. 33 (London: Heinemann, 1924), 37.

31. Ibid.

32. Stevenson, hearing that Gladstone had enjoyed his *Treasure Island*, acerbically noted that the prime minister should better have "attended to the imperial affairs of England."

33. Thomas Carlyle calls the West Indies a "black Ireland" and explicitly compares the political and economic failures of the two British "colonies" (Thomas Carlyle, "Occasional Discourse on the Negro Question," *Fraser's Magazine* [Dec. 1849]: 527–38). For more on anti-Irish prejudice, see L.P. Curtis, *Anglo-Saxons and Celts: A Study of Anti-Irish Prejudice in Victorian England* (Bridgeport: New York University Press, 1968) and L. P. Curtis, *Apes and Angels: The Irishman in Victorian Caricature* (Washington, DC: Smithsonian Books, 1971).

34. H. Bellyse Baildon, *Robert Louis Stevenson: A Life Study in Criticism* (London: Chatto & Windus, 1901), 50.

35. T. C. Livingstone, introduction, *The New Arabian Nights and The Dynamiter* (London: Collins, 1953), 15.

36. Frank McLynn, *Robert Louis Stevenson: A Biography* (New York: Random House, 1994), 235. McLynn also suggests Louis was himself aware of Fanny's questionable literary talent and "allowed many of the weak passages in [*The Dynamiter*] to stand out of deference to Fanny" (ibid., 420).

37. Ibid., 237.

38. Quoted in Nellie Van de Grift Sanchez, *The Life of Mrs. Robert Louis Stevenson* (London: Chatto & Windus, 1920), 118.

39. McLynn, *Robert Louis Stevenson*, 235.

40. Ibid., 235.

41. Kiely, *Robert Louis Stevenson*, 129.

42. See Charles T. Davis and Henry Louis Gates, Jr., eds. *The Slave's Narrative* (New York: Oxford University Press, 1985), xi–xii and John Sekora, "Black Message/White Envelope: Genre, Authenticity, and Authority in the Antebellum Slave Narrative" *Callalloo* 10 (1989): 497.

Works Cited

Adrian, Arthur. "Dickens on American Slavery: A Carlylean Slant." *PMLA* 67 (1952): 315–29.

Altick, Richard. *The English Common Reader: A Social History of the Mass Reading Public, 1800–1900*. Columbus: Ohio State University Press, 1998.

———. *Punch: The Lively Youth of a British Institution 1841–1851*. Columbus: Ohio State University Press, 1997.

Anderson, Benedict. *Imagined Communities: Reflections on the Origin and Spread of Nationalism*. New York: Verso, 1991.

Andrews, William L. "The Representation of Slavery and Afro-American Literary Realism." *African American Autobiography: A Collection of Critical Essays*. Englewood Cliffs, NJ: Prentice Hall, 1993.

Andrews, William L., and Frances Smith Foster. *Witnessing Slavery*. London: Greenwood Press, 1979.

Appiah, Kwame Anthony. "Cosmopolitan Patriots." *Critical Inquiry* 23 (1997): 617–39.

Armstrong, Nancy, and Leonard Tennenhouse. *The Imaginary Puritan: Literature, Intellectual Labor, and the Origins of Personal Life*. Berkeley: University of California Press, 1992.

Austen, Jane. *Emma*. New York: Norton, 2000.

Baildon, H. Bellyse. *Robert Louis Stevenson: A Life Study in Criticism*. London: Chatto & Windus, 1901.

Bailey, Ronald. "The Slave(ry) Trade and the Development of Capitalism in the United States: The Textile Industry in New England." *The Atlantic Slave Trade*, ed. Joseph E. Inikori and Stanley L. Engerman. Durham, NC: Duke University Press, 1992.

Bakhtin, M. M. *The Dialogic Imagination: Four Essays*. Ed. Michael Holquist. Trans. Caryl Emerson and Michael Holquist. Austin: University of Texas Press, 1981.

Baudrillard, Jean. *The Transparency of Evil: Essays on Extreme Phenomena*. London: Verso, 1992.

Beckles, Hilary. "Plantation Production and White 'Proto-Slavery': White Indentured Servants and the Colonisation of the English West Indies, 1624–1645." *The Americas* 41 (1985): 21–45.

Berthold, Dennis. "Class Acts: The Astor Place Riots and Melville's 'The Two Temples.' *American Literature* 71 (1999): 429–61.

Blackett, R. J. M. *Building an Antislavery Wall: Black Americans in the Atlantic Abolitionist Movement, 1830–1860.* Baton Rouge: Louisiana State University Press, 1983.

———. *Divided Hearts: Britain and the American Civil War.* Baton Rouge: Louisiana State University Press, 2001.

——— Foreword. *Running a Thousand Miles to Freedom.* Baton Rouge: Louisiana State University Press, 1999.

———. "The Odyssey of William and Ellen Craft." *Running a Thousand Miles to Freedom.* Baton Rouge: Louisiana State University Press, 1999.

Blassingame, John W. *The Slave Community: Plantation Life in the Antebellum South.* New York: Oxford University Press, 1979.

Blassingame, John W., et al. *The Frederick Douglass Papers: Series One— Speeches, Debates, and Interviews,* 5 vols. New Haven: Yale University Press, 1979.

Bodenheimer, Rosemarie. "*North and South:* A Permanent State of Change." *Nineteenth-Century Fiction* 34 (1979): 281–301.

———. *The Politics of Story in Victorian Social Fiction.* Ithaca: Cornell University Press, 1988.

Bolster, W. Jeffrey. *Black Jacks: African American Seamen in the Age of Sail.* Cambridge: Harvard University Press, 1997.

Bontemps, Arna Wendell. Introduction. *Great Slave Narratives.* Boston: Beacon Press, 1969.

Brantlinger, Patrick. *The Spirit of Reform: British Literature and Politics, 1832–1867.* Cambridge: Harvard University Press, 1977.

Breton, Rob. "Ghosts in the Machina: Plotting in Chartist and Working-Class Fiction." *Victorian Studies* 47 (2005): 557–75.

Brontë, Charlotte. "An American Tale" (9 September 1929). *Juvenilia: 1829–1835.* New York: Penguin, 1997.

——— *Jane Eyre.* Ed. Richard J. Dunn. New York: Norton, 2000.

———. *The Letters of Charlotte Brontë.* Ed. Margaret Smith. 3 vols. Oxford: Clarendon, 1995–c.2004.

Brooks, Daphne A. *Bodies in Dissent: Spectacular Performance of Race and Freedom: 1850–1910.* Durham, NC: Duke University Press, 2006.

Brooks, Peter. "Repetition, Repression, and Return: *Great Expectations* and the Study of Plot." *New Literary History* 11 (1980): 503–26.

Brown, William Wells. *Three Years in Europe or, Places I Have Seen and People I Have Met.* London: Charles Gilpin, 1852.

Bugg, John. "The Other Interesting Narrative: Olaudah Equiano's Public Book Tour." *PMLA* 121 (2006): 1424–42.

Burton, Anthony. *The Rise and Fall of King Cotton.* London: BBC, 1984.

Carlyle, Thomas. *Centenary Edition of the Works of Thomas Carlyle in Thirty Volumes.* London: Chapman and Hall, 1896.

———. "Occasional Discourse on the Negro Question." *Fraser's Magazine* (Dec. 1849): 527–38.

Carretta, Vincent. *Equiano, the African: Biography of a Self-Made Man.* New York: Penguin, 2007.

Cazamian, Louis. *The Social Novel in England* (1903). Trans. Martin Fido. London and Boston: Routledge and Kegan Paul, 1973.

Claybaugh, Amanda. *The Novel of Purpose: Literature and Social Reform in the Anglo-American World.* Ithaca, NY: Cornell University Press, 2006.

———. "Toward a New Transatlanticism: Dickens in the United States." *Victorian Studies* 48 (2006): 439–60.

Cohen, Margaret. "Traveling Genres." *New Literary History* 34 (2003): 481–99.

Conacher, J. B. "British Policy in the Anglo-American Enlistment Crisis of 1855–1856." *Proceedings of the American Philosophical Society* 136 (1992): 533–76.

Cowper, William. "Charity." *The Poems of William Cowper*. Ed. John D. Baird and Charles Ryskamp. 3 vols. New York: Oxford University Press, 1980–1995.

Craft, William and Ellen. *Running a Thousand Miles to Freedom*. Baton Rouge: Louisiana State University Press, 1999.

Craik, W. A. *Elizabeth Gaskell and the English Provincial Novel*. London: Methuen, 1975.

Crawford, Iain. "Pip and the Monster: The Joys of Bondage." *Studies in English Literature* 28 (1988): 625–58.

Cugoano, Ottobah. *The Narrative of the Enslavement of Ottobah Cugoano, a Native of Africa, Published by Himself, In the Year 1787*. London: Hatchard and Company, 1825.

Curtis, L. P. *Anglo-Saxons and Celts: A Study of Anti-Irish Prejudice in Victorian England*. Bridgeport: New York University Press, 1968.

———. *Apes and Angels: The Irishman in Victorian Caricature*. Washington, D.C.: Smithsonian Books, 1971.

David, Deirdre. *Fictions of Resolution in Three Victorian Novels*. New York: Columbia University Press, 1981.

Davis, Charles T. and Henry Louis Gates, Jr., eds. *The Slave's Narrative*. New York: Oxford University Press, 1985.

Davis, David Brion. *The Problem of Slavery in the Age of Revolution, 1770–1823*. New York: Oxford University Press, 1999.

———. *The Problem of Slavery in Western Culture*. New York: Oxford University Press, 1988.

Derrida, Jacques, "The Law of Genre." Trans. Avital Ronell. *Critical Inquiry* 7 (1980): 55–81.

Dickens, Charles and Henry Morley. "North American Slavery." *Household Words*. Sep 1852.

Dickens, Charles. *American Notes For General Circulation*. New York: Penguin, 2000.

———. *Bleak House*. New York: Penguin, 2003.

———. *Great Expectations*. Ed. Angus Calder. New York: Penguin, 1985.

———. "In Memoriam," *Cornhill Magazine* (Feb 1864). *Thackeray: The Critical Heritage*. Ed. Geoffrey Tillotson and Donald Hawes. London: Routledge, 1966.

———. *Martin Chuzzlewit*. New York: Penguin, 2000.

———. *The Letters of Charles Dickens*. Ed. Madeline House, Graham Storey, and Kathleen Tillotson. 12 vols. New York: Oxford University Press, 1965–2002.

Dodge, Bertha. *The Plant That Would Be King*. Austin: University of Texas Press, 1984.

Douglass, Frederick. *Frederick Douglass: Selected Speeches and Writings*. Ed. Philip S. Foner and Yuval Taylor. Chicago: Lawrence Hill Books, 2000.

———. *Life and Times of Frederick Douglass*. New York: Collier, 1967.

———. *My Bondage and My Freedom*. New York: Miller, Orton, and Mulligan, 1855.

———. *Narrative of the Life of Frederick Douglass, An American Slave*. New York: Signet, 1968.

———. "Speech on American Slavery, September 24, 1847. *The Frederick Douglass Papers: Volume 2, Seriers One: Speeches, Debates, and Interviews, 1847–1854*. New Haven: Yale University Press, 1982.

Du Bois, W. E. B. *The Souls of Black Folk*, ed. Henry Louis Gates and Terri Hume Oliver. New York: Norton, 1999.

Edwards, Brent Hayes. *The Practice of Diaspora: Literature, Translation, and the Rise of Black Internationalism*. Cambridge: Harvard University Press, 2003.

Findlay, J. R. "Thackeray," *Scotsman* (18 Dec 1850). *Thackeray: The Critical Heritage*. Ed. Geoffrey Tillotson and Donald Hawes. London: Routledge, 1966.

Fisch, Audrey. *American Slaves in Victorian England: Abolitionist Politics in Popular Literature and Culture*. New York: Cambridge University Press, 2000.

Fogleman, Aaron S. "From Slaves, Convicts, and Servants to Free Passengers: the Transformation of Immigration in the Era of the American Revolution." *The Journal of American History* 85 (1998): 43–76.

Foner, Philip S. *British Labor and the American Civil War*. New York: Holmes and Meier, 1981.

Forster, John. "Thackeray," *Examiner* (13 Nov 1852). *Thackeray: The Critical Heritage*. Ed. Geoffrey Tillotson and DonaldHawes. London: Routledge, 1966.

Foster, Frances Smith. *Witnessing Slavery: The Development of Ante-Bellum Slave Narratives*. Madison: University of Wisconsin Press, 1994.

Fraser, Rebecca. *Charlotte Brontë: A Writer's Life*. London: Methuen, 1998.

Freedgood, Elaine. "Realism, Fetishism, and Genocide: 'Negro Head' Tobacco in and around *Great Expectations*." *Novel: A Forum on Fiction* 36 (2002).

Frost, Lucy and Hamish Maxwell-Stewart. Introduction. *Chain Letters: Narrating Convict Lives*. Melbourne: Melbourne University Press, 2001.

Fryer, Peter. *Staying Power: The History of Black People in Britain*. London: Pluto, 1984.

Gallagher, Catherine. *The Industrial Reformation of English Fiction: Social Discourse and Narrative Form 1832–1867*. Chicago: University of Chicago Press, 1985.

Garber, Marjorie. *Vested Interests: Cross-Dressing and Cultural Anxiety*. London: Routledge, 1997.

Gaskell, Elizabeth. *Further Letters of Mrs. Gaskell*. Ed. John Chapple and Alan Shelston. Manchester: Manchester University Press, 2000.

———. *The Letters of Mrs. Gaskell*. Ed. J. A. V. Chapple and Arthur Pollard. Cambridge: Harvard University Press, 1966.

———. "The Grey Woman." *Gothic Tales*. New York: Penguin, 2004.

———. *The Life of Charlotte Brontë*. New York: Penguin, 1997.

———. "Lois the Witch." *Gothic Tales*. New York: Penguin, 2004.

———. *My Lady Ludlow*. Charleston: BookSurge Classics, 2004.

———. *North and South*. Elizabeth Gaskell, *North and South*. Ed. Alan Shelston. New York: Norton, 2005.

———. *Sylvia's Lovers*. New York: Penguin, 1997.

Gates, Henry Louis, Jr. *The Signifying Monkey: A Theory of African-American Literary Criticism*. New York: Oxford University Press, 1989.

Gawthrop, Humphrey. "Slavery: *Idée Fixe* of Emily and Charlotte Brontë." *Brontë Studies* 28 (2003): 113–21.

Gilbert, Sandra and Susan Gubar. *The Madwoman in the Attic: The Woman Writer and the Nineteenth-Century Literary Imagination*. New Haven: Yale University Press, 2000.

Giles, Paul. "Narrative Reversals and Power Exchanges: Frederick Douglass and British Culture." *American Literature* 73 (2001): 779–810.

———. *Transatlantic Insurrections: British Culture and the Formation of American Literature, 1730–1860*. Philadelphia: University of Pennsylania Press, 2001.

———. *Virtual Americas: Transnational Fictions and the Transatlantic Imaginary*. Durham, NC: Duke University Press, 2002.

Gilroy, Paul. *The Black Atlantic: Modernity and Double Consciousness*. Cambridge: Harvard University Press, 1993.

Goldberg, Michael. "From Bentham to Carlyle: Dickens' Political Development." *Journal of the History of Ideas* 33 (1972): 61–76.

Grandy, Moses. *Narrative of the Life of Moses Grandy; Late a Slave in the United States of America*. London: C. Gilpin, 1843.

Greenspan, Ezra. *The Cambridge Companion to Walt Whitman*. Cambridge: Cambridge University Press, 1995.

Grossman, Jonathan. *The Art of Alibi: English Law Courts and the Novel*. Baltimore: Johns Hopkins Press, 2002.

Hammon, Briton. *A Narrative of the Uncommon Sufferings, and Surpizing Deliverance of Briton Hammon, A Negro Man*. Boston: Green and Russell, 1760.

Heglar, Charles. *Rethinking the Slave Narrative*. Westport, Conn.: Greenwood Press, 2001.

Henson, Josiah. *The Life of Josiah Henson, Formerly a Slave, Now an Inhabitant of Canada, As Narrated by Himself*. Boston: Arthur D. Phelps, 1849.

Howes, Craig. "Pendennis and the Controversy on the 'Dignity of Literature.'" *Nineteenth-Century Literature*. 41 (1986): 269–98.

Ingham, Patricia. Introduction. *American Notes For General Circulation*. New York: Penguin, 2000.

Jacobs, Harriet. *Incidents in the Life of a Slave Girl, Written by Herself*. Ed. Jean Fagan Yellin. Cambridge: Harvard University Press, 2000.

Jaffe, Audrey. *Vanishing Points: Dickens, Narrative, and the Study of Omniscience*. Berkeley: University of California Press, 1991.

Jakobson, Roman. "Two Aspects of Language." *The Norton Anthology of Theory and Criticism*, ed. Vincent B. Leitch. New York: Norton, 2001.

Jeffers, Thomas L. "Thackeray's Pendennis: Son and Gentleman." *Nineteenth-Century Fiction* 33 (1978): 175–93.

Kiely, Robert. *Robert Louis Stevenson and the Fiction of Adventure*. Cambridge: Harvard University Press, 1965.

Kiernan, V. G. *The Lords of Human Kind: European Attitudes Towards the Outside World in the Imperial Age*. London: Weidenfeld & Nicolson, 1969.

Kingsley, Henry. "Thackeray." *Macmillan's* Feb 1864. *Thackeray: The Critical Heritage*, ed. Geoffrey Tillotson and Donald Hawes. London: Routledge, 1966.

Laqueur, Thomas. *Religion and Respectability: Sunday Schools and Working Class Culture, 1780–1850*. New Haven: Yale University Press, 1976.

Leatheley, Mary. *Large Pictures with Little Stories*. London: Darton, *c*. 1855.

Lee, Debbie. *Slavery and the Romantic Imagination*. Philadelphia: University of Pennsylvania Press, 2002.

Livingstone, T. C. Introduction. *The New Arabian Nights and The Dynamiter*. London: Collins, 1953.

Lorimer, Douglas. *Colour, Class and the Victorians*. Bristol (England): Leicester University Press, 1978.

Lott, Eric. *Blackface Minstrelsy and the American Working Class*. New York: Oxford University Press, 1993.

Susan Manning and Andrew Taylor, Ed. *Transatlantic Literary Studies: A Reader*. Baltimore: Johns Hopkins University Press, 2007.

Marcus, Sharon. "The Profession of the Author: Abstraction, Advertising, and *Jane Eyre*." *PMLA* 110 (1995): 206–19.

Markovits, Stefanie. "*North and South*, East and West: Elizabeth Gaskell, the Crimean War, and the Condition of England." *Nineteenth-Century Literature* 59 (2005): 463–93.

Marrant, John and William Aldridge. *A Narrative of the Lord's Wonderful Dealings with John Marrant, a Black*. London: Gilbert and Plummer, 1785.

Martin, Theodore. *Westminster Review* (April 1853). *Thackeray: The Critical Heritage*. Ed. Geoffrey Tillotson and Donald Hawes. London: Routledge, 1966.

Masson, David. "Thackeray," *North British Review* (May 1851). *Thackeray: The Critical Heritage*. Ed. Geoffrey Tillotson and Donald Hawes. London: Routledge, 1966.

Mayhew, Henry. *London Labour and the London Poor*. 4 vols. London: Dover, 1968.

Mays, Kelly J. "When a 'Speck' Begins to Read." *Reading Sites: Social Difference and Reader Response*. Ed. Patrocinio P. Schweickart and Elizabeth A. Flynn. New York: MLA, 2004.

McGill, Meredith. *American Literature and the Culture of Reprinting, 1834–1853*. Philadelphia: University of Pennsylvania Press, 2003.

McLemore, Sarah. "Dynamite Terror and the Textual Landscape of London." Unpublished dissertation. University of California, Santa Barbara, 2007.

McLynn, Frank. *Robert Louis Stevenson: A Biography*. New York: Random House, 1994.

McPherson, James. *The Abolitionist Legacy: From Reconstruction to the NAACP*. Princeton: Princeton University Press, 1975.

Meckier, Jerome. *Innocent Abroad: Charles Dickens's American Engagements*. Lexington: University of Kentucky Press, 1990.

Meyer, Susan. *Imperialism at Home: Race and Victorian Women's Fiction*. Ithaca, NY: Cornell University Press, 1996.

Midgley, Claire. *Women Against Slavery: the British Campaigns, 1780–1870*. New York: Routledge, 1992.

Montégut, Emile. "Le Roman de Moeurs Industrielles," *Revue des Deux Mondes*, 1 October 1855, XII (new period, second series). Trans. Anne-Marie Hutchings. *North and South*. Ed. Alan Shelston New York: Norton, 2005.

Moretti, Franco. *The Way of the World: The Bildungsroman in European Culture*. New York: Verso, 2000.

Moss, Sidney P. *Charles Dickens' Quarrel with America*. Troy: Whitson, 1984.

———. "South Carolina Contemplates Banning Dickens's *American Notes*." *Dickensian* 80 (1984): 157–62.

Nicholas, Stephen. "The Convict Labour Market." *Convict Workers: Reinterpreting Australia's Past*. New York: Cambridge University Press, 1988.

Nichols, Charles H. *Many Thousand Gone: The Ex-Slaves Account of Their Bondage and Freedom*. Bloomington: Indiana University Press, 1969.

———. "Who Read the Slave Narratives?" The Phylon Quarterly 20 (1959): 149–62.

Northup, Solomon. *Twelve Years a Slave: Narrative of Solomon Northup, a Citizen of New-York, Kidnapped in Washington City in 1841, and Rescued in 1853*. Auburn: Derby and Miller, 1853.

Olney, James. "'I was born': Slave Narratives, Their Status as Autobiography and as Literature." *Calalloo* 20 (1984): 46–73.

Patterson, Orlando. *Slavery and Social Death: A Comparative Study*. Cambridge: Harvard University Press, 1982.

Peters, Catherine. *Thackeray's Universe*. Boston: Faber and Faber, 1987.

Pratt, Mary Louise. *Imperial Eyes: Travel Writing and Transculturation*. New York: Routledge, 1992.

Pybus, Cassandra. 'the d—Yankee quill-driver.' *Chain Letters: Narrating Convict Lives*. Melbourne: Melbourne University Press, 2001.

Pyckett, Lyn. "The Newgate Novel and Sensation Fiction, 1830–1868." *The Cambridge Companion to Crime Fiction*. Ed. Martin Priestman. Cambridge: Cambridge University Press, 2003.

Ray, Gordon. *Thackeray: The Age of Wisdom 1847–1863*. New York: McGraw-Hill, 1958.

Ray, Gordon, and Edgar Harden, eds. *The Letters and Private Papers of William Makepeace Thackeray*. Cambridge: Harvard University Press, 1946.

Richards, I. A. *The Philosophy of Rhetoric*. New York: Oxford University Press, 1965.

Richardson, Alan. *Literature, Education, and Romanticism: Reading as Social Practice, 1780–1832*. Cambridge: Cambridge University Press, 2004.

Rigby, Elizabeth. "*Vanity Fair* and *Jane Eyre*." *Quarterly Review* 84:167 (December 1848).

Rintoul, R. S. "Thackeray's *Pendennis*," *Spectator* (21 Dec 1850). *Thackeray: The Critical Heritage*. Ed. Geoffrey Tillotson and Donald Hawes. London: Routledge, 1966.

Ripley, C. Peter, et al. *The Black Abolitionist Papers*, 5 vols. Chapel Hill: University of North Carolina Press, 1985–1992.

Roach, Joseph. *Cities of the Dead*. New York: Columbia University Press, 1996.

Rohrbach, Augusta. *Truth Stranger Than Fiction: Race, Realism, and the U.S. Literary Marketplace*. New York: Palgrave, 2002.

Roper, Moses. *Narrative of the Adventures and Escape of Moses Roper, from American Slavery*. London: Warder Office, 1839.

Ruskin, John. *Modern Painters*. New York: John Wiley and Son, 1866.

Said, Edward W. *Culture and Imperialism*. New York: Knopf, 1993.

Sanchez, Nellie Van de Grift. *The Life of Mrs. Robert Louis Stevenson*. London: Chatto & Windus, 1920.

Schama, Simon. "The Patriot: Turner and the Drama of History." *The New Yorker*. September 24, 2007.

Schor, Hilary. *Scheherezade in the Market-Place: Elizabeth Gaskell and the Victorian Novel*. New York and Oxford: Oxford University Press, 1992.

Sekora, John. "Black Message/White Envelope: Genre, Authenticity, and Authority in the Antebellum Slave Narrative." *Callalloo* 10 (1989): 482–515.

Sharpe, Jenny. *Allegories of Empire: The Figure of Woman in the Colonial Text*. Minneapolis: University of Minnesota Press, 1993.

Shillingsburg, Peter. *William Mackepeace Thackeray: A Literary Life*. New York: Palgrave, 2001.

———. *Pegasus in Harness: Victorian Publishing and W. M. Thackeray*. Charlottesville: University of Virginia Press, 1992.

Short, K. R. M. *The Dynamite War: Irish American Bombers in Victorian Britain*. Dublin: Gill and MacMillan, 1979.

Sollors, Werner. *Neither Black Nor White Yet Both: Thematic Explorations of Interracial Literature*. New York: Oxford University Press, 1997.

Spivak, Gayatri Chakravorty. "Three Women's Texts and a Critique of Imperialism." *Critical Inquiry* 12 (1985): 243–61.

Starling, Marion Wilson. *The Slave Narrative: Its Place in American History*. Washington: Howard University Press, 1988.

Stauffer, John. *The Black Hearts of Men: Radical Abolitionists and the Transformation of Race*. Cambridge: Harvard University Press, 2002.

Sternlieb, Lisa. *Hazarding Confidences: The Female Narrator in the British Novel*. New York: Palgrave, 2002.

Stevenson, Fanny Van De Grift. Prefatory Note. *The Dynamiter*. London: Heinemann, 1923–24.

Stevenson, Robert Louis. *The Letters of Robert Louis Stevenson*. Ed. Bradford A. Booth and Ernest Mayhew. 5 vols. New Haven: Yale University Press, 1995.

———. *The Works of Robert Louis Stevenson*. Tusitala Edition, 35 vols. London: Heinemann, 1924.

Robert Louis Stevenson and Fanny Stevenson. *The Dynamiter*. Fairfield, Iowa: 1st World Publishing, 2004.

Stone, Harry. "Dickens and Harriet Beecher Stowe." *Nineteenth-Century Fiction* 12 (1957): 188–202.

Stone, Lawrence. "Literature and Education in England, 1640–1900." *Past and Present* 42 (1969) 60–139.

Stoneman, Patsy. *Elizabeth Gaskell*. Bloomington and Indianapolis: Indiana University Press, 1987.

Stowe, Harriet Beecher. *The Key to 'Uncle Tom's Cabin.'* Boston: John P. Jewett, 1853.

———. *Uncle Tom's Cabin*. New York: Norton, 1994.

Sutherland, John. "Thackeray as Victorian Racialist." *Essays in Criticism* 20 (1970) 441–45.

———. *Thackeray at Work*. London: Athlone Press, 1974.

Taylor, Clare. *British and American Abolitionists: An Episode in Transatlantic Understanding*. Edinburgh: Edinburgh University Press, 1974.

Taylor, Mary. *Mary Taylor, Friend of Charlotte Brontë: Letters from New Zealand*. Ed. Joan Stevens. Wellington: Oxford University Press, 1972.

Temperley, Howard. *British Antislavery 1833–1870*. London: Longman, 1972.

Thackeray, W. M. *The Adventures of Philip*. London: Smith, Elder, & Company, 1887.

———. *The Book of Snobs*. Ed. John Sutherland. New York: St. Martin's, 1978.

————. *Letters and Private Papers of William Makepeace Thackeray*, 4 vols. Ed. Gordon N. Ray and Edgar Harden. London: Oxford University Press, 1945–46.

————. *The History of Pendennis*. Ed. Peter Shillingsburg. New York: Garland, 1991.

————. *Vanity Fair*. Ed. Peter Shillingsburg. New York: Norton, 1994.

Thomas, Deborah A. *Thackeray and Slavery*. Athens: Ohio University Press, 1993.

Thomas, Helen. *Romanticism and Slave Narratives: Transatlantic Testimonies*. Cambridge: Cambridge University Press, 2000.

Tillotson, Geoffrey and Donald Hawes, eds. *Thackeray: The Critical Heritage*. New York: Barnes and Noble, 1968.

Trollope, Frances. *Domestic Manners of the Americans*. New York: Penguin, 1997.

Turley, David. *The Culture of English Antislavery, 1780–1860*. New York: Routledge, 1991.

Uglow, Jenny. *Elizabeth Gaskell: A Habit of Stories*. Boston: Faber and Faber, 1993.

[Unsigned Article]. "English Authors—American Booksellers." *Punch, or the London Charivari*, Jan-Jun 1847: 178.

[Unsigned Review]. *Athenaeum* (7 Dec 1850). In Geoffrey Tillotson and Donald Hawes, ed., *Thackeray: The Critical Heritage*. London: Routledge, 1966.

Wallace, Diana. "Uncanny Stories: The Ghost Story as Female Gothic." *Gothic Studies* 6 (2004): 57–68.

Ward, A. W. "Introduction to *North and South*," in *The Works of Mrs. Gaskell, Volume IV*. London: Smith, Elder & Co., 1906.

Wardrop, Daneen. "'While I am Writing': Webster's 1825 Spelling Book, the Ell, and Frederick Douglass's Positions of Language. *African American Review* 32 (1998): 649–60.

Watson, J. R. "'Round the Sofa': Elizabeth Gaskell Tells Stories." *The Yearbook of English Studies* 26 (1996): 89–99.

Weisbuch, Robert. *Atlantic Double-Cross: American Literature and British Influence in the Age of Emerson*. Chicago: University of Chicago Press, 1986.

Welsh, Alexander. *From Copyright to Copperfield*. Cambridge: Harvard University Press, 1987.

Williams, James. *Narrative of James Williams, An American Slave who was, For Several Years a Driver on a Cotton Plantation in Alabama*. New York: The American Antislavery Society, 1838.

Williams, Raymond. *Culture and Society 1780–1950*. New York: Columbia University Press, 1958.

Winks, Robin W., et al., eds. *Four Fugitive Slave Narratives*. Reading: Addison-Wesley, 1969.

Winter, Kari J. *Subjects of Slavery, Agents of Change: Women and Power in Gothic Novels and Slave Narratives, 1790–1865*. Athens: University of Georgia Press, 1995.

Woloch, Alex. *The One vs. the Many*. Princeton: Princeton University Press, 2003.

Wood, Marcus. *Blind Memory: Visual Representations of Slavery in England and America, 1780–1865*. Manchester: Manchester University Press, 2000.

———. *Slavery, Empathy, and Pornography*. New York: Oxford University Press, 2002.

Wright, Edgar. *Mrs. Gaskell: The Basis for Reassessment*. New York: Oxford University Press, 1965.

Yeazell, Ruth. "More true than real: Jane Eyre's 'Mysterious Summons.'" *Nineteenth Century Fiction* 29 (1974): 127–43.

Yellin, Jean Fagan. *Harriet Jacobs: A Life*. New York: Basic Civitas Books, 2004.

———. "Incidents Abroad: Harriet Jacobs and the Transatlantic Movement" in *Women's Rights and Transatlantic Slavery in the Era of Emancipation*. Ed. Kathryn Kish Sklar and James Brewer Stewart (New Haven: Yale University Press, 2007).

Index

imperialism, 8, 20–21, 25–26, 41, 125, 141
    and *Jane Eyre*, 25–26, 41
impressment, 101
indentured servitude, 115, 124, 132
Ingham, Patricia, 114
interabolition period, 10, 13
Ireland, 10, 61, 62, 138, 139
Irish National Invincibles, 138
Irish Rebublican Brotherhood, 138, 139, 141

Jacobs, Harriet, 23, 78–83, 87, 128
Jamaica, 61, 62, 132
Jeffers, Thomas L., 62
Jim Crow, 131

Kentucky minstrels, 11
Kiely, Robert, 134, 143
Kingsley, Henry, 53, 54, 74

Lancashire, 99, 100, 102, 105, 110
Leatheley, Mary, 67, 71
Leeds *Mercury*, 28, 84
Leeds Music Hall, 28
liberalism, 54, 55, 63
The *Liberator*, 14, 80
Liberia, 114
Lincoln, Abraham, 129, 131
literacy, 22, 23, 30, 31, 34, 39, 48–52, 107, 116, 118, 120
    slave, 9, 13, 23, 77, 90–95, 117, 120, 124, 134
    working-class, 23, 77, 90–95, 120–122, 127
    See also education
"literary nigritudes," 10, 15, 17
Liverpool Mercury, 84
Livingstone, T. C., 142
London Labour and the London Poor, 11
Lorimer, Douglas, 8, 128–129, 132

Macmillan's, 53
Macready, William Charles, 3, 114, 129
Markovits, Stefanie, 97, 104
Martin, Theodore, 54
Martineau, Harriet, 11, 18, 26
Massachussetts Slavery Question, 115

Masson, David, 55
Mauger, Matthew, 117
Mayhew, Henry, 11
McGill, Meredith, 16, 64
McLemore, Sarah, 139
McLynn, Frank, 142, 143
McPherson, James, 131
Meckier, Jerome, 113
Memoirs of Archy Moore, 14
Methodists, 26
metonymic networks, 9, 15, 16, 21, 22, 41, 99, 102, 107, 108, 115, 121–122
    of genre, 16, 21, 22, 99, 108
    in *Great Expectations*, 115, 121–122
    of slavery, 9, 15, 16, 21, 22, 41, 99, 102
Meyer, Susan, 25, 26, 41
Midgley, Claire, 11
Miller, Linus, 117
minstrelsy, 11
miscegenation, 17, 78, 82–83
Monroe Doctrine, 99
Montégut, Émile, 99
Morant Bay Rebellion, 132
Moretti, Franco, 65
Morgan, Elisha, 129
Moss, Sidney, 113
Muller, Salomé, 87

narrative, convict, 117
narrative, slave, 8, 17, 27, 28, 105
    audience of, 11–13, 105
    authenticity of, 14
    circulation of, 10, 64, 105
    and contiguous genres, 117
    generic features of, 9, 13, 107
    and lecture tours, 10–11, 27, 28
    and metonymic networks, 9, 16
    phases of, 13–14, 132
    and textual contact zones, 19
    veracity of, 14
    and Victorian novelists, 8–9, 20
narrative, spiritual. *See* autobiography, spiritual
Nat Turner's Rebellion (1831), 72, 83
nationalism, 15, 109, 132, 138, 140
Navy, British. *See* Royal Navy
negrophobia, 8, 73